Finding God

AT BYU

RELIGIOUS STUDIES CENTER PUBLICATIONS

BOOK OF MORMON SYMPOSIUM SERIES

The Book of Mormon: The Keystone Scripture

The Book of Mormon: First Nephi, The Doctrinal Foundation

The Book of Mormon: Second Nephi, The Doctrinal Structure

The Book of Mormon: Jacob through Words of Mormon, To Learn with Joy

The Book of Mormon: Mosiah, Salvation Only through Christ

The Book of Mormon: Alma, The Testimony of the Word

The Book of Mormon: Helaman through 3 Nephi 8, According to Thy Word

The Book of Mormon: 3 Nephi 9–30, This Is My Gospel

The Book of Mormon: Fourth Nephi through Moroni, From Zion to Destruction

MONOGRAPH SERIES

Nibley on the Timely and the Timeless

Deity and Death

The Glory of God Is Intelligence

Reflections on Mormonism

Literature of Belief

The Words of Joseph Smith

Book of Mormon Authorship

Mormons and Muslims

The Temple in Antiquity

Isaiah and the Prophets

Scriptures for the Modern World

The Joseph Smith Translation: The Restoration of Plain and Precious Things

Apocryphal Writings and the Latter-day Saints

The Pearl of Great Price: Revelations from God

The Lectures on Faith in Historical Perspective

Mormon Redress Petitions: Documents of the 1833–1838 Missouri Conflict

Joseph Smith: The Prophet, the Man

Historicity and the Latter-day Saint Scriptures

SPECIALIZED MONOGRAPH SERIES

Supporting Saints: Life Stories of Nineteenth-Century Mormons

The Call of Zion: The Story of the First Welsh Mormon Emigration

The Religion and Family Connection: Social Science Perspectives

Welsh Mormon Writings from 1844 to 1862: A Historical Bibliography

Peter and the Popes

John Lyon: The Life of a Pioneer Poet

Latter-day Prophets and the United States Constitution

View of the Hebrews: 1825 2nd Edition

Book of Mormon Authors: Their Words and Messages

Prophet of the Jubilee

Manuscript Found: The Complete Original "Spaulding Manuscript"

Latter-day Saint Social Life: Social Research on the LDS Church and Its Members

From Jerusalem to Zarahemla: Literary and Historical Studies of the Book of Mormon

Religion, Mental Health, and the Latter-day Saints

OCCASIONAL PAPERS

Excavations at Seila, Egypt

Christopher Columbus: A Latter-day Saint Perspective

Church History in Black and White: George Edward Anderson's Photographic Mission to Latter-day Saint Historical Sites

California Saints: A 150-Year Legacy in the Golden State

A Woman's View: Helen Mar Whitney's Reminiscences of Early Church History

Joseph Smith Portraits: A Search for the Prophet's Likeness

A Descriptive Bibliography of the Mormon Church

Brigham Young: Images of a Mormon Prophet

Prophets and Apostles of the Last Dispensation

The Restored Gospel and the Message of the Four Gospels

Finding God at BYU

Finding God

AT BYU

Cover image © 2001 PhotoDisc, Inc.

Cover design by Covenant Communications, Inc.

Distributed by Covenant Communications, Inc.
American Fork, Utah

Printed in the United States of America
First Printing: October 2001

08 07 06 05 04 03 02 01   10 9 8 7 6 5 4 3 2 1

ISBN 1-57734-929-6

Contents

Introduction
Finding God at BYU

> *Each experience and encounter with people*
> *of faith is for me . . . a religious*
> *experience. — Rabbi David Rosen*

Near Luxor, Egypt, the magnificent temple of Hatshepsut rises against the western cliffs of the Nile valley. Hatshepsut, a woman king, followed the practice of rulers of the time and commissioned a burial place for herself that included bas-relief paintings of scenes from her life. Now, gazing across centuries, we wonder at the art and the hands that created it. It's the idea that intrigues us — the idea of building a place for burial while one is still alive, the idea of choosing events from one's life to decorate the walls of a burial place. What events would you choose? Would BYU be there? We began to think that there are stories to tell. This book is about finding God and strengthening faith. Though some have written about how they joined The Church of Jesus Christ of Latter-day Saints, it is not a book of conversion stories. When we began the effort three years ago to find persons with interesting stories to tell about how BYU intertwined with their lives and affected their faith, we expected to see two kinds of influences come together. The first, we thought naively, would consist of meaningful encounters with religious values in the classrooms of BYU. That is, we imagined that the intellectual and academic influences of the classroom would lead to reflections on faith. We also anticipated that those encounters would lead to a blossoming curiosity which could only be satisfied when the individual joined the LDS Church, or became more active and committed if already a member. We were wrong. Instead, we found experiences that were much richer and wondrously more complex.

We freely admit that we draw inspiration for this collection of stories from a work titled *Finding God at Harvard*, which was edited by Kelly Monroe and appeared in 1996. Monroe's book offers to readers a rich array of stories that explore a variety of personal responses to religion, particularly as one can find religion at Harvard University, a bastion of secular education. A person immediately senses, of course, the motivation for collecting stories about faith at a university that is unabashedly secular. So why a book about faith at BYU? Is it not one of the chief purposes of BYU to strengthen faith, to assist students and others to find God? After all, the published mission statement since 1981 states that "all students at BYU should be taught the truths of the gospel of Jesus Christ." Hence, one expects BYU to provide a classroom atmosphere in which faith finds strength and the name of God brings respect. So why a book on finding God at BYU? Experiences are likely to be predictable and, in a general way, pretty much the same. We were wrong again.

Instead, the variety of personal experience among the authors points to a high degree of both reward and frustration. For some, BYU was not an easy place to come to. In fact, for them it posed powerful personal challenges almost from the first day. For others, the spiritual and personal rewards for coming to campus were immediate. The essays of Patricia Holland and Terry EchoHawk are of individuals who as young teenagers were deeply touched by their first contact with the University. They came expecting a wonderful influence and found it. Because of Earl Kauffman's visits to other universities during his senior year in high school, he also came away from his first contact sensing an unusual, special dimension to the campus.

In contrast, overtly or subtly, for others the atmosphere at BYU apparently demands that they decide how to respond to the openly religious campus environment. The stories of Vivian Mushahwar and Kevin Giddens reflect this dimension of life at BYU. Each came as a student who had grown up in a very different atmosphere and had no idea what campus life in an LDS setting would be like. Their transitions to life on campus were challenging. It was similarly challenging for Benoy Tamang, who attended BYU-Hawaii as an undergraduate from Nepal. For Julie Boerio-Goates, who is married to a Latter-day Saint whose family has deep ties with BYU, there were few surprises. But the intensity of the atmosphere forced her, as it were, to decide how she felt about her own faith.

As we have hinted, our biggest surprise arose from what we didn't find. We were surprised at the almost total lack of reference to classroom experiences as life-changing. Rather, crucial differences arose either because of interaction with other individuals or because of the general religious environment at the University. From the reflections of those whose essays follow, it is clear that for many either the BYU *community* or a particular *individual* associated with BYU was far more important and formative than the BYU *classroom*. Thus, a person — his priests quorum adviser — made a difference in the life of Larry EchoHawk. An old man in India, and then later a BYU professor, brought God into the life of Karandeep Singh and effectively kept Him there. Initially, a religion professor opened Steve Clements's heart to God, and his fiancée kept it open. For Charles Metten, it has been students — individually — who have made a positive difference in his long teaching career. As a student, Allen Bergin followed the woman he loved to Provo and was never the same thereafter, personally or professionally.

For a few, by contrast, a task serendipitously brought them to a point where contact with the University or the Church meant something to them. That is the case with Rabbi David Rosen, who traveled to Salt Lake City to meet with Church leaders about the BYU Jerusalem Center, and with Johnny Bahbah, who was moved spiritually when translating a General Conference talk into Arabic.

Four faculty members came to appreciate the unique spiritual characteristics of BYU only after they had joined the faculty. Bruce Christensen sees the University differently and in a more reflective way because of leaving and then returning. Kate Kirkham, who arrived as a faculty member with high expectations, appreciates the University because of divine help in surmounting difficulties encountered there. Van Gessel, who came with few expectations but from a strong LDS background, was surprised by the effect that freedom to speak in the classroom about spiritual matters had on him. Robert Patterson, who for much of his career avoided association with BYU, found God in day-to-day interactions with colleagues and students that took on a sacred hue.

Others who wrote knew to a substantial degree what awaited them at the University and were not surprised by its emphasis on religious matters. But their essays reveal a rich texture of religious life at BYU. Melinda Cameron, daughter of a famous actor, came from Beverly Hills High School looking for a career in theater but also looking for something that only BYU might be able to offer. Lita Giddens, already a member of the Church, came to BYU because of a promise in a blessing. Eula Monroe joined the faculty after teaching at Western Kentucky University for years and now advises the Baptist Student Union on campus. Both Frank Rothaermel of Germany and Fredy Gantner of Switzerland knew of BYU's connections to the Church before attending graduate school but found that the University fostered deeper spiritual meaning than they had expected. Michael Young, a Latter-day Saint before he came to BYU, was one of the few who reported unusual stimulation in a classroom setting.

We return to the image created by Hatshepsut's monument in Upper Egypt. She chose to feature certain events from her life on the walls of her monument. In a similar way, our authors have done likewise. In each of their life stories, BYU has played a significant part.

We thank sincerely the authors whose essays appear in this book. It has been a privilege for us to work with them, and we consider it a sacred task to bring their stories to the public. On one level, these individuals have reproduced a significant part of their life histories. On another, they have permanently enriched our lives, as well as our perspectives on finding God at BYU.

On another note, we offer thanks to some who wrote for us but whose stories do not appear in these pages. There are regions in the world where people do not enjoy much freedom. For sensitive political and personal reasons, we agreed with those authors not to print their stories. We sincerely hope that time and circumstance will improve so that their essays might yet see the light of day.

Finally, we wish to express gratitude to Pat Ward, administrative assistant in Ancient Studies, who helped us tremendously in the workaday tasks associated with stitching this book together. And we thank the staff of the Religious Studies Center for bringing it to light.

S. Kent Brown
Kaye T. Hanson
James R. Kearl

Beginnings

*Know therefore this day, and consider it in thine heart,
that the Lord he is God in heaven above, and upon
the earth beneath: there is none else. Thou shalt keep
therefore his statutes, and his commandments, which
I command thee this day, that it may go well with thee,
and with thy children after thee, and that thou mayest
prolong thy days upon the earth, which the Lord thy
God giveth thee, for ever (Deuteronomy 4:39–40).*

First Things First

Patricia Terry Holland

Patricia Terry Holland is a native of St. George, Utah. A talented musician, she has had specialized training in voice and piano, including study under the direction of a member of the faculty from the Julliard School of Music in New York City. It was the study of music that first brought her to Brigham Young University, though she has returned over the years in several different capacities. She is active in church and community service and has served in the general presidency of the Young Women of The Church of Jesus Christ of Latter-day Saints and on the board of directors of the Deseret Book Company. Currently she is serving on the Primary Children's Medical Center Board. She is the coauthor, with her husband, of ON EARTH AS IT IS IN HEAVEN. Mrs. Holland is married to Elder Jeffrey R. Holland, a member of the Quorum of the Twelve Apostles of The Church of Jesus Christ of Latter-day Saints and former president of Brigham Young University. They have three children and six grandchildren.

I first came to BYU as a sixteen year old, when my parents enrolled me in a music camp for young people. Typically, the summer music camps were two to three weeks long. But because I didn't have exposure to specialized teachers in the small town where I grew up, my parents arranged for me to stay the entire summer. So I had a full summer of exposure to Brigham Young University. It was in that summer that I first fell in love with the University, its mission, and the spirit it held for me. It had a great impact on me. The first thing that had a great and lasting impact on me was seeing students pray over their meals. That's just not something you usually saw young people do at that age in such a public way. The impression added greatly to my own spiritual growth, building on a foundation laid by deeply religious parents whose whole motivation in life is the spiritual. Seeing other young people being motivated by the Spirit and understanding that it was important to them to pray, even over a hamburger, awakened something within me and began to create spiritual depth and resolve.

I was alone. I was young. I didn't have any friends. I lived with an older woman off campus. I would get up early in the morning and practice the organ and the piano. I had a lot of time to myself, and I remember the scriptures became very important to me then. I started reading the scriptures that summer because of the influence of watching the students. I prayed with more sincerity because I saw the sincerity with which I thought I saw them praying. I could hear them praying. And they were just enough older than I was that I looked up to all of them. I thought, "Here are all these wonderful BYU students, and look what they do." The minute I started to study my scriptures daily, they became all-important to me. I have learned that the more I study, the more I want to study. The more I feel the spirit of the Holy Ghost, the more I want that with me continually.

Because they were all older than I was, the students with whom I associated that summer were great role models for me. One young woman, a pianist, particularly impressed me. I remember deciding that summer that I was going to set goals so that by the time I was a college-age student, I could become as competent as she was and play with the kind of touch, feeling, emotion, and passion that I saw in her performances. Others, indeed the entire community of music students, impressed me greatly because it was easy for me to see their religious devotion intertwined with their devotion to their music. Watching other students reading their scriptures, meeting a lot of returned missionaries, and sensing the spirituality at the "Y" motivated me to want to become more like those students.

During the prior academic year, I met Jeff. He was a year older than I in our high school. We had dated once or twice, and he wrote me during the summer. I remember writing him and telling him what a wonderful place the BYU community was, how it inspired me, and motivated me, and gave me great dreams. I wanted to set higher goals, and I wanted him to be a part of that. I wanted him to experience that sort of thing. But every member of his family had gone to the University of Utah. I think that I probably had an influence on him, at least in the beginning, to think about going to BYU someday. I think my enthusiasm for it spilled over into his thinking, though it did take some time before he was fully convinced that he was going to go to BYU. He had intended to be a physician from the time he was a little boy. The "U" had a wonderful medical program, so he had always intended to attend the University of Utah.

Over the next year Jeff and I became better friends. And we started to date more seriously — very seriously, in fact! He went on a mission, and we continued to write. I went to Dixie College. When he returned I wanted to further my music training, so I went east and studied music. While I was in New York, he spent an additional year at Dixie. Then he decided to cast his lot with BYU. And he convinced me to come home. Teachers there were trying to convince me to stay, but he was a lot more persuasive than they were. I returned home, we were married in June, and we both enrolled at BYU in the fall of 1963 as a young married couple.

We were very, very poor and eventually one of us had to work full time. I chose to work because we both knew Jeff's career wasn't just for Jeff, it was for our family. I worked full time in the State Bank of Utah, took evening classes, and went to summer school. Sometimes we made enough money so I could go a full semester. Just as he was about to graduate, Jeff was asked to teach for a year in what was then called the College of Religion. He was getting his degree in English, but university administrators had decided to try an experiment with two students fresh out of their undergraduate work. They wanted to choose two students who had no experience in teaching religion classes but who they thought were natural teachers. I remember Robert K. Thomas, who was then the academic vice president, and Dean Wes Belnap talking about this with my husband and a student friend of his, Quinn Gardner. They asked these two if they would stay an extra year, work on a master's degree, and teach several sections of the Book of Mormon. They both agreed to do so.

Jeff fell in love with teaching the Book of Mormon. He had already had a wonderful awakening to the Book of Mormon from his mission president, Elder Marion D. Hanks. As mission president, he wanted his missionaries to know and love the Book of Mormon. So Jeff's training as a missionary and his natural ability to teach were a wonderful combination. To be in the classroom with the Book of Mormon — he loved it! Every night he would come home so excited, saying, "Oh I love this more and more. The more I teach it, the more I see it affecting the students, and the more I love doing it."

At the time, he wasn't sure what he wanted to do for a career. He had decided not to go into medicine. He loved English, he loved writing, and he loved teaching. He had some encouragement to consider going into the practice of law. But after teaching the Book of Mormon for a year, he fell in love with teaching it. He came home one night and said, "Should we give this a try?" I knew spiritually that was what we were to do. It was just one of those moments when I knew the answer was yes.

So we left BYU, and Jeff took a position with the Church Educational System, teaching in the institute program. Our first assignment was in the Bay Area in California. Jeff taught there for a year, and then CES had an opening for a director at the University of Washington in Seattle. It was a big institute with two student wards. There were some challenges. The program was faltering. Given Jeff's age and inexperience it was a real gamble on the part of the CES leaders, but they asked him if he would like to take that position. We said, "Yes!" and moved to Seattle. He was called into the bishopric the first Sunday we were in town, and six months later he was made the bishop. The institute students responded to his interest and efforts. In a matter of months the classes were bulging at the seams.

The longer Jeff taught the more he knew he loved to teach. But we knew that if he were to teach to the height of his ability, he needed graduate training. Due to a very spiritual experience Jeff had one evening in the BYU library, he had known for several years that he should go to Yale University. While in Seattle, Jeff had been taking classes at the University of Washington, only to discover that one of the faculty members in English literature was a distinguished graduate from Yale. He offered to write a letter of recommendation if Jeff applied to Yale. He applied, was accepted, and we moved to New Haven, where Jeff enrolled in the American Studies program. We lived across the street from the Divinity School, and he often sat in on some of the lectures there. He was looking for everything that would help prepare him to be a better teacher of the gospel of Jesus Christ. While at Yale, he was called to serve in the presidency of the Hartford Connecticut Stake. He taught two institute classes while we were there — one at Yale and one at Amherst University, which was a 180-mile round-trip drive each week for our whole time there. Jeff finished a four-year program in three years. They were intense years, but we were truly blessed.

While he was busy, I was a Relief Society president and the mother of two small children. Because of the time, energy, and emotion that church service took, it disciplined and humbled us. We had some very discouraging moments. There was one period when we didn't have any money. I had to borrow money once from friends to buy enough milk to get through the week. I was also sick. I had pneumonia, and my little girl had pneumonia for nearly eight weeks. It was just a very depressing time, a very discouraging time.

I remember at one point actually being so discouraged that I believed Jeff should quit and we should just find a job. We didn't have enough money to do anything but survive; we were stretched so thin. In the most difficult moments of this period, I remember Jeff saying to me, "If you will read your scriptures every day, you will be able to survive this a lot better." I remember thinking, "Oh sure, how is just reading the scriptures going to give us enough money to get through the week and more energy to get through the month?" It sounded like trivial advice, and I let it pass. A few days later he said, "I promise that if you will read your scriptures it will really make a difference." He said it so earnestly, I didn't dismiss it this time. I could see he was grasping for any and every help we could get. I remember thinking, "I have read my scriptures all my life." Well, I thought I was reading them, but I was reading them once a week, or on Sundays, or whatever.

One day I was just so down, so blue, that I decided to fast and pray. Toward the end of the day, just before I was closing my fast, Jeff's counsel about reading the scriptures daily kept coming back into my mind. In fact, he had given me a beautiful new set — a triple combination — for Christmas with money he really didn't have. This must have been February by now. Those scriptures had sat on my nightstand just looking beautiful. I walked over, picked them up, and randomly opened the triple combination. The book opened to section 84 of the Doctrine and Covenants, and my eyes fell on the words, "Your minds in times past have been darkened . . . because you have treated lightly the things you have received . . . even the Book of Mormon and the former commandments which I have given" (D&C 84:54, 57). I thought, "That is just too specific." I thought I had read the scriptures, but I could not remember reading "your minds [being] darkened" because of treating lightly the Book of Mormon. Well, my mind had certainly been "darkened." I knew that was revelation. In a nearby passage, it reads, "For the word of the Lord is truth, and whatsoever is truth is light, and whatsoever is light is Spirit, even the Spirit of Jesus Christ" (D&C 84:45). And I knew if I had that light, truth, spirit, even Jesus Christ with me, it would make a great difference every day.

So I put that to a test. I would not begin a day without reading until I felt the Spirit of Jesus Christ. It's not that the problems went away; they didn't. We were still poor. We still had those demanding church callings. But they seemed easier. I had more energy. Somebody gave us an old, second car. Blessings sort of poured from heaven. I attribute it to reading the scriptures. Now I can't live a day without it. It would be like going without food. It's like starving for me if I have a day that doesn't start with the scriptures.

We had to have the help of the Lord to make it through those years. It was a real walk by faith for us poor, struggling married students to get through that experience successfully. It *had* to be a walk of faith. I think all of this was a preparatory time for Jeff to become the president of BYU, and it prepared me to support and work with him on a spiritual basis.

While we were at Yale, BYU courted us, but Jeff had a contract with CES to return to teaching in the institute program. We returned to Salt Lake City, and Jeff taught at the institute at the University of Utah. We had only been in Salt Lake City for about three months when he was asked to become the director of the Melchizedek Priesthood MIA, a new program that had been instituted by President Harold B. Lee to help the single adults in the church, including college-age students. Jeff continued to teach institute at night and worked with the Melchizedek Priesthood MIA. After two years of this, he was asked by BYU President Dallin H. Oaks to become the dean of Religious Instruction. BYU once again came into our lives.

President Thomas S. Monson interviewed Jeff for that job. In the course of the interview, he happened to say to him, "It's like we're throwing young Daniel into the lion's den, Jeff, so you had better go prayerfully." He did go just that way. After we were at

BYU for only a little while, I remember Jeff coming home and saying, "You know, these faculty members are great people, but they don't seem to have much fun. We need to do some hosting and have the faculty members over. We need to have people enjoy this work." So we hosted a lot, and had a lot of brown bag lunches with faculty members. Those faculty members were wonderful people, and they would have supported anybody, but we felt a distance when we first arrived. Jeff was young. He was from the outside. He hadn't earned his spurs with the old-timers. So it was a challenge. But I remember Jeff saying, "This is a great assignment at a great university. Let's work on this." We invited faculty members to our home, and he spent a lot of time listening. He was blessed. A spirit of conviviality seemed to come. His personality was contagious. He loved them, and they knew it. However, two years after being named dean, the Church commissioner of education position became open when Elder Maxwell, then the commissioner, was asked to give his full time to General Authority assignments. Jeff was called by President Spencer W. Kimball to fill that position. We moved back to Salt Lake City.

Four years into this position, Jeff became the executive secretary of the General Authority search committee, chaired by Elder Gordon B. Hinckley. The committee was charged to find a new president for BYU when President Oaks retired. Jeff threw himself into the task, never thinking that his name was going to be submitted. After only three days of effort, he was called in by the First Presidency to make a report. He dutifully appeared and showed them the long list of names he had begun to compile. President Kimball, President Tanner, and President Romney looked at him, smiled, and then President Kimball said, "Very nice. This has been wonderful work, but we are calling you to be the president of BYU." Unbelieving, Jeff responded: "You're kidding!" President Kimball looked around the room and with everyone smiling said, "We don't do a lot of kidding in this room, President Holland."

I had mixed feelings about this call and what it would mean for our family. It was probably the happiest time in my life to that point. We had our first home in Bountiful, and my children were at wonderful ages. I was just learning how to be a homemaker. In fact, the day the call was extended I was making my first strawberry jam. Then I received this telephone call from Jeff. Interestingly enough, while he was working for the search committee looking for a new president, I had received my own spiritual promptings that he was going to be called to be the president of BYU. So I was not as surprised as he was, and that helped me a great deal. But when the call was extended, I thought, "Oh no. My children—we have moved them around so many times, and we finally have roots." We were out of school, we were living a normal life, and they were happy. They had friends—each of their equivalent ages—who lived up and down the same street. I thought, "I can't put them in that environment. I can't have them live in a fishbowl and have them live such an abnormal life."

I also had no idea what that would mean for me. I remember lying awake nights worrying about that. In fact, in one of our exchanges with the First Presidency, I had asked if we could live off campus, if there was a possibility that we could live in a normal neighborhood and live a normal life. They were very willing, but Jeff felt strongly that we should live in the president's home on campus. He knew it would be a challenge, but he thoroughly intended to be a "parent" to those students. He wanted them to know where we lived and that BYU was their home. While he thought our children would do well in this environment, it was a big anxiety for me. And then finally one day I just thought, "Well, your children are going to be your children no matter how you live or where you live. It's what you do inside the walls of your own home that's going to make the difference." We had a little chat with our family and said, "This is going to be a family experience. We will see it as a family calling. We are all to serve the Lord and represent the gospel and do our missionary work and do the best we can." They were willing and that was the approach we all took to this new assignment.

When Jeff was set apart, sweet President Kimball said to me, "I'm not going to set you apart for this calling, but I feel that you need a special blessing." He had a vision for women which came out in that blessing. It was really quite remarkable. While I don't remember the exact words, the sense was, "I bless you that you will have the energy and the desire to serve alongside your husband. You will give everything you can give to serving the University and to serving the Lord in this capacity." I took his blessing seriously. I felt that a prophet had asked me to do a certain work, and I believed that we do what prophets ask us to do.

It was a very humbling time for me. It was very frightening. I was extremely shy — I still am. One would think, after all those years at the University and in the Young Women General Presidency and everything else that I've done, I would have overcome my shyness. But it was a very humbling time for me. I also remember thinking, "If I go to the temple once a week and live the covenants I have made, there are promises that go with those covenants." Isaiah promises us that though "the mountains shall depart, and the hills be removed, . . . [his] kindness shall not depart from [us]" (Isa. 54:10). My greatest concern was my children: "Will I lose my children with all of this enormous responsibility? Will they resent it?" I remember reading Isaiah's promise that if you keep your covenants, your children will all be taught of the Lord, and great shall be the peace of your children (Isa. 54:13). I also remember getting up early and going to the wonderful Provo Temple and thinking, "If I am just true to these covenants, I will be worthy of those blessings." It was a humbling time for both of us.

I can now say with deep gratitude that for our children, it turned out to be one of the greatest things that ever happened to them. Whatever life you are asked to live, ultimately you are responsible for what you make of it. Early on we said, "We will concentrate on the good in this and make it a positive experience." My children tried to focus on the good. They had wonderful opportunities and privileges, and they learned so much. It truly was a blessing for us in every conceivable way. One of the things we do now as a family is talk about the many people whom we hosted in our home and the wonderful influence that they brought. I think of people like Madeleine L'Engle, who wrote wonderful children's literature, Alex Haley, and Chaim Potok, to name a few. And every year we hosted General Authorities. They brought a great spirit into our home and took a genuine interest in our children. It was a wonderful kind of exposure for our children to have dinner conversations with people like this. They have all said that since leaving — and now they are all experienced university students at other universities — they really miss the special spirit, the Spirit of the Lord, that was always a part of our life on the BYU campus.

Students also had a great influence in our children's lives. When they woke up Sunday mornings and saw thousands of young people dressed in their very best, carrying their scriptures, and looking happy, acting happy, bouncing across the campus toward a church meeting, they couldn't help but be influenced. And they couldn't miss seeing them.

I recall one person in particular who was influenced by the spirit of the University in a special way. He was a bus driver. It happened the night that we won an important NCAA tournament game when Danny Ainge made his last-second basket against Notre Dame. Our children were old enough that we had left them at home when we accompanied the team. We told BYU security that they were there. Security personnel were always good to drive around and keep an eye on the house. But that night a great horde of people came out of their apartments, out of the Marriott Center, out of the Wilkinson Center, out of everywhere. Towns-people came out of their nearby homes and congregated on the campus. They were celebrating, running everywhere on campus. Finally, they said, "Let's all go congratulate Jeff and Pat." So they all came over to the president's home. Our children were looking out the window, and they were absolutely terrified because there were four or five thousand people descending upon our home, climbing over the surrounding walls, and sending up Cougar cheers. But of course no harm came to our children, and no harm was done to our home.

The bus driver had brought some people to the University, and he had listened to the game. He was a member of another faith. He heard us win and then saw what happened on the campus, parked as he was in one of the parking lots. He was impressed that this huge body of students could have so much fun, and celebrate so joyously and buoyantly, but not cause any problems and not destroy anything. He was so impressed that when he returned to his home in Colorado, he called the Mormon missionaries and said, "I want to know more about the Church because of what I saw on the BYU campus." He joined the Church, and we later heard this story from him personally.

Jeff decided early on that the best thing that he could do for the University was to put the gospel at the "hub of the wheel" and make it a great university *because* of our gospel foundation, not in spite of it. What some over the years had seen as our disadvantage, he saw as our truest and greatest advantage. Our LDS values and doctrines, our unique, wonderful view of truth would make us a truly distinguished university. It was the University of The Church of Jesus Christ of Latter-day Saints. The Savior was central to Jeff's life, and he wanted the Savior, the Great Teacher, to be central to the University. So he worked very hard, we both did, at trying to keep that image before the University. I participated with Jeff as much as I could, which was something I wouldn't have done had it not been for the blessing and clarion call from President Kimball. President Kimball felt that way about his own wife. He felt very strongly that she should participate with him.

One thing Jeff felt strongly about was speaking directly to the students at the start of each semester. And he asked me to join him in that — again something of the parent image. Those devotional addresses wouldn't be possible, I think, at any other university, but at BYU they were always wonderfully well attended. I look back on those addresses as some of the most important my husband has ever given. Also, although it terrified me, I appreciated my chance to tell the students I loved them.

Most people don't know that Jeff taught a class every semester he was at BYU, usually a Book of Mormon class. He said it kept him close to the life of both faculty members and students. He loved it. It energized him. Most of the long-term, close student associations he had as president came from regular contact with those students in those classes.

He loved the time with his associates in the administration. Some of the most wonderful memories I have are the nights we all went to the temple together to start each semester. Then we would come back to the president's home for a bowl of soup and fresh cornbread, or some such snack. Those were wonderful nights, wonderful days. I am so sorry that not every university has a temple and gospel principles to unite it, to bind its president to the administrators and faculty and students. Jeff always said Provo is as Nauvoo was originally planned to be — an LDS community with a temple and a university at its center. A temple and a university! That was the ideal city of Zion for Joseph Smith, and it was the ideal city of Zion for Jeffrey Holland.

Of course two of my husband's most enduring, long-term contributions were made off campus — the building of the Jerusalem Center for Near Eastern Studies and the publication of the five-volume *Encyclopedia of Mormonism* by the Macmillan Publishing Company. No book could do justice to what Jeff went through getting the Jerusalem Center built, but someday perhaps that story will be told. From such threatening and difficult beginnings, it has become one of the must-see attractions in the Holy Land. And it has blessed thousands of students' lives. He loves that building and what it represents. To him it is an integral part of what BYU is saying to the world about Christ and the prophets. For all of its challenge, the success of the Center is one of the true joys of his BYU years.

The *Encyclopedia of Mormonism*, on the other hand, serves both Latter-day Saints and non–Latter-day Saints around the world. With a talented, devoted team of editors and literally hundreds of writers, this encyclopedia gave us a great chance — maybe our first real chance — to tell our own doctrine and history, rather than have someone else tell it. Its influence for the Church will go on for many years, and such a project could have been undertaken only at a university like BYU. In that sense it is like other unique BYU services, such as the Missionary Training Center. Without the University, its resources, and its personnel, many of these essential church services could not be provided — at least not on such a large scale. It really is the Lord's University in the sense that it is sustained by his tithing and directed by his prophets. His Spirit is there for those who are searching for it and looking for it. God's hand *is* over that university. He uses it. We see that now in the most profound ways.

While Jeff was president, the late King Hussein of Jordan invited us to visit him when he and others saw us doing so much in Israel. While we were there on one particular visit, we were able to secure a building in the name of the University for university work and for church services. While we couldn't meet as a church officially, we could hold our services if we didn't proselyte. There were perhaps four or five church members in Amman when this building was secured. In 1998 when we visited Amman again at the invitation of the government, my husband was now a member of the Quorum of the Twelve. We visited this little branch. There were over 130 people in attendance at a midweek fireside! They are sending out their own missionaries! We were also able to meet the then Crown Prince, His Majesty Prince Hassan, King Hussein's brother. Because of his interest in education, he was very cordial to us and listened to our view of the Church. He was very warm and wonderful. And he said on this last visit, "You can have anything you want, really. We won't let you come in and proselyte our Muslim people, but you can proselyte the Christian community. We'll recognize your church." Jeff said, "We are probably going to have to have some legal work done to formalize that." The Prince said, "Fine." He picked up the phone and called his legal officers. He then said, "We shall work with yours when you get back to the United States."

This could never have happened without Brigham Young University. In many ways, we would not have much influence in China if it were not for BYU entertaining groups and a host of faculty members going into China, building those relationships and showing the Chinese what the Church of Jesus Christ can do for their young people. The University is a major tool in the hands of the Lord in building the Kingdom of God.

When students and faculty members see the University the way it should be seen, as a tool in the hands of the Lord to teach the gospel and to build up the Kingdom of God, God sort of sets them apart, and they become ambassadors for the University. There is a special countenance given them, and a special ability, which make a big difference. That is *real* learning. I have been able to witness the work of such people literally by the hundreds; by the thousands, I guess. BYU will always be the Lord's University to me.

Yea, I tell thee, that thou mayest know that there is none else save God that knowest thy thoughts and the intents of thy heart (D&C 6:16).

Chance

Frank T. Rothaermel

Frank T. Rothaermel is a native of Butzbach, Germany. After high school, he completed a vocational training degree in wholesale and retailing and played semiprofessional hockey. At the point where he had to choose what he would do as his life's work, he left the hockey team, to the dismay of many, and continued study for undergraduate and master's degrees in economics and history at Duisburg, Germany. He studied for an academic year at Sheffield Hallam University in the United Kingdom before he entered the MBA program at BYU, where he met the Church. He has now completed his Ph.D. in strategic management and economics at the University of Washington. He is an assistant professor at the Eli Broad Graduate School of Management at Michigan State University. Dr. Rothaermel married Kelleyn Quinn in August 1997, and they are the parents of one child.

I was born and raised in the rural, small-town community of Butzbach, Germany, near Frankfurt. I grew up in the Protestant (Lutheran) faith. I remember my mother reading the scriptures to my sister and me at night when we were little. She used a Bible written for little children; I still clearly remember the brown linen cover with golden print. This service of love by my mother planted the seed in my heart which eventually developed into a knowledge that Jesus is the Christ. Since my earliest childhood I had a testimony of the divinity of Jesus Christ. Subsequently, in my youth I was quite active in our Protestant church. I recall that I could feel the Holy Ghost quite strongly at times. I indeed had a fairytale childhood, growing up in a loving home where my mother chose to be a homemaker and my father provided well for our family. However, this beautiful family life was interrupted by a sudden tragedy.

When I was thirteen years of age my father died unexpectedly. Suddenly, my mother was a young widow in her early thirties with two young children and a large mortgage on our home. The years to follow were the hardest of our lives. Unfortunately, my mother received little support from our extended family or from anyone else. Being a young boy, I could not fathom why this happened to us. I could not comprehend why God took my father and why we had to experience so much hardship. I loved my father very much, and I lost him at a time when a boy needs a father perhaps more than at any other time in his life. Subsequently, my interest in active church attendance waned. During the next few years, I attended church only at Christmas, often only to do my mother a favor. But in my heart I still believed in Christ.

After graduation from high school, I became more serious about life. I started to focus first on my sports career playing ice hockey in semiprofessional German leagues and later on my academic goals. At this time something interesting happened. The question "What is the purpose of life?" came into my mind and would not leave me. I even asked some of my closest friends what they thought the purpose of life was. However, their answers were not satisfying. I also felt that there had to be more to life than the life I had known or observed in the people around me. But I did not know what I was searching for.

Besides my career in ice hockey, I was enrolled at the Gerhard-Mercator University in Duisburg, Germany, to study business and economics. During my undergraduate studies, however, I focused more on my sports career than on academics. I was basically unable to attend any classes during the winter semesters since my team practiced twice a day, and we played about sixty games a season, often three games a week. During my four and a half years as an ice-hockey player, I was traded several times. During those years, I experienced the best and the worst of human behavior. Due to my focus on sports, I neglected my studies. But at age twenty-four, I decided to quit ice hockey in order to complete my undergraduate degree. This was one of the hardest decisions in my life, because I loved the sport and considered it to be in some way an inheritance from my father, since he had introduced the game to me. However, it was the correct choice, and I did very well in school. Subsequently, the dean of the school,

Professor Cassel, hired me as a research assistant. Through the opportunity to work for him, I started to discover my love for learning.

In the meantime, I had completed my undergraduate studies and enrolled in a master's program in economics and economic and social history at the same university. After a year as an exchange student in England, I returned to Germany with the intent to pursue an M.B.A. degree in the United States after completing my master's degree. I talked about my idea with Professor Cassel, my former mentor, and he was surprisingly supportive, given that I had just been gone for a year. He said he would talk to one of his friends. This friend, Professor Bryson, a professor at Brigham Young University, happened to be in Germany on a sabbatical. Within weeks after my return from England, Professor Bryson and I met in Duisburg to discuss my future academic plans. He was the first LDS member I ever knowingly met, which is not surprising in a country with eighty million inhabitants and only about thirty thousand Latter-day Saints. Professor Bryson conducted that interview very professionally and focused on academic matters only. However, I was very much touched by his spirituality and had a strong desire to know more about his church. Indeed, I asked him questions about the Church and the gospel and also asked for a copy of the Book of Mormon. A few weeks later, he presented me a copy in German and prefaced it with a beautiful dedication in German. Translated into English, parts of his dedication read: "Dear Herr Rothaermel! I'm delighted to have the privilege to present you with this book. It is the most important book in my life. I have read Keynes and Schumpeter once. However, I have read this book about fifty times. I know through better methods (Moroni 10:3–5) than the scientific method that this book is true and from God. If you follow the principles of this book, you will discover the true purpose of life." After reading that dedication, I opened the Book of Mormon for the first time and read the marked passage in Moroni 10. After reading that passage, I instantly felt in my heart that the Book of Mormon was true and that indeed it contained the word of God.

My meeting and further correspondence with Professor Bryson sparked such an interest in me about the restored gospel that I decided to apply to BYU for a master's in business administration (M.B.A.), not only to pursue an academic degree but also to continue and intensify my investigation of the Church. I had a strong academic record, and I would have been accepted into many different MBA programs throughout the United States. However, I was eager to study at a school which aspired to such honorable principles as does BYU. I had learned much about BYU by studying its catalogues, including the Honor Code in which some of the principles for which the school stands are explained. In reading the Honor Code, I was particularly impressed by the thirteenth Article of Faith: "We believe in being honest, true, chaste, benevolent, virtuous, and in doing good to all men. . . . If there is anything virtuous, lovely, or of good report or praiseworthy, we seek after these things." I even attended a night class in Germany conducted by a stake president. I felt a strong desire in my heart to study, live, and associate with people who aspired to such honorable goals and values. I wanted to be part of a community whose explicit goal for the individual member is to follow Christ and to strive to be one's best in all endeavors. During this time, I also started praying off and on.

Finally, I decided that I would apply only to BYU and reasoned that if the Lord wanted me to find out more about the restored gospel, I would be accepted. I was subsequently very excited to learn that I had been admitted into the highly competitive Marriott School of Management.

I came to BYU in August 1993 with a strong desire to learn more about the Church and the restored gospel, and with the personal resolution to live a better life. Friends picked me up from the airport in Salt Lake City when I first arrived. On our way to Provo we stopped at Temple Square. I was overwhelmed by the beauty of the buildings and by the beauty of the people serving at Temple Square. I felt at that moment a strong desire to be baptized and to become a member of the Church. I did not know why I felt that way, but today I feel that the Spirit had testified to me. I did not act upon this prompting, however.

At BYU I began to transform my life to one of applying gospel principles. But the extremely competitive environment in graduate school was completely new for me. In Germany, students are not graded on a curve but on absolute performance. One year, for example, five students in a class may receive an A and the next year no one would. Students are graded compared to an absolute ideal and not relative to one another. Therefore, the first few weeks in MBA school were very frustrating for me. Not only was I not sure whether I would measure up in the program, but also the very competitive atmosphere among students was intense. In addition, my living conditions in the dormitory were not ideal. Those were very stressful weeks for me. In general, coming to a foreign country to attend graduate school is always a challenge. However, I adjusted, and I started praying again regularly and reading the scriptures off and on.

Shortly after the semester started, the missionaries visited me with a professor of mine in the business school, Dr. Ned C. Hill, who himself had served his mission in Germany. I was very touched that he would take time out of his busy schedule to visit me with the missionaries in my dormitory room. That night, Dr. Hill and the missionaries bore powerful testimonies. At the end of the visit they asked me to offer a word of prayer. This was my first vocal prayer in more than twenty years, and I could feel the Holy Ghost very strongly.

In the meantime, I had also made good friends in the MBA program. Many of my friends were returned missionaries from Germany. Those friends truly fellowshipped me, which helped through the difficult adjustment period at the beginning of my stay at BYU. In addition, I found the cultural understanding prevalent at BYU amazing. Not only did quite a few of my fellow students and professors understand the culture and language of my home country, but the entire BYU campus was permeated by a cosmopolitan culture. As a student from outside the country, I found this to be very comforting.

With one of my very good friends I began attending church shortly after the semester started. On my first Sunday, I had such an incredible spiritual experience that I could not wait for the next Sunday to come. Sundays instantly became my favorite day of the week. In my heart, I had long before made the decision to be baptized, but in my mind I was reluctant to act on my promptings. I decided to put off my decision whether to be baptized until the Christmas break when I would have more time to think about it than during a crazy first semester in graduate school. I promised the missionaries to start taking the discussions then. However, Thanksgiving came around, and I became very ill. I was by myself in my dormitory room. On top of that, there were problems with the heating, and I felt very lonely and miserable. So I decided to purchase a ticket to fly home to Germany for Christmas rather than spend the time in Provo. I knew that I would be happy to be back home for Christmas. But I felt I would be betraying the missionaries because I had promised them that I would take the discussions in Provo over the Christmas break. I shared this dilemma with one of my good friends in the MBA program, and it so happened that his father was currently serving as the mission president of the Germany Frankfurt Mission. So he said to me, "No problem, I will talk to my father, and he will arrange the discussions for you in Germany." This friend was a very special friend to me during my time at BYU. He truly exemplified humility. It was not until much later that I got to know from someone else that he is the grandson of President Benson. He himself would never have mentioned it.

I took the discussions in Germany in the Frankfurt mission home as well as in my own home in Butzbach. My friend from the MBA program was also able to attend the discussions with me, since he was visiting his parents in Frankfurt over Christmas. I also had the opportunity to talk to my mother about my intended baptism while we were on a train ride back from Duisburg, where I had been awarded a prize by the university for my master's thesis. It was very difficult to tell my mother that I wanted to join the LDS Church. People in Germany do not know much about the Church, and parents often feel they have lost their children once they join. My mother was not happy, to say the least, as I shared with her my desire to be baptized. She was really worried about me, and she did not understand. As a matter of fact, when I invited her to attend my baptism, she said: "I have baptized you into the Protestant church, this now you must do on your own." Despite her unhappiness, I felt I needed to go forth with faith. I knew I needed to be baptized since I had felt the truthfulness of the restored gospel with all my heart. I could not deny this feeling.

I was baptized on the BYU campus in January of 1994. What a special day it was for me, and how grateful I was for the many friends who attended my baptism and who made me feel so special and loved! I had felt the Spirit off and on before my baptism. At my baptism I felt the Spirit more powerfully than ever before, particularly when I was confirmed a member of the Church and given the gift of the Holy Ghost.

Looking back, I realize that it was a tremendous blessing to be at BYU during the crucial time after my baptism. In few places in the world is it possible to partake of an education that combines spiritual and temporal learning. Not only did I have a great exposure to doctrine, but I could also observe strong LDS families and communities first hand. For example, one of my professors from the Marriott School of Management, Dr. Robert J. Parsons, basically adopted me as his son. In his home I saw and experienced the workings of a family who truly lives the gospel. Not only did my classmates and wonderful professors inspire me, but the devotionals and firesides where I had the chance to hear the inspired words of modern-day prophets particularly touched me.

It is impossible for me to name all the people who influenced me at BYU. However, I would like to express my gratitude for President Rex E. Lee. The first time I met him was shortly after my arrival at BYU as I attended a reception for a friend of mine. During the following two years, I saw him several times on campus. Even though his illness must have been extremely painful, he was always cheerful and said "Hi" to me every time he saw me. He truly exemplified the meaning of living a Christlike life. What a privilege it was for me to attend one of his last receptions at my graduation. President Lee gave me a big hug, a moment I shall never forget.

Professor Janet Howard nurtured me like a mother after I underwent two knee surgeries following a skiing accident. She truly taught me what selfless service means. I was also touched by the brief visit I had with President Bateman. Shortly after my own baptism, I was baptized by Dr. Parsons for my deceased father in the Provo Temple. There we ran into President Bateman. Brother Parsons introduced me to him. President Bateman took some time to talk with me and, when he asked where I was from, I replied "a small town near Frankfurt." He interrupted and asked, "Frankfort, Kentucky?" This was his way to compliment me on my English. All these outstanding individuals were role models for me, and even now I try to emulate them since they truly exhibited Christlike attributes.

Through constant repentance, fasting, prayer, searching the scriptures, and trying hard to keep the commandments, the Savior helped me to become a better person. He helped me to heal, to change my heart, and to be closer to him. Exactly one year after my baptism, I received my endowment in the Salt Lake Temple. This was a day I will never forget. I was fasting and was well prepared. I felt the Spirit stronger than ever before. As a pioneer in my family, I had no family member with me. Even so, it was a very joyful day for me. Later, I had the privilege to stand as proxy in an endowment ceremony for my deceased father. On that occasion in the temple, I felt I was able to communicate with him. I once again could feel how it felt when he hugged me when I was a little boy. This brought much joy to my heart. Subsequently, I did the genealogy for deceased members of my family and performed the temple work on their behalf—what a privilege!

Eventually, I completed my graduate work at BYU. Shortly after my graduation, I even had the chance to visit with President Gordon B. Hinckley for a short while. My family was visiting me for graduation, and the following Sunday my sister and I attended a sacrament meeting in the Joseph Smith Memorial Building near Temple Square. My family and I had just enjoyed the Mormon Tabernacle Choir. My sister, who is not a member, and I attended that sacrament meeting, which President Hinckley also attended. After the meeting, President Hinckley visited with several members of the congregation. I thought that this might be a good opportunity to shake the prophet's hand and have my sister do the same so that she might feel that President Hinckley is indeed a prophet of God. Graciously, he shook both of our hands. However, to my complete surprise he then began a conversation with me. Later I understood why. It was I who needed a stronger testimony of the divine calling of President Hinckley. What a highlight that was during my stay at BYU.

Before leaving BYU I spent the summer attending classes in the religion department. My goal was to get a thorough understanding of the Book of Mormon. Brothers Judd and Wilson both did an excellent job teaching the Book of Mormon. So after graduating from the MBA program I spent the summer studying the Book of Mormon for several hours each day. Not only did I receive a wonderful temporal education at BYU, but I found God at BYU and, through God, found myself. This is a priceless possession which I will cherish throughout eternity.

I marvel sometimes how these things came to pass. Why was I so lucky? I know that these things did not happen by chance. I know that the Savior's hand guided my search for happiness.

Y

How beautiful upon the mountains are the feet of those that bring glad tidings of good things (D&C 128:19).

At the Precipice

Madison U. Sowell

Madison U. Sowell is a professor of Italian and Comparative Literature at BYU and currently serves as the president of the Italy Milan Mission. He was born and reared in Piggott, Arkansas. He has published widely in his own discipline, in particular on Dante, and has also written for more general audiences, including for Church publications. Dr. Sowell has been active as a leader in the Rocky Mountain Medieval and Renaissance Association and has served as an editor of its journal. He was chair of the Department of French and Italian from 1989 to 1998, when he was called as mission president. He has also chaired the Faculty General Education Council and served on the University Strategic Planning and Self-Study Committee. He has received honors from colleagues and students alike for his teaching skills. Dr. Sowell and his wife, Debra, are the parents of two daughters.

I often reflect on the significance of archetypal images — potent symbols found in literature and life that deal with fundamental issues. These images can teach us much if we will engage them and ponder their personal significance. One of my favorite images is that of the mountain or hill, and I am hardly alone in this fondness. The ancient Greeks had numerous mountains that doubled as evocative symbols. Mount Olympus represented the pantheon of the gods, and Mount Parnassus, sacred to the nine muses, stood for artistic inspiration. The Bible's mountains and hills are legion and include Mount Sinai and Mount Zion in the Old Testament and the Mount of Olives and the Mount of Transfiguration in the New Testament. We could easily add to this impressive list the Hill of Calvary and the Hill Cumorah. Dante, aware of the tradition-steeped Greek mountains and sacred biblical mounts, envisioned Purgatory as a seven-storied mountain surrounded by a vast expanse of water. In most of these cases, mountains and hills symbolically link the earthly and the heavenly, the human and the divine, this world and the next. Reaching high into the sky, mountains, like the steeples on our churches and temples, naturally draw our minds heavenward toward God.

Not by chance I believe, BYU is nestled at the foot of mountains, in a liminal space befitting a Zion university, a sacred space where valley floor rises to abut mountain foothills. Above them, mountain peaks reach upward and can be seen from all angles of campus, epitomizing what can transpire at Brigham Young University. As a consequence, the BYU community naturally draws inspiration and strength from the majesty of the surrounding Wasatch Range. As one of our hymns exclaims in exultation, "For the strength of the hills we bless thee, / Our God, our fathers' God; / Thou hast made thy children mighty / By the touch of the mountain sod" (Hymn 35).

My affinity for mountains runs deep. The last photograph taken of my father and me was on a family trip to the Ozark Mountains in Arkansas one month before he was killed in a car accident. In the photo I am eight years old, and we stand next to each other on a lookout point. The mountain setting reminds me to this day of an idyllic time from long ago. And so it happened, almost from the day I set foot on the BYU campus in August 1970, as a freshman and LDS convert of fifteen months, that I aspired to climb Y Mountain. I yearned to hike all the way to the top and survey the valley's panorama. I found particularly intriguing a majestic evergreen, two-thirds of the way up the mountain and to the far left of the block Y, that appeared to have two tops. I made one half-hearted attempt to reach the mysterious tree with freshmen dormmates George and Gene in the winter semester, but we started too late in the day and ended up spending the night about halfway up, huddled around a meager campfire and warding off a wild animal that smelled our food and approached in the dead of the night. Eventually it became so cold that George and I zipped our sleeping bags together for additional warmth, while the more corpulent Gene snoozed unaffected by the cold. The next morning we were too enervated and chilled to continue, and so we returned to Helaman Halls without accomplishing our goal.

In the summer term following my freshman year I had another roommate, Scott. I had received a mission call to the Italy North Mission, and he had become engaged to marry. I was to leave on my mission in September, the same month of his wedding. Jointly we decided it would be fun to have our very own bachelor party one summer afternoon by climbing Y Mountain. He got off work at noon. We had a quick lunch, packed snacks and cream soda (but nothing so mundane as water), bid adieu to his somewhat lachrymose fiancée, and took off with determination to conquer the mountain. Before we left we offered a routine prayer for the Lord's protection and a safe return. His fiancée was nervous about our proposed hike, but we confidently assured her that we would be fine and would return before dark.

The trek up the mountain was hotter and more arduous than we had expected, but we persevered with the dogged determination of teenagers. Once through the scrub oaks that dotted the lower mountainside, we set our sights for the mysterious, twin-topped tree. When we finally reached it, we discovered that it was actually two pines growing together. Previous hikers had left a glass vial with a stopper hanging from one of the branches. Inside were messages written for those who came afterwards. Scott and I composed a few light-hearted verses of encouragement, neither of us fathoming that — but for the hand of God — those could have been the last written record we ever left behind. We briefly surveyed the valley floor. It was mid-afternoon, and the sun was well past its zenith but still fairly high in the sky. Surely there was time to make it to the top well before sundown.

Without pausing to eat, we scampered toward the top third of the mountain, which we found to be full of cliffs and rocks and much more challenging. This was not so much hiking as rock climbing. Being without ropes and mountain-climbing equipment and lacking expertise in scaling cliffs, we decided it would be prudent to take as few risks as possible. Besides, Scott and I had, respectively, a marriage and a mission to look forward to. We had full lives that we wanted to live, books to read, foreign lands to discover. This bachelors' hike was intended as a divertissement, a light interlude before far weightier matters began to complicate our lives. We looked for paths around and crevices through the rocks, and eventually with no little effort we found and navigated them.

The view from the mountaintop proved to be spectacular. The sun was starting to set, and its rays glistened on a shimmering Utah Lake. A mountain breeze refreshed us. The air was clean. We sat down on a smooth slab and were astonished to see fossilized seashells and seahorses encased in the rock beneath us. We were sitting thousands of feet high on what was once an ocean floor. The thought of water made us realize that we were incredibly thirsty, almost dehydrated. Scott pulled out the two cream sodas which had been well-shaken in his backpack on the half-day trip up the mountain. As he opened his, the pressure was so great that the can fairly exploded and a bubbling soda splattered over his face and hands. He was drenched with a sweet stickiness, and drinking the hot soda only seemed to make him thirstier. I guffawed and promptly recreated the cream soda experience for myself by opening my pressurized can. Surely this was the good life, laughing at our silliness and enjoying the beauties of nature.

Scott and I gazed at God's handiwork and talked of the coming changes in our lives. What effect would a mission have on me? How would marriage change him? Where would we each be in one year's time? We chatted and watched the sun sink lower. The buildings on the BYU campus that loomed so large from the ground were minuscule from where we sat. It seemed such a shame to leave this perch, high above all our earthly cares, far from the pressures of the exams that soon would be upon us. We decided to have another prayer before making our descent. This prayer was much more heartfelt and sincere; it was a prayer of gratitude. We were grateful for our friendship, for the restored Church, for our Savior, for our families, for this experience. The prayer concluded, we took in Utah Valley at dusk. Lights were beginning to come on, creating a new effect, but it was still light enough to see easily the way down the mountain. We reasoned that it would take us very little time to make the descent in the waning light of day. But then one of us suggested that we take an alternate route home, down the back side of the mountain into the breathtakingly beautiful Rock Canyon. It would be so much more picturesque. We gazed at Squaw Peak and contemplated studying the layers of sedimentary rock on the opposing wall of the canyon as we descended. It seemed like such a great idea, and we had few clues as to what lay ahead of us.

The descent went rapidly at first, but we were surprised at how much darker it was on the northeastern side of Y Mountain. The setting rays of the sun did not penetrate here, and it was quite shady. At first I was in the lead. Gradually I began to slow down my pace, proceeding rather prudently, and then Scott suggested that he take us down at a faster pace. Otherwise we might be stuck in the dark on the mountain all night. I became uneasy as I realized that I could no longer see well in the shadows and really had slowed down my pace considerably. I placed my hand on a low bush to steady myself and was unnerved when a bird flew out without warning. Even faster than our descent was the descent of eventide. In a matter of minutes twilight became night. Then it was pitch dark, and there was no moon yet in sight. The little flashlight we had brought got weaker and weaker until finally it was of no use and was turned off to allow us to use both hands to scoot down the rocky mountainside. We kept going, but at an ever slower pace. Suddenly Scott stopped and said he had a feeling that we should catch our breath.

By this point I could not see even two feet in front of me, nor could he. I knew he was there because I could hear him speaking. We could tell that we were on a steep incline that appeared to be a rock slide. Scott felt around and found a fairly large rock to sit on. He plopped down on it, and it came loose and slipped out from under him. To this day I can remember the sound of that rock as it slid and scraped against the rocks on the ground for a yard or so. Then, strangely, the scraping sound stopped; there was an abrupt and eerie silence, followed by the distant sound of the rock crashing against other rocks many, many yards below. We had descended to the very edge of a steep cliff. We both picked up pebbles and threw them in front of us. Once again, silence was followed by the faint sound of our pebbles striking other rocks quite a distance below us. Had we not stopped when we did, it would have been our bodies crashing at the base of the cliff. Scott's impression to halt our descent had been inspired. We trembled as we contemplated what would have happened had we pressed forward with the foolhardiness that had characterized much of our day together.

I sat down and, feeling my way with my hand, carefully edged myself to the left. I felt a perpendicular wall of solid rock. Behind us was the steep slope we had just come down. Scott edged himself to the right and encountered a thick outcropping of scrub oak, seemingly impenetrable. It appeared that we were on a sloping ledge that led to a dramatic precipice. Exhausted and shaken, neither of us had the desire to crawl back up the mountain.

Adrenalin was flowing through our veins, making us sweat, but we were also being chilled by the night air. What were we to do? We huddled together and concluded that it was time to offer a third prayer, but this one with "sincere heart, with real intent" (Moroni 10:4). And so two nineteen-year-old BYU students knelt in the dark, on the edge of an abyss, and poured out their hearts to God, seeking forgiveness for foolishness and inspiration as to how to get out of this self-created predicament. We each prayed in turn. Then we waited. We waited and listened for a response. We had faith that it would come. We saw God's hand in stopping us before disaster had struck. We knew we had missions to accomplish before we died.

God answers prayers and gives revelations in diverse ways. He has done so via theophanies, appearing personally to Moses and Joseph Smith; he has done so via angels and heavenly messengers, such as Gabriel and Moroni; he has done so through an audible voice and by writing with his finger; he has done so through the instrumentality of other persons. But most often it is through "a small voice," a distinct and comforting impression that when followed leads to a stronger confirmation of his will. And so it was on that dark night. We both felt impressed to turn right and head into the scrub oak, Scott leading and I holding on to his belt to try to prevent him from falling. We tried the flashlight again and were amazed and delighted to discover that the battery seemed to have been recharged; the light shone more brightly than before. Deeply sobered and profoundly grateful, we proceeded cautiously and prayerfully. Before long we made it to the floor of the canyon, and within an hour or so we were back in our dorm room, eager to offer further prayers of gratitude.

In the intervening thirty years, I have reflected often on the power of prayer and how essential it is that we learn to pray with sincerity and specificity. I felt then, as I do now, that "in nothing doth man offend God, or against none is his wrath kindled, save those who confess not his hand in all things, and obey not his commandments" (D&C 59:21). I have also often reflected on the almost unique juxtaposition of Y Mountain and BYU that creates an environment wherein a couple of college freshman who found themselves in difficulty, even if of their own making, would turn to their Father in Heaven in prayer for assistance. Scott now serves as a bishop in a ward in the eastern United States. I now serve in an overseas missionary assignment. Both of us live far from Y Mountain, and almost three decades separate us from that night when we learned to find God through heartfelt prayer. Yet we still draw on that experience every time we listen to the still, small voice, whether we are counseling ward members or exhorting missionaries to press forward with faith. It was a sacred moment for us, and it illustrates the need we all have to climb every mountain that life presents us and to learn from every experience, bitter or sweet.

Mountains can symbolize either adventure or adversity, a goal to reach or an obstacle to overcome. Ideally, our encounters with life's mountains provide catalysts for change. For me, both as a student and as a professor, learning to progress and evolve is what a Zion education is all about. Y Mountain always reminds me of that verity, and so I am grateful for BYU's location and the direction it points me — upward toward God.

Throughout my adult years I have attempted to put into practice what I discovered that dark, prayerful night as I descended into Rock Canyon. The lesson learned about the necessity of calling on God for illumination, if we would be saved, has rescued me and others from more than one peril at key junctures in my personal, professional, and ecclesiastical life. Sometimes the dangers I have faced were hidden perils; at other times the dangers were not so much my own as those of others with whom I worked. I should like to illustrate, with a trio of vignettes, that prayer and attention to the Spirit can help one conquer any mountain and navigate around any cliff.

As a returned missionary facing graduation from BYU, I consulted with trusted mentors, analyzed pros and cons, and then prayed sincerely and specifically for guidance as to which graduate school I should attend. I had received flattering offers from a few universities that would have paid me generously to attend and enroll in their doctoral programs. I also had been accepted to a graduate program at another well-established school, but without any offer of financial aid for the first two years. All the programs were academically solid, had distinguished libraries, and appeared comparable in terms of placing their graduates. Given the increasingly poor job market for new Ph.D. graduates in foreign language and literature that characterized the late 1970s, finance-based logic strongly suggested avoiding the costliness of a private university. After much pondering, however, the undeniable impressions of the Spirit were that I should attend the costly private school whose department had a policy against offering teaching assistantships to beginning graduate students.

From my limited perspective, the danger was that of paying for an expensive program and then not finding an academic post upon completion of my Ph.D.; i.e., going to school for years, falling into debt, and then being without a job in my field. Nevertheless, based on the clear answer to my prayers about how to proceed, I took a leap of faith and turned down the offers from the other schools. Almost immediately miracles began to happen to confirm the rightness of my decision. A relative who had come into an inheritance sent me an unsolicited check that covered much of the first year's tuition. Soon after arriving on the campus where I was to study, I was invited by an elderly retired professor and his wife to live with them; they set rent at only a dollar per day, including utilities, in exchange for the assurance that if they needed anyone in the middle of the night they could call on me. Because their house was across from the LDS chapel and only a few minutes from campus, I did not need a car and could forego that expense. And so it went, with similar miracles each year I was in graduate school. When I graduated, I had not accumulated a penny of educational debt. I had climbed another mountain; the trick now was to get down without falling off.

As the decade of the 1970s drew to a close, the academic job market worsened. When it came time to apply for a teaching job, I found that positions were few and far between. But what had also happened was that in this worsening market for job candidates, degrees from my school were relatively more desirable: colleges and universities that were hiring were favoring, all other things being equal, job candidates from the long-established institutions. And so I ended up with more than one enticing professorial post being offered me. I came to realize that the danger I had faced upon graduating from BYU — the hidden precipice I had not seen — really had not been that of going into debt by attending an expensive school and then failing to obtain a job, but rather that of selecting an ostensibly comparable graduate program that in the end would have shortchanged me in a quickly evolving and highly discriminating job market. Listening to the quiet voice of the Spirit had paid, once again, an important dividend.

This brings me to my next vignette. Once established at BYU, I developed a pleasant and satisfying association with the Honor Code Office. In fact, one of the reasons I elected to teach at BYU was because of the code of conduct to which students subscribed, including the dress and grooming standards. I served as the first faculty mentor to the Honor Code Council, made up of students, and for many years I have included a statement supporting the Honor Code and dress and grooming standards in my course syllabi. Most students appreciate my staunch and enthusiastic support of the code and the standards, but occasionally I have encountered a student who did not share my enthusiasm. A returned missionary whom I will call Jim was one who fell into the latter category.

Jim came from a family whose parents were divorced and whose father was not LDS. He had served a two-year mission but had been plagued with health problems. He carried a chip on his shoulder. Tall and smartly dressed, he appeared in my Italian class on the first day of the semester with his handsome brown hair cascading over his ears and shirt collar. I did not say anything to him personally about the grooming standards, but I made a point of sharing a statement about how I expected all my students to be persons of integrity and to maintain their agreements to abide by the University's dress and grooming standards. In the past I had found that this was usually enough to correct most problems. At the next class period, however, I saw that Jim's hair was uncut. When the class ended, I spoke with him briefly and informed him cordially that he needed to get a haircut in order to be in compliance with the University standards. He did not take my comment well. The next time he came with his hair brushed and combed in such a way that it was not as obvious that he was still violating the grooming standards; nevertheless I knew that he was not being compliant, and he knew that I knew. Unaccustomed to outright defiance, I decided to invite Jim to see me in my office.

Our interview was not an easy one for either of us. He was as determined to keep his hair at the length he deemed fashionable as I was to see him conform to BYU standards. After a number of chats before and after class, in the corridors, and in my office, and without any notable success on my part in convincing him that a person of integrity would abide by what he had promised to do when he applied to BYU, I reported Jim to the Honor Code Office. He was summoned to appear before a counselor and was told to cut his hair or withdraw from the University. He cut his hair. His sulking presence in class the next day made a negative impression on all present. He glared at me, he smirked at me, and he made it clear that he was not happy. Nevertheless he remained in the class, completed his assignments, and received a passing grade.

Although Jim did not take any other class from me, our paths crossed frequently in subsequent semesters because of the particular part-time campus job he had. Like Samson, he grew his hair longer and longer. I would remind him of his Honor Code commitments when I would see him. He would not do anything about his hair. I would report him to the Honor Code Office. He would receive another ultimatum and then cut his hair. This scenario repeated itself more times than I care to remember. Several years passed and Jim graduated from BYU and found employment in Utah County. I lost direct contact with him.

One night just before 10 P.M., my home phone rang. The voice on the other end said, "This is Jim. I need help. I am surrounded by darkness." At first I did not know who it was because of the commonness of his name, but then it dawned that it was my former student. He had been deeply depressed and had not eaten for a couple of days. He was too weak to drive his car. I asked him where he was and told him I would retrieve him. I brought him home, and my wife prepared a simple meal for him and then left us alone to talk. Metaphorically speaking, he had been crawling down the backside of his own mountain in the darkness of bad choices. After breaking up with his girlfriend, he had stopped just short of a gaping abyss. He feared falling or throwing himself into the black hole, but he did not know how to get out of the dangerous predicament in which he found himself. He asked me to help him. I asked why he had called me, the professor who had repeatedly reported him to the Honor Code Office. He looked at me and stated simply, "I always knew that you cared."

By chance, the bishop of the young adult ward in whose boundaries Jim was living was a campus colleague and my trusted friend. I introduced them, and my former student began the long road back to full activity in the Church. One of the happiest days of my teaching career occurred over a year later when Jim asked me to accompany him to the temple, his first time back in five years. As we sat in the celestial room of the Provo Temple, not far from the mouth of Rock Canyon, I felt the sweet spirit of the Holy Ghost — the same Comforter that I had felt many years before when my roommate and I had paused to pray while facing our own precipice.

The final story I share involves my experience as bishop of a BYU off-campus ward and illustrates perhaps most pointedly what I learned about our need to seek direction from God, not only for ourselves but also for those for whom we have stewardship responsibilities. For four years I served simultaneously as both a bishop and a BYU department chair. In this dual role I interacted closely with hundreds of students, as a minister and as an administrator. Many times students and ward members who came to see me would sit in a chair in my office directly in front of a large window that looked out on Y Mountain. I would look at them, listen to their problems or concerns, and then gaze beyond them to the mountain I had climbed many years before.

December always brought the largest number of students to my office. During the day I had students petitioning for various matters, and at night I had ward members coming in for tithing settlement. Time at home became rarer and more precious. One late wintry afternoon, after tithing settlement had ended for the year and final exams had been graded, I found myself hurrying to finish my last bit of paperwork so I could go home and be with my family. The sun was casting its setting rays on Y Mountain. I was nurturing a prayer in my heart that my ward members would make it home safely for the holidays. By then, all should have left for Christmas break. Suddenly a clear impression of the Spirit came that I should drive through my ward boundaries *south* of campus before heading *north* of campus to my home. I dismissed the thought for two reasons: first, I wanted to be home with my family; second, it was likely that none of my ward members would be in the apartment area south of campus which lay within my ward. The impression came a second time, and I brushed it off as I packed my briefcase. When the words "Go to your ward boundaries" lodged in my mind a third time, I decided to obey.

I drove through the block containing my ward but did not see anyone outside or inside the apartments. My first thought was, "Why did I come?" The answer came, "Park the car and get out." I did and walked around the parking lot in the middle of a block of houses and apartment buildings. I surveyed the scene once more and was preparing to leave when I noticed a light inside an apartment on the top floor of one of the buildings. I felt drawn to the light even though I could not remember who lived in that particular apartment. I knocked on the door, and a middle-aged woman whom I did not recognize opened the door. I introduced myself as Bishop Sowell, and she seemed startled—almost as if she were seeing a ghost. She turned around and emotionally exclaimed to her daughter, a young woman whom I recognized as a non-BYU student living in my ward, "It's your bishop!"

I was ushered in, and soon I knew why I had been so strongly impressed to drive south rather than north and seek them out. The student was pregnant out of wedlock and had informed her heartbroken mother who was praying fervently for help. The daughter was deciding what to do about the pregnancy, and the mother—a faithful LDS woman—was desperate for her child to make the right decision, perhaps the most important of her life. The mother told me, "I had just asked my daughter whom she trusted to advise her, and then you knocked on the door. Bishop, thank you for coming at this precise moment." Deeply humbled, I sat down and lovingly counseled the daughter. Because my wife and I have adopted a child, I was able to bear personal testimony of the rightness of placing a child for adoption when the biological parents do not or cannot marry. I also explained the repentance process and the way back to God. Because of my miraculous appearance at just the right time, the daughter was more receptive to counsel. In the end, she chose to give birth to the child and placed the baby for adoption with a worthy LDS couple. The young woman had stumbled to the edge of a precipice, but she did not fall into the abyss.

As I left the student apartment, I discovered that night had fallen. Soon the moon would rise and shine on a snow-covered Y Mountain. While driving home, I expressed a prayer of gratitude in my heart. The lesson I had learned as a BYU freshman almost three decades previously about prayer and our need to follow the dictates of the Spirit had once again born fruit and, in this case, saved someone else.

Y

O Lord, thou hast searched me, and known me. Thou knowest my downsitting and mine uprising, thou understandest my thought afar off. Thou compassest my path and my lying down, and art acquainted with all my ways (Psalms 139:1–3).

Hard Choices

Steve Clements

Steve Clements was born in Houston, Texas, and reared in Huntsville, Texas, where he had a stellar high school football career and was named to the Parade All-America team in 1989. He also became the 1989 Gatorade player of the year for Texas. Between 1986 and 1989 he set the record for the most passing yards in a high school career in Texas with 8,204 yards. He attended the University of Texas at Austin and then Brigham Young University, where he graduated with a bachelor of science degree in special education in 1995. He is married to Emily Stevens, and they have one daughter. They live in Lehi, Utah, where Mr. Clements is a resource teacher and head football coach at Lehi High School.

Choices are made everyday by people. A young child decides whether to eat a cookie after being told not to touch the cookie jar. A teenager decides whether to join a gang, smoke, or drink alcohol. A young man or woman tries to determine what the meaning of life is. This story is about the choice that I made to attend Brigham Young University and how my choice to come to Provo was instrumental in my quest to discover a whole new life.

My first experience with the city of Provo, Utah, came in the summer of 1986. As a youth, I had competed in the high jump event of track and field and had done very well. I was invited to Provo, where the national youth finals were held for all track and field participants. As I later reflected back on that weekend, a few things struck me as different. First, I noticed few minorities. Coming from the South, this was a new scene for me. Second, while driving through town I realized that there were no large buildings. Because I lived only seventy miles from the fourth largest city in the United States (Houston), this too was different, almost weird.

As I progressed through my teenage years, my development as a high school quarterback began to attract the attention of college football recruiters across the nation. By then, I was a student at Huntsville High School in Huntsville, Texas. During my junior year I began to receive letters from various colleges expressing interest in my attending school on a football scholarship. Letters came from UCLA, the University of Alabama, the University of Miami, the University of Texas, Louisiana State University, and Brigham Young University, to name a few. My choices began to narrow during my senior year. I compiled my "top five" list, seeing that an athlete could receive only five paid recruiting trips to colleges interested in the athlete's services. These schools were Alabama, UCLA, LSU, Texas, and BYU.

Why these schools? My early choice of Alabama stemmed from two things: a conversation between a coach and my father, who was my high school coach, and an Alabama football game that I attended. After watching me play in a game during my junior year, Homer Smith, then the offensive coordinator at Alabama, told my father that I was one of the best high school quarterbacks he had seen. The football game I attended was the 1989 Sugar Bowl, where Alabama shocked football fans by beating the highly favored Miami Hurricanes. I was impressed.

UCLA was tops on my list because of its high-profile status. Who wouldn't want to experience summer nine months out of the year? And then there was the enticement of Hollywood and Beverly Hills, and of seeing one's favorite movie stars, in person!

Louisiana State University caught my eye because its games were on television in my area, and I had the thrill of walking inside its stadium when I was a junior. The television announcers would always comment on the diehard character of the fans. And there seemed to be only one time when all eighty-five thousand people were not cheering for the Tigers — halftime. That made my heart beat a little bit quicker.

I was, however, pretty partial to the University of Texas, for good reason. My father had played quarterback there from 1954 to 1958. My mother was the first female head cheerleader at the University. My brother had graduated from there with a bachelor's degree in liberal arts. My grandmother was an active member in many organizations at the University, and her husband was elected into the Hall of Honor as a baseball coach. In addition, uncles, aunts, and three cousins had attended and graduated from the University of Texas. No pressure, right?

I included Brigham Young University on this list as well, in large part because of the national championship that the team had won in 1984. Not only did that honor put the university on the football map, but it brought a lot of attention to the quarterback position, which I was extremely interested in because I had aspirations of becoming a quarterback in the National Football League. I knew that BYU liked to pass the football. Hence, the quarterback became the most famous person on campus. I wondered what it would be like to be the next Jim McMahon or Steve Young. That was enticing to me.

My decision to attend the University of Texas at Austin was not the toughest choice I have had to make in my life, but leaving was. I had come to UT on the assumption that I would have an opportunity to contribute as an underclassman. I redshirted my first year (1990–91) but played well in spring practices. It looked promising for me, or so I thought. But not only had the coaches placed me third on the depth chart, they seemed to be not keeping their promise to change the team's offense in ways that would optimize my skills. The University of Texas was traditionally a run-oriented football team but "was going to throw the ball a lot more," as a coach from the University had told me during the recruiting process.

After discussing with my parents my frustrations and intention to further my career at another college, I decided to transfer to Brigham Young University. I wanted to pursue my dream of becoming a quarterback in the NFL, and BYU was now the avenue to get me there. My education would be paid for, and as athletes believed, all universities allowed athletes a little more leniency in the matter of grades than the general student population. So I was not worried about that aspect of college. I wanted to play football, period.

My knowledge of BYU was actually quite shallow. Through the grapevine, I knew Mormons to be "weird." The Honor Code was an absolute shock. Although it was discussed while I was being recruited by BYU, I did not take it seriously, nor did I believe it to be viable. Jim McMahon had somehow found a way to stay eligible and get through school. Why couldn't someone from a small town in Texas do the same thing?

Once on campus, I sought out those with whom I had the most in common, and they became my friends. Although I had many LDS and non-LDS friends, my closest friends were non-members or members who thought the Honor Code to be a joke and did not adhere to its principles. The closer I grew to those friends, the more resentful I became toward members of the LDS Church. In a way, I began to persecute the Church. For instance, my friends and I used to discuss why people, especially in poverty-stricken countries, joined the Church. We concluded that those people joined because of the Church's welfare program. I believed that some people joined the Church for the sole purpose of being helped; it was not because of what they believed, but because they wanted things handed to them.

One day a friend and I were driving along Ninth East in Provo, which runs on the east side of campus. As we passed the playing fields east of the Harmon Building we yelled, "Hurry, run away, they're brainwashing you! Get out while you still have a chance!" I even used to carry a Bible into the training room of the Smith Fieldhouse because I wanted to "show" people that I was not a Mormon.

Other things angered me. First, I found it difficult to believe that a university would require every student, LDS or not, to take religion classes. I believed this to be ludicrous because I felt BYU forcing me to learn a religion I did not believe in. Second, most of the students assumed that you were LDS. Of course, the odds were in their favor since 98.6 percent of the students at the time were members. This still upset me, though. Two employees at BYU, however, began to alter my way of thinking by their examples and their behavior toward me.

Brother Alan Parrish taught a religion class exclusively for non–Latter-day Saints, which introduced Mormonism and its roots. I was not at all interested in anything he had to say concerning the Church, but he taught it in a way that was not offensive to me. As I continued to go to class and listen to the things Brother Parrish had to say, I began to gain respect for him. It was not the substance but the approach. He was careful not to step on anyone's toes. I sensed that he truly believed in what he was teaching, and his passion for it drew me to him. However, my testimony was not triggered until the second semester of my sophomore year.

I enrolled in a class on the Book of Mormon. Again, Brother Parrish was the teacher. (By this time I decided to enroll only in religion classes that he taught, if possible.) As a class we examined two people and their stories that led me to start asking questions of myself. In the class, we began with the history of the Book of Mormon and progressed into the book of Alma. As was my custom in most classes, especially religion classes, I sat in one of the desks closest to the door. This allowed me to be the first one to leave class when the bell rang. I did not want to converse with anyone and mill around after classes talking to students not of my faith. (I was Presbyterian, but inactive.)

Part of the purpose of the class was to discuss the history of the Book of Mormon, which included the story of Joseph Smith. As we studied, those in the class — excluding me — discussed this amazing story. Surprisingly, I started to think about the subject of angels and scripture translation. As Brother Parrish presented the material in his clear-cut manner, the one thought that bore down upon me and, in my opinion, defines The Church of Jesus Christ of Latter-day Saints was, "Either Joseph Smith translated the Book of Mormon, or he didn't." The more I wondered and thought about this event, the more I believed it to be true. Of course this dawning was deeply personal, and I kept it to myself. My testimony had begun. Small, yes, but a start nonetheless.

Probably the most influential character in the Book of Mormon for me was, and continues to be, King Benjamin. He is first introduced in the book of Omni, but the record of his works is more complete in the book of Mosiah. It was during the discussions of King Benjamin's reign that I began to understand and appreciate what this man had done for others. King Benjamin taught the true importance of charity and service. This is best illustrated in Mosiah 2:17: "When ye are in the service of your fellow beings ye are only in the service of your God." This was and to this day still is my favorite scripture. I was fortunate to have Brother Parrish to open my eyes, so to speak. Although I tried not to hear what was said, I was subconsciously listening.

During my years at BYU, I became very fond of Sherry Nielsen, the secretary in the athletic training room of the Smith Fieldhouse. I would compare her to a den mother in that I think she was a second mother to most of the student-athletes. In my case, she was no exception. Not only did I see her on a daily basis, but I learned that she dealt with others unconditionally. She treated everyone the same. We were all on an even playing field in her eyes. Sherry was genuine to all: black, white, LDS, or not. She allowed me to vent my frustrations, and I did so often. Sherry would listen patiently and then give me sound advice. Whether it was my lack of playing time on the football team or the issue of dating, Sherry always knew the right thing to say. What impressed me most about her, and aided in my investigation of the Church my senior year, was that she never pushed the Church on me. Sherry never said, "Why don't you take the discussions from the missionaries and just see what you think?" or "Why don't you read a little bit of the Book of Mormon and form an opinion?" She never pushed, prodded, forced, or coerced. She just listened and responded with genuine interest. For those attributes and qualities I am truly grateful for Sherry Nielsen.

During my sophomore year I received firsthand knowledge of what a priesthood blessing was. I had dislocated my shoulder in a game against the University of Hawaii and was preparing to undergo surgery in a few days. Unbeknownst to me, LaVell Edwards, the head football coach, received a telephone call from my mother. Someone had told her that blessings from a priesthood member in the LDS Church could be given to those in need, and she asked Coach Edwards if he would mind giving me one. Coach Edwards did give a blessing to me with the help of Mike King, the associate to the athletic director. My shoulder surgery was a success, and I felt that my shoulder was stronger after the surgery than it had been before I was injured. This event only added to the small testimony I had.

At this point, I probably had more of a testimony than some have when they join the Church. But I was not about to act on it. There were too many influences pushing me in other directions. My friends in Texas already thought I was nuts for going to Provo, Utah, to attend college. What would they think if I was baptized? No thank you. More importantly, what would my family think? Again, I'd pass.

All this changed during the summer before my senior year. Every summer I went back home to work and be with my friends and family. This summer was an exception. I needed a few more credits if I was to graduate on time. Staying in Provo was the best decision that I had made.

While I was taking summer classes I also worked for NuSkin at a warehouse in south Provo. My title was Assembly Line Supervisor. Each supervisor was in charge of a table at which there were approximately six workers. The supervisors were to oversee the quality of products that employees produced at each table. Most employees were temporaries who wanted to work only three to six months. I noticed a young woman, Emily Stevens, and was immediately attracted to her. But one thing was wrong: she was a Mormon. It was during our third date that I realized I wanted a more serious relationship. We had begun to date one another exclusively through the summer.

After finishing the needed classes, I went home for six weeks where my biggest challenge awaited. My mother had heard plenty of negative things about the LDS Church, and she was worried about her son, who was dating a Church member. Shortly before I returned to Provo, she showed me a video entitled *The Godmakers*. This video was produced by persons attempting to discredit the beliefs, principles, and members of the Church. In short, the portrait of the Church illustrated in the video consisted of half-truths. This video had a great impact on me because it "packed a lot of punch." It raised many disturbing questions in my mind and put me in a predicament. What was I supposed to believe? This video or the good examples demonstrated by my girlfriend's family?

My experience with her family was, and still is, tremendously influential. They had convinced me that a person did not need to swear to get a point across or blame someone else for one's downfalls. Prayer is vital. Communication should be the backbone of a relationship. Serving others helps not only those in need but aids in one's growth, mentally and spiritually. All these things began to dawn on me then, and this family has continued to have an impact on my life. The more I spent time with them the more I saw the fallacies created by the anti-Mormon group that produced the video. The things portrayed there were false and without merit. As we learn in 2 Nephi 2, there is opposition in all things, even to what is good and true. Through this family I had learned about the temple, baptisms for the dead, family prayer, and many other gospel principles.

I finally told Emily that after the football season I would take the discussions from the missionaries. Luckily for me, I did not say exactly how soon after the season. Apprehension began to set in, and I procrastinated. But Emily's impatience overcame both my apprehension and my procrastination, and I started taking the discussions in January of 1995.

The missionary lessons were an educational experience, but that was about it. I was in love and wanted to marry Emily soon. Nobody was going to stop me. But I had to face the reality of becoming a Latter-day Saint. It was something that seemed inevitable. I understood this from the many discussions Emily and I had during our courtship. She would not have it any other way. I was baptized on 26 February 1995.

That morning, around 6:30 A.M., I received a telephone call from a former bishop who had been excommunicated from the Church. My mother had asked him to call me. The purpose of the call was to warn me of the hardships that I would face if I was baptized. Because he woke me up, I was half asleep. I patiently listened, placed the phone down after he had finished, and went back to sleep. Closing my eyes, though, did not bring closure to the phone call. When I awakened, the message was still there, "Don't do it! You don't know what you're getting yourself into!" I began to have a little doubt as to what I was doing. Did I really know what I was getting myself into? And then I remembered what the missionaries had told me during our discussions. They had said, "There is opposition in all things that are right and true." I felt that this was the very circumstance that they had described. I was baptized.

I know I was probably baptized for the wrong reason, but what a blessing it has been! Understanding temple work, I can now be baptized for deceased family members. My wife and my children and I are sealed for all eternity. And because of honest tithe paying, I will be given that which is sufficient for my needs. Most importantly, though, I truly understand the meaning and role of the family in today's twisted society. These blessings and knowledge would not have come if I had not joined The Church of Jesus Christ of Latter-day Saints.

It is hard to describe in a few words my family's feelings about my joining the Church. My mother strongly disapproved, but there is certainly no loss of love between us. I deeply respect her desire to protect her son. She will always be my mother, no matter what kind of disagreements we may have concerning my faith. My father and younger brother are fence-sitters, which means they have neither supported nor rejected my baptism. My younger sister, who sustained damage to her brain at birth, is unable to form an opinion because of her condition. My older brother, ten years my senior, has supported me in my decision from the beginning. Oddly enough, he is agnostic. I remember him telling me regarding my decision to be baptized, "Do whatever makes you happy." Being baptized has given me a new sense of hope. How can a person not be happy when he or she has hope? I am truly happy.

My dream of becoming a professional football player lasted but a short while. I played for the San Antonio Texans, then part of the Canadian Football League, for half of the 1995 season. After being released, my desire to be a professional football player also lessened considerably. Because I had not played much at BYU, no one really knew if I was any good or not. There was not much evidence of my ability on film. I came to realize that I was not supposed to play professional football. I was to do something else, and that was to teach. That profession has given me the deep, personal satisfaction that I have looked for in my life.

Am I bitter? No. Rather I feel that a person does not always get what he or she wants. In contrast, I have come to the conclusion that I should build on what I have. Because of the influence of the Church, I now know that things happen to us for a reason, and sometimes that reason is hidden for a while. In my case, I was to teach, not play football. I have accepted that without regrets.

Coming to Brigham Young University allowed me to explore my inner self, and I found what I know to be true. It began with religion classes, which candidly I objected to, and ended with meeting my beautiful wife and her family and eventually being baptized a member of The Church of Jesus Christ of Latter-day Saints. BYU opened a window of opportunity and knowledge for me, as I know it has done for many others. Did I feel out of place? Yes. Do I think it was worth it? Yes. Do I have a testimony? Yes. Did I find God? Yes.

Y

Surprises

That I may be comforted together with you by the mutual faith both of you and me (Romans 1:12).

A Catholic Rediscovers God

Juliana Boerio-Goates

Juliana Boerio-Goates is a professor of chemistry at BYU. She is a native of Latrobe, Pennsylvania, and received her undergraduate degree in chemistry from Seton Hill College, a Catholic women's college in Greensburg, Pennsylvania, and an M.S. and Ph.D. in physical chemistry from the University of Michigan. She has been a visiting scientist at the Argonne National Laboratory, MIT, and Oxford University and has been recognized for her contributions as a young scholar by an award from the principal professional organization in her discipline. At BYU she was named a Karl G. Maeser Professor of General Education for her contributions in the classroom. Dr. Boerio-Goates belongs to the St. Francis of Assisi Catholic Church in Orem, where she has been active in leadership positions, including coordinator of the first Christmas Eve Midnight Mass celebrated at the Provo LDS Tabernacle. She and her husband, Steven R. Goates, are the parents of two children.

"Why would a Catholic want to teach at BYU?" That is the question I am most often asked when I tell my general education physical science students that I am not a member of the dominant religion on the Brigham Young University campus. "Because the experience makes me a better Catholic," is my answer, which often is more of a surprise than the initial revelation of my religious affiliation. But it is an answer which reflects my own growth as a committed Catholic living in Utah Valley and working on the BYU campus, a growth which was unexpected when I decided to come to BYU, but one which has had a valued outcome.

I am a product of sixteen years of Catholic education, from first grade through college, and I have always been an active participant in the sacramental life of my church. Some of my earliest and fondest memories are of attending church with my family, and especially with my grandmother. As a young child, I remember falling asleep each evening to the recitation of the rosary. As I got older, Friday evening Benediction, Forty Hours Devotion, and the Easter Triduum were all events which formed my spiritual base. Then, in high school and college, my religion classes gave me a theological and intellectual framework from which to support, explain, and nurture the rich emotional and spiritual tapestry which the early participation in sacred rituals had produced. My formal education, conducted in parochial schools, also introduced me to the notion that a strong secular education could be provided within a religious setting in which artificial boundaries need not be erected between faith and reason.

However, all of these experiences were obtained in a safe environment in which a majority of my friends, neighbors, and associates shared my religious allegiance. I was never challenged nor called upon to explain why I believed a certain principle nor given an opportunity for reflection upon different theological viewpoints to explore the true levels of my faith and commitment to it. Then, as a graduate and postdoctoral student, the demands of my education provided excuses to reduce my level of formal religious participation.

During the summer following my junior year as an undergraduate, I met and fell in love with a young LDS man who was an undergraduate at BYU. For three years we continued to see each other, although for much of two years we were separated by long distances, while we decided whether two very strongly held but very different religious beliefs could be brought together in a successful marriage. While naively underestimating the difficulties, we decided to marry, and I began the journey which ultimately led me to BYU. Following graduate school and postdoctoral experiences, we began to search for employment. Knowing that it was going to be difficult to find two academic positions in the same department, we nevertheless applied to the chemistry department at BYU. Fortunately for us, the general area of my research (thermodynamics) was one in which BYU had had a longstanding strength, but my specialty (low-temperature heat capacities and thermodynamics of solids) was not represented in the department. My husband, a laser spectroscopist, was in an area into which the department wished to expand.

My preemployment interactions with members of the chemistry department, university administration, and Elder Paul H. Dunn, the General Authority who conducted my faculty interview, were all very positive. I was struck by the universal concern of the interviewers. There was more emphasis on whether I could be happy in the unique environment of BYU rather than if I would be objectionable or unsuitable. When offers of employment came to both of us, we were encouraged to accept by an LDS institute director who told us that he thought we each had a mission to fulfill there.

From my earliest days on campus, it was clear to me that religion was an important part of the BYU experience. The theme of the university conference which opened my first academic semester at BYU was "Unto Whom Much Is Given, Much Is Expected." For some time, I had had an inner conviction that I should make use of my God-given talents, and so I resonated to this theme and took it to be an affirmation of my decision to come. The themes of the next few university conferences also set out very clearly that being employed as a faculty member at BYU was more than just a job. (For this reason, I am somewhat surprised now to hear some talk as though BYU in those years — early to mid-eighties — was too secular an institution.)

In the course of the last fifteen years, I have rediscovered God — at BYU. This rediscovery has occurred on two levels: in a renewed and deepened commitment to an image of God, that is, to a particular set of theological principles and conceptions; and in a deeper involvement with the organized church which embodies that theology. I suppose that change on the first level does not presume a parallel change in the second, but in my case it did. There are several general themes which can be drawn from the myriad experiences which have led to my renewed commitment. These include my experience as a member of the religious minority, the encouragement to consider in a sophisticated way the relationship of faith and reason, and the opportunity to see good examples of their integration. Working with women and men of both deep faith and outstanding academic abilities, and discussing religious beliefs with them and with students, has transformed the experience from being a purely academic, intellectual one to a life-changing one. Moreover, the opportunities provided to work in leadership roles at the parish level of my church have provided a motivation as well.

Being a member of a religious minority in a culture and society dominated by a majority religion has presented numerous opportunities for growth. I find that I am constantly examining religious ideas expressed by my LDS colleagues, students, and neighbors in the light of my own understanding and image of God. This process of conscious comparison means that I must continually examine what it is that I believe. Things which I took for granted throughout my youth and young adult life, I now consider carefully for their implications. For example, the liturgical ritual of the Mass and especially the Divine Presence in the Blessed Sacrament has become deeply important to me after attendance at Mormon sacrament meetings.

On the other hand, the Mormon expectation that all people assume church responsibilities was a major factor leading me to return to a greater participation in the various activities of my own church. In fifteen years, I have served as lector, eucharistic minister, faculty advisor to the Catholic Newman Club for students at BYU and the local community college, member and president of the Parish Council, and most recently, as director of liturgy for the parish. Each of these activities has caused me to grow in my faith. For example, my involvement with the liturgy has enabled me to learn more of the theology that motivates the various rituals of the Church's liturgical year.

The constant testing of ideas associated with the minority experience might have been present were I teaching at one of the state institutions of higher education in Utah, but probably would not have been grounded at such a deep intellectual level. At BYU, I have taken advantage of resources like *The Pope Speaks,* a compilation of major papal addresses and writings, and a wide range of Catholic periodicals which are available in the BYU library because of the research interests of the faculty.

Perhaps one of the most focused opportunities for this growth came through my preparation to teach a general education physical science class required of many BYU students. I saw this class as an opportunity to synthesize the fundamental and unifying ideas of physics, chemistry, and geology, to put them into a historical and philosophical perspective, and to build a basis from which a faithful person could view science. Because of this latter objective, I became better grounded in several well-known historical examples of the tension which exists between science and religion, for example, Galileo and Darwin. I also renewed an earlier interest in Pierre Teilhard de Chardin, a French Jesuit paleontologist who sought to show that evolution was a divinely instituted force which leads nature to higher and higher states of being. My early introduction to his writings and his life gave me an example that one could unite a deep love for science and a strong religious faith. For example, Teilhard has written, "There is a communion with God, a communion with the earth, and a communion with God through the earth."[1] Teilhard had a deep reverence for nature and the world of matter and saw in the study of nature an opportunity to come to know its divine Creator. During a great portion of his scientific and theological career, Teilhard, like Galileo, was asked by Rome to cease publication of his writings on this perspective. However, the ban was lifted after his death, and his writings exhibited a strong influence in the 1960s and 1970s on many Catholic theologians.

In addition, because of this teaching assignment, I was fortunate to have the opportunity to sit in on classes taught by Jae Ballif, professor of physics and astronomy and former provost of BYU. I found him to be a master at incorporating religious considerations into a science class without sentimentalizing the religion or watering down the science. He transmitted his deep commitment to his LDS faith by introducing scriptural quotations when they were pertinent to the subject matter and by occasional statements of his personal beliefs. For example, as an introduction to the discussion of reason, he began with a citation from the Doctrine and Covenants (D&C 50:10–11) and led students to see that reasoning is useful if you start from the right place and use correct principles.

During the first lecture of this physical science class each semester, I announce to the class that I am Catholic. However, I also reassure them of my commitment to present them with official LDS positions on potentially controversial topics. I joke with them that if they had wanted the Catholic perspective they would have gone to Notre Dame, and I tell them that my sources have impeccable LDS credentials. In addition to the citations from scripture borrowed from Professor Ballif, I include quotations from the famous LDS scientist Henry Eyring, including ones from his book *The Faith of a Scientist*. On the last day of class, however, as we review the ideas of Newton, Galileo, DNA synthesis, plate tectonics, and cosmology, I take the opportunity to talk of my own beliefs and faith. I introduce Teilhard and cite him as another modern example of a scientist who had profound faith. I read a few sections from the Catholic catechism on faith and reason and end by showing a *B.C.* cartoon in which the strip's characters observe the fireworks of a volcano, a shooting star, a rainbow, and other magnificent natural phenomena and then reflect upon the divine origins of the universe. I encourage students to develop a sense of wonder and curiosity for the natural world around them and to use this as a springboard for a greater appreciation of the divine Intellect whose work this is.

I have also been influenced by interactions with my research students. The nature of my research occasionally requires working late into the night overseeing data collection from a computer-automated set of instruments. When things are going well and the equipment requires minimal intervention, these evenings provide valuable chances to get to know my students and to share beliefs and questions. From these young men and women, I have come to a better understanding of how culture can shape one's expressions of faith. Many are returned missionaries who have served in South or Central America. During these late-night sessions, they have shared with me their perceptions of Catholicism gleaned from their work in Catholic countries. Their frank statements of their impressions have helped me to look at Catholicism from an outsider's point of view. I will never forget the relief one student expressed when I explained that certain folk-cultural aspects of South American Catholicism were not church dogma and were not practices in which I engaged. He had found it hard to reconcile my scholarly image with what he thought Catholics had to believe from his missionary experiences. However, he found the post–Vatican II faith, which I professed, to be compatible with the professional image he had of me. He, in turn, was surprised to learn of the perceptions held by many non-Mormons about the LDS Church that make it hard for them to understand how an intellectual could accept the religious tenets of his church.

For the three years I was associate dean of general education and honors, I had the good fortune to work with some of the brightest and most thoughtful students at the University through the honors program. Twice I was invited to present devotionals at the weekly honors "morning sides" held in the Maeser Building, and I attended devotionals given by other faculty, visitors, and general authorities. Those morning devotionals were reminiscent of my undergraduate years, during which I frequently attended daily Mass with some of my professors. The devotionals often were a source of great spiritual insights. For example, BYU associate academic vice president John Tanner's meditation on the prayers used to bless the sacrament in LDS services made me reflect on the parallels and divergences between the LDS sacrament and the Catholic concept of the Divine Presence in the Eucharist.

I have already alluded to the influence of Professor Jae Ballif in strengthening my conviction that faith, reason, and science were not mutually incompatible. I have found many others like Jae, women and men of deep yet intellectual faith, who are unashamed to speak of their beliefs and the importance of those beliefs in their lives. Those are scholars well grounded in their disciplines, and many have made professional sacrifices to accept positions at BYU. While faculty members at BYU are with few exceptions LDS, those colleagues bring expertise and insights from their disciplines to our religious discussions. From Donna Lee Bowen of the political science department and her knowledge of Islam and Muslims I have gained some perspective on a non-Christian tradition. John Tanner, through a chance reference to a poem by T. S. Eliot, introduced me to a piece of literature which has enriched my perspective on Holy Week. James Faulconer, then dean of general education and honors and a philosopher, shared with me a favorite article that has provided rich food for thought on the Catholic concept of Eucharist. With my husband, Steven, there is a continued discussion of the essential elements of our two faiths, a sharing of religious activities where possible, a gracious acceptance of the differences, and a generous freedom to worship as we each believe. Engagements in scholarly, yet faith-filled, discussions of religious topics with those and other faculty continue to deepen not only my faith but my appreciation and respect for the sincerity of theirs.

When I first told friends and scientific colleagues that I was going to take a job at BYU, there were many skeptics who doubted that I could forgo the cup of hot coffee which usually accompanied my forays into the air-conditioned calorimetry lab and others who predicted that I would be made miserable by the insistent pressure to become Mormon, or that I would find BYU to be too provincial. I will admit that there are times when a freshly brewed cup of coffee would make the day go better, that I have been hurt by those who are unwilling to accept my deep commitment to Catholicism and feel the need to send the missionaries around one more time, and that there are a few narrow-minded students, faculty, and administrators at BYU. But, the richness and variety of my spiritual, personal, and professional experiences at BYU have provided times of great joy and happiness. Freeman Dyson suggests in his book *Infinite in All Directions* that the ideal environment for life is one which is comfortable, but not too comfortable. At BYU, I have found a place where my faith is challenged because of the majority religion but where I can be comfortable and find support so that my faith continues to grow and strengthen.

Note

1. "Cosmic Life," in *Writings in Time of War* (London: Collins, 1968).

Marvel not that all mankind, yea, men and women, all nations, kindreds, tongues and people, must be born again; yea, born of God, changed from their carnal and fallen state, to a state of righteousness, being redeemed of God, becoming his sons and daughters; and thus they become new creatures (Mosiah 27:25–26).

Knocking at the Door

Alfred Gantner

Alfred (Fredy) Gantner was born and reared in Switzerland, where he attended school, served in the Swiss Army, and completed his diploma from the Zurich Business School before he entered the MBA program in the Marriott School of Management at BYU. After graduation, he joined Goldman, Sachs, & Co., where he worked at assignments in New York and London before he transferred to Zurich. There he is cofounder and CEO of Partners Group, an international venture capital/private equity investment manager. Fredy and his wife, Cornelia, are the parents of four children.

BYU is a very special place for me, as it is for many others. I did not find my spouse there. I did not even attend classes at BYU when I first came. But more important, I found God.

I first came to know the Church in Switzerland when I was fourteen. My older sister dated a member of the Church and started to attend meetings on Sundays. They married, and some time later my sister decided to get baptized. Occasionally I would attend sacrament meetings when my sister or my brother-in-law gave a talk. Although my parents belong to a Protestant church, our family did not attend church meetings regularly. However, my parents had taught their children about the existence of our Heavenly Father. I was probably one of the few students who enjoyed my religion classes in junior high school. I showed vivid interest in different religious denominations, and over time I investigated the Roman Catholic Church, the Jehovah's Witnesses, some of the Free Churches, as well as the LDS Church. I found interesting aspects of truth in all of them. A good friend of mine was Muslim, and I had high esteem for him and his religious beliefs as well. In a German literature class in high school we read a German classic, *Nathan the Wise*, written by Gotthold E. Lessing during the period of the Enlightenment. While we will look more closely at this story later on, the basic message is that there is no true church, that all religions have some truth, and that the true church was probably lost a long time ago. I was very much impressed by this thought, and my own searching for truth seemed to confirm Lessing's philosophy.

It was against this background that several missionary couples taught me. It was very interesting to hear about a restored gospel that seemed to offer more than the many different kinds of reformation that I had studied so far. I read in the Book of Mormon and had interesting discussions with the missionaries and members of the Church. I gained a favorable impression of the Church and had a very positive feeling when reading in the Book of Mormon and when discussing it with missionaries and members. Today I know about the fine, whispering voice of the Holy Ghost. But then I did not recognize it as such. I was still very liberal in my thinking. Many of the laws, such as the Word of Wisdom or the law of chastity, seemed to be very old-fashioned and behind so-called modern times. Also, there were no people my age in the branch with whom I could associate besides the white-shirt/black-tie missionaries, who seemed to live such a different life. So for many years I was a friend of the Church but showed little interest in joining. Among the missionaries I was already known as a "professional investigator." Nevertheless, the many hours of studying and teaching started to bear fruit. The priorities in my life changed as I began to understand gospel principles.

In my mid-twenties I was working as a trader at the Zurich Stock Exchange when I felt the need to deepen my business education. My brother-in-law suggested that I should consider the Marriott School of Management, which has an excellent reputation for its international business program. He sent my résumé to a friend of his who is a faculty member at BYU, who in turn passed it to the business school. The response was very positive, and the faculty member suggested that I should consider the MBA program. The application procedure would only be a formality, since the MBA program had already expressed a strong interest in my admission. Based on this encouraging news and the prospect of attending a reputable two-year post-graduate program in business administration, I resigned from my job by the year's end. Starting the following January, I had to serve another four months of military duty as a lieutenant in the Swiss Army. But I had only two weeks of service left when a rather devastating letter from BYU arrived.

I was told that I could not be admitted into a graduate program at BYU since my educational background would not fulfill the necessary requirements. Great! Two weeks of service left, no job anymore, no apartment, luggage packed, ticket bought to Salt Lake City. I decided that I might as well just go there anyway and discuss this mess with the people who caused it.

I had been invited to stay with friends of my brother-in-law, the Barrus family, which was a fantastic experience. For the first time in my life I experienced the blessing of the priesthood in a home and the wonderful bonding experience of regular family prayers. This family is still an example to me. After two weeks I found housing in an apartment complex called King Henry. I shared rooms with three other students who all became my great friends. The first Sunday they invited me to church and then took me along for the ward prayer in the clubhouse that same evening. I was more than amazed by these young people. There were only single students attending the ward, and all the different callings (except the bishopric) were carried by the students themselves. I witnessed powerful sacrament and testimony meetings, and interesting and spiritual Sunday School and priesthood classes. Especially the ward prayers touched me deeply every time. I felt the love and care those young people had for each other. Nobody forced them, nobody told them, nobody supervised them. They truly did serve each other out of an inner conviction that they are all brothers and sisters in Christ. What a powerful experience for somebody who grew up in a country where the wooden church benches are empty on Sundays, people under sixty-five are rarely seen at mass, and no young men can be found to fill the vacant priest positions.

I remember one Saturday morning when two of my roommates were called by sisters of the ward to give a sick sister a blessing. I was invited to go along, and I was again more than impressed. I felt the spirit and the faith of the people who had gathered in that room to ask the Lord in a very direct way for a very specific blessing. I also participated in many fun ward activities and in the weekly family home evening program. While there were no members my age in the branch back home, I was now able to affiliate with many young Latter-day Saints from different parts of the United States and from other countries all over the world. Most of them had come to BYU to receive a good education. But equally important, they came to grow spiritually through the values taught and practiced at the University and among the student body itself. Who would believe that more than thirty-thousand young people voluntarily commit themselves to a very stringent moral and ethical behavior code in order to be admitted to a university? More important, most of those students do not live those values for the rules' sake but out of a deep religious conviction. What an incredible testimony of the restored gospel! What force could move so many young hearts to forsake many of the great temptations of modern society? BYU and its students are an enormous living testimony of our Lord Jesus Christ and his restored Church on the earth.

After about two months of pondering the Book of Mormon and other Church literature, uncountable hours of discussion with friends, and many intense personal prayers, I was baptized and ordained to the Aaronic Priesthood in November 1991. After three months at BYU, I was asked to tell my conversion story in a sacrament meeting the day before my departure back to Switzerland. The following is the talk I gave on that occasion. I think that it best reflects the feelings of my heart about how I found God at BYU.

> Many of you have served a mission. You went from door to door, talked with people in the street, and taught them the gospel. I met my first missionaries about seven years ago in Switzerland through my sister and brother-in-law who are members of the Church. They and other missionaries taught me a long time and with a lot of patience. I often felt a good and even a strong feeling, but I struggled to accept the gospel. Nevertheless, I started thinking about my life and the purpose in life. I realized that my job as a stock-exchange trader gave me a nice salary and earthly comfort, but not a real personal satisfaction. Finally, I decided to quit my job and go back to school to try to go through an MBA program. My choice was BYU. I wanted to find out more about these strange people who had such an important influence on my life.

> When the plane was landing over Salt Lake City and I saw the mountains, it was a little bit like a coming home. This feeling has not left me from that moment on. I have been amazed at how many friendly and helpful people I have met in this valley. I have never

felt as a stranger because of the spontaneous help and love of a lot of people. Again I was deeply touched by the way the members of this Church are and live.

In ninth grade in high school we read a play with a religious background. It is called *Nathan the Wise*, written by Gotthold Ephraim Lessing, who lived in the eighteenth century and is one of the most important German philosophers of the Enlightenment. A wise Jewish man named Nathan is called by the Sultan, a Muslim, who gives him a test by asking the question, "Which religion—Jewish, Muslim, or Christian—might be the right one?" Nathan answers this question with a tale that has become famous in German literature as the Ring Parable:

> In days of yore, there dwelt in eastern lands
> A man who had a ring of priceless worth
> Received from hands beloved. The stone it held,
> An opal, shed a hundred colors fair,
> And had the magic power that he who wore it,
> Trusting its strength, was loved of God and men. . . .
> At last this ring, passed on from son to son,
> Descended to a father of three sons;
> All three of whom were duly dutiful,
> All three of whom in consequence he needs
> Must love alike. . . .
>
> And so to each
> He promised it, in pious frailty.
> This lasted while it might.—Then came the time
> For dying, and the loving father finds
> Himself embarrassed. . . .
>
> He orders two more rings, in pattern like
> His own, and bids him spare no cost nor toil
> To make them in all points identical. . . .
>
> In glee and joy he calls his sons to him,
> Each by himself, confers on him his blessing—
> His ring as well—and dies. . . .
>
> . . . What ensues is wholly obvious.—
> Scarce is the father dead when all three sons
> Appear, each with his ring, and each would be
> The reigning prince. They seek the facts, they quarrel,
> Accuse. . . .
>
> The sons preferred complaint;
> And each swore to the judge, he had received
> The ring directly from his father's hand.—

As was the truth!—And long before had had
His father's promise, one day to enjoy
The privilege of the ring.—No less than truth!—
His father, each asserted, could not have
Been false to him; and sooner than suspect
This thing of him, of such a loving father;
He must accuse his brothers. . . .

 Thus said the judge: unless you swiftly bring
Your father here to me, I'll bid you leave
My judgment seat. Think you that I am here
For solving riddles? Would you wait, perhaps,
Until the genuine ring should rise and speak?—
But stop! I hear the genuine ring enjoys
The magic power to make its wearer loved,
Beloved of God and men. That must decide!
For spurious rings can surely not do that!—
Whom then do two of you love most? Quick, speak!
You're mute? The rings' effect is only backward,
Not outward? Each one loves himself the most?—
O then you are, all three, deceived deceivers!
Your rings are false, all three. The genuine ring
No doubt got lost. To hide the grievous loss,
To make it good, the father caused three rings
To serve for one. . . .

All three he loved; and loved alike;
Since two of you he'd not humiliate
To favor one.—Well then! Let each aspire
To emulate his father's unbeguiled,
Unprejudiced affection! Let each strive
To match the rest in bringing to the fore
The magic of the opal in his ring![1]

I asked myself: Did I just find some of that magic of the opal ring among the members of this church? This question stayed in my mind, and I found it again in the Book of Mormon, Moroni 7:5: "For I remember the word of God which saith by their works ye shall know them; for if their works be good, then they are good also." After some more time there was no doubt in me that this church had an amazingly positive influence on people, that it had the magic of the opal. Or was it even the true ring that had been found again?

After my first two weeks in Provo I made an important decision to live in the King Henry apartments. That gave me the chance to know all of you and to share the wonderful Forty-fifth Ward. I want to let you know that I feel a deep love for you in this ward. I thank you for your friendship and for the wonderful time that you have shared with me. Your way of living and your love for each other let me understand what the word charity — the opal of the ring — means. I know that it is caused by the power and influence of God through your strong faith in Jesus Christ. But I was still looking for my personal testimony. Sometimes on Sundays I felt awkward in church because everybody would share his testimony, and I seemed to be the only person who could not figure out that the Church was true. I had really tried hard to find the truth when, about four weeks ago, everything seemed to turn against me. There was almost no hope anymore of being admitted to the BYU MBA program, I had problems finding housing (fall semester had started), and I had a lot of unanswered questions. I knelt down and started to pray to Heavenly Father for him to give me a clear sign. I was waiting for thunder, and nothing happened.

Today I know that he answered my prayers in a much more powerful way. The next day I met a wonderful person and we started to talk extensively about the Church and my concerns. From our conversation I took the assignment to read Alma 32 the next day. I want to read verses 17, 18, and 21 with you: "Yea, there are many who do say: If thou wilt show unto us a sign from heaven, then we shall know of a surety; then we shall believe. Now I ask, is this faith? Behold, I say unto you, Nay; for if a man knoweth a thing he hath no cause to believe, for he knoweth it. And now as I said concerning faith — faith is not to have a perfect knowledge of things; therefore if ye have faith ye hope for things which are not seen, which are true."

I realized that it was wrong to wait for thunder, for a miracle, for earthly proof. The next day we read Moroni 7:26, and for the first time I started to really trust God that I would receive an answer to my prayers. Some days later I had an appointment with our bishop, who is an extraordinary man, followed by a personal blessing. We read Moroni 10:4-5 together: "And when ye shall receive these things, I would exhort you that ye would ask God, the Eternal Father, in the name of Christ, if these things are not true; and if ye shall ask with a sincere heart, with real intent, having faith in Christ, he will manifest the truth of it unto you, by the power of the Holy Ghost. And by the power of the Holy Ghost ye may know the truth of all things."

I had struggled for two years and finally found the truth in just three short weeks when I started to trust in God. I am so thankful for all the many people who helped me to make the most important decision of my life. I will stay close to them my whole life through deep gratitude, love, and prayers for them. All of you have had an influence on my decision through your daily examples. You can see through my experience that your work is not done after your missions. You are missionaries your whole life long. I felt the gospel in you and through you. You have been wonderful missionaries. I thank you with my entire heart and I want to let you know that there will be a friend of yours in Switzerland.

I am proud to stand in front of you and testify that I know with certainty that this church is the true and only true Church upon the face of this earth and that the gospel has been restored through Joseph Smith, a modern-day prophet of God. You have testified of the Book of Mormon and the Book of Mormon has testified of you, my friends. I testify to you that this book is holy scripture and is another witness of our Redeemer and Savior, Jesus Christ.

The next day I flew back to Switzerland and began to understand just what it was my Father in Heaven had in mind for me. I began to see why I had not been admitted immediately to BYU's MBA program, and I began to see that I was being prepared for a most marvelous blessing.

First, I registered in school to take some additional classes so I would fill BYU's requirements for entry into graduate school. Second, I began attending my home branch. While I had been in Provo, Cornelia had moved to our Swiss branch. We got to know each other, fell in love, and were married six months later. The Lord had prepared me at BYU to meet her, but she had to get to the right place for that to happen. We got married on a beautiful day in May and left for Utah in August of 1992.

In the spring of 1994 I graduated from business school and Cornelia, my wife, finished her bachelor's degree in broadcast communication during the following summer. I was offered a job by Goldman, Sachs & Co. — an American investment bank — and was trained in New York and London before being transferred to Zurich in 1995. In 1996, two of my colleagues and I left Goldman to establish our own venture capital/private equity investment company.

Some years have passed since we left Utah Valley. Cornelia has given birth to three boys and one girl. We both serve in our branch in Switzerland. Cornelia is the Young Womens president and seminary teacher, while I am currently serving in the branch presidency. I am grateful to my Heavenly Father for the opportunity to serve in his Church and for all the many blessings that I have received over the past few years, especially for my wonderful wife and our children.

We spent two wonderful years at BYU. I think of many positive classroom experiences that expanded beyond academic matters, including social and spiritual aspects of business and life in general. Many of the campus devotionals with Church leaders will be memories of a lifetime. But most important, we met many wonderful people who share with us a common vision about building up the Lord's kingdom upon this beautiful planet earth. Today I know that he is everywhere, but it took going to BYU to find it out. BYU is more than an educational institution. It is a most important place where young people can grow strong in the gospel of Jesus Christ. It was a great privilege for me to study and grow spiritually at the school of the Lord. I hope that BYU students never forget that they enter to learn and go forth to serve.

Note

1. Gotthold Ephraim Lessing, *Nathan the Wise: A Dramatic Poem in Five Acts,* trans. Bayard Quincy Morgan (New York: Frederick Ungar Publishing, 1955), 75–79.

I say unto you, even as you desire of me so it shall be unto you; and if you desire, you shall be the means of doing much good in this generation (D&C 6:8).

A Frog in the Well

Van C. Gessel

Van C. Gessel is a professor of Japanese and dean of the College of Humanities at Brigham Young University. He has served on the faculties of Columbia University, Notre Dame University, and the University of California at Berkeley. He joined the faculty at BYU in 1990. Dr. Gessel's publications include THE STING OF LIFE: THREE CONTEMPORARY JAPANESE NOVELISTS *(Columbia University Press, 1989) and* THREE MODERN NOVELISTS: SŌSEKI, TANIZAKI, KAWABATA *(Kodansha International, 1985). He has published six translations of works by the Japanese Christian novelist Endō Shōsaku and has furthered Japanese literary education at BYU by serving as advisor to the Milwaukee Repertory Theater's production of a stage adaptation of Endō's* SILENCE, *by American playwright Steven Dietz, which was performed at BYU in the fall of 1998. Professor Gessel is married to Elizabeth Darley, and they are the parents of two children.*

"The frog in the well knows nothing of the great ocean," according to a Japanese proverb. My professional career—and, in particular, the manner in which I scrupulously avoided affiliation with BYU until I was ready for the experience—has persuaded me that the obverse is also true: a frog who has wandered from one ocean to another can only come to understand the comforts and rewards of the well after much meandering.

As I consider the four opportunities I had to become associated with BYU, and the three I rejected out of hand, I have come to realize that the problem for me was not one of "finding God at BYU." It was, rather, that of "finding that God is at BYU," and, more specifically, that of "finding that God wanted me at BYU." This is not to suggest that I have not had significant personal encounters with God since coming to BYU in 1990; a couple of those I will detail below. But my personal journey has been much more a discovery of the role the University could play in my life, and I in its. That will be my focus in the ruminations which follow.

I grew up a Baptist in Salt Lake City and joined the Church only a month into the beginning of my college career at the University of Utah. My conversion to the gospel was not accompanied by any pentecostal promptings to transfer to the Church's University in Provo. I had a four-year scholarship to the "U" in hand; besides, it was the late 1960s, and there were few things more important to my generation than the right to choose our own lengths of both skirt and stubble (neither of which I personally wore, by the way). Not many of my LDS high school chums chose BYU. My wife-to-be, who had introduced me to the Church, was certainly not going to kneel to have her hems measured. So like many of my friends, I lived at home in Salt Lake City and became a resident Ute.

I thus blissfully avoided giving BYU consideration for my own education. Even after returning from a mission to Japan to discover that the language department at the U of U had no advanced-level Japanese courses to offer and treated my request for lower-division language credit with a goodly measure of scorn, I could see no reason to forfeit my scholarship. The idea of trading in my red sweaters for blue never appeared as even a faint blip on my radar screen.

A desire to pursue graduate study of Japanese language and literature took me and my new bride on a meandering journey through educational Sinai. We lived in Manhattan for three years while I worked on my Ph.D. at Columbia University, then a year in Tokyo while I pursued my dissertation research. I taught at Columbia for a year after receiving my degree, then spent two interesting years as a Latter-day Saint on the faculty at Notre Dame. (Parenthetically, I listen in dumb amazement to conversations about whether BYU should try to become a "Mormon Notre Dame." When I lived in South Bend from 1980 to 1982, well over *half* the Notre Dame faculty was non-Catholic. I never heard any discussion about integrating Catholic beliefs with secular study. And the only real conversation about the religious nature of the institution came as part of a feeble effort to define what it meant for the University to be "Catholic with a lower-case c." The only way BYU could become a Latter-day Saint version of Notre Dame would be to abandon its religious mission altogether.) I subsequently spent eight years at the University of California at Berkeley, where I received tenure the year before I came to BYU.

Interspersed in that chronology, however, were two failed attempts by BYU to recruit me. Both times, I could not see how coming to Provo would "further my career." In fact, on the second occasion, I consciously defined the choice between an offer from Berkeley and an offer from BYU as options to establish myself as a scholar in my discipline or to make whatever contribution I could to the Church's educational system. When I opted for Berkeley, I convinced myself that there were many ways to serve in and serve the Church, and that whatever ecclesiastical roles I could fill in "the mission field" would be acceptable to the Lord. I'm still somewhat persuaded by that logic and am certain it is a completely worthy choice for most people at most times of their lives. And I am persuaded that I made the right decision for that particular time in my life and career.

But lives and careers are dynamic, and I think the Lord uses that shift and flux to mold and change and make best use of us. No one I knew, either personally or professionally, could have conceived of the possibility that I might resign a newly tenured position at a prestigious university like Berkeley, abandoning the fame of name and the privilege of working with graduate students, in order to come to BYU. I was the most convinced of anyone that I would never get or desire another opportunity to make that choice.

My job-interview trip to Provo in early 1990 was, in fact, almost comically painful to me. A determined department chair and dean at BYU had labored mightily to locate a faculty slot for me, but it seemed to me that their efforts had come a bit too late. Just six months earlier I had, after considerable tribulation, attained a tenured position at one of the most renowned (if, admittedly, radical) public institutions in the nation. Psychologically, it was time for me to settle in, to finally nestle into an academic and emotional home for my work. Berkeley had just afforded me that opportunity, and it seemed madness to consider uprooting my career and my family once again. Yet, a sense of both gratitude and duty dictated that I at least acknowledge the earnest efforts of the BYU chair and dean and go through the motions of a campus interview. Then I could politely decline when and if an offer was made.

The interviews went smoothly, and the campus visit was pleasant. Still, when I returned to California I told my wife that I felt as though I had misused tithing funds by allowing the University to pay my expenses for a job-hunting trip that I had no intention of taking seriously. I was convinced that an offer from BYU could not be made to appear attractive to me. Little David in Provo could not begin to find stones large enough to fell the Goliath that towered over the academic world just as the Campanile dominates the Berkeley campus.

Three previous times I had snubbed, ignored, or discounted what BYU had to offer. Granted, there was every likelihood that those "offerings" had increased in value, and in personal significance for me, with the passage of time. In retrospect, however, I now view the processes of my life not as random episodes linked only by their accidental association with me as an individual, but as part of a training program to prepare me for roles and duties and relationships that I could never have anticipated for myself.

In my more whimsical moments, I surmise that the Lord had a hand in raising the fees for faculty parking at Berkeley, knowing it would be the final straw that broke the back of my intellectual pride. (I no longer consider it a coincidence that I experienced three brushes with BYU and can locate the admonition "Be thou humble" three distinct times in my patriarchal blessing.) While I am not convinced that God is actually responsible for dismantling before my very eyes what had once been a thriving Japanese program at Berkeley, I do know of a certainty that he demolished my illusions about the importance of university name recognition, and that the eroding away of every reason I had tenaciously embraced as my excuses to remain at Berkeley finally drove me to that most risky of actions — to actually pray about whether I should accept what turned out in all ways to be an attractive offer from BYU.

I never did unearth any really logical reasons why I should leave Berkeley. The ninety-minute-one-way commute so I couldn't locate a campus parking space that I was paying sixty dollars a month for the privilege of not finding was an irritation, but it was not a *reasonable* reason to abandon ship. All I can affirm is that the Lord changed my heart and that of my family, and in my wicked moments I suspect he even hardened the hearts of the bureaucratic pharaohs at Berkeley who refused to counter BYU's offer to me with anything but insults. In any case, I had contracts with BYU and with Ryder Truck within the space of a couple of weeks. The frog had seen both oceans, and after determining that the opportunity to taste the living water in the well far surpassed the vistas on either coastline — which were, admittedly, wide but ultimately not spiritually nourishing — he opted for the well.

Many perspectives have changed for me since coming to BYU. My approach to teaching has changed significantly, and that is not unrelated to the dramatically different ways that I look at my students. I first learned the meaning of academic freedom not at that secular bastion of same, Berkeley, but at BYU. I had not realized, until I began teaching my field of Japanese Christian literature to a room full of Christians, that I had never previously felt at liberty to discuss the Christian messages, symbols, and purport of the texts with my students. Teaching religious novels (in my case, works such as *Silence* and *The Samurai* by the Japanese Catholic author Endō Shūsaku) at Berkeley and even, interestingly enough, at Notre Dame had been an intellectual exercise in fuzzy obfuscation. Obviously religious features of texts were diluted in class discussions to abstractly "cultural" features, and the conflicts were not defined in terms of right vs. wrong, temptation vs. moral choices, but pared down into politically acceptable declarations about the differences between civilizations East and West. The attempt to teach Christian fiction in the rarefied secular air at Berkeley was akin to describing Michelangelo's Sistine paintings as "depictions of mythical encounters with figures from legend and superstition."

I thrilled at the expansive realization, as I hesitantly introduced religious dialogue into my Japanese literature classes at BYU, that my students had more than a passing interest in those topics. In fact, reading in *Silence* about a Catholic missionary in seventeenth-century Japan who struggles to defeat his own Eurocentric ego while enduring tortures that are ultimately the means by which he discovers the depths of his own faith in Christ, my classes — populated predominantly by returned missionaries from Japan — could relate with such personal intensity to such novels that our level of conversation about the very topics I could not introduce at other universities transformed many classes into moments of simultaneous literary and spiritual discovery. Hearing a returned missionary from Japan confess that he, like the semifictional Catholic priest of three centuries earlier, had harbored feelings of cultural and spiritual superiority to the people he had been called to love and serve opened my eyes to some of the challenges and opportunities available to me, in my role as a BYU faculty member, to help refine the raw ore that a missionary carried home from Japan.

My goal as a teacher at previous institutions had been to impart knowledge and information about my discipline of Japanese literature to my students. Coming to BYU — where I experienced for the first time the exhilarating emancipation that comes from being able to talk about who I am as an individual of faith and to discuss literature from a perspective that is, for me, inextricably tied to the spiritual experiences I have had in and with Japan — has not obliterated that goal of imparting knowledge. But it has expanded and enriched my pedagogical aims as I have sensed divine confirmation that I can help add value to the knowledge my students already have of Japan from their mission experience and can thereby assist in molding them into even better emissaries of the gospel message as they continue their associations with the Japanese people. The great majority of our students of Japanese do not pursue the academic study of the country in graduate programs but rather branch out into fields such as law, business, medicine, and so forth. But I suspect that most of them will continue to have contacts with Japan, either through work in the country or in companies that have contacts there.

And so, from my perspective, they have not completed their missions. Or, rather, they have the opportunity, as part of the education we provide them at BYU, to serve unofficial second missions as they pursue their secular careers. If I am doing my job properly in the classroom, students will have learned more of nations, kindreds, tongues, and peoples. With that expanded knowledge and sensitivity, they ought to be even more effective carriers of the Word, and from that higher plateau they are virtually *impelled* to be so. They leave Provo with a charge to preach the gospel from a new summit of discernment, a new depth of sensitivity, a new awareness of cultural qualities and idiosyncracies, a new facility with words. They should, in short, leave BYU more fluent in the language of redeeming love. In the Doctrine and Covenants, after the Lord has instructed all of us to study things in heaven and on earth, including a knowledge of countries and of kingdoms, I find it interesting that in the very next verse he seems to be speaking very specifically to graduates of BYU: "That ye may be prepared in all things when I shall send you *again* to magnify the calling whereunto I have called you, and the mission with which I have commissioned you" (D&C 88:80; emphasis added).

I think I was rather slow in learning this new definition of my role as a teacher at BYU. While the campus-wide conversations about integrating knowledge and faith interested me from the outset, the discussion of literary works all but totally removed from the Western Christian tradition seemed at first to offer little that could facilitate my teaching in that mode. I supposed I could assign a Japanese novel and then bear testimony after we had discussed it that my students should avoid modeling their behavior after the lives of these fictional characters. But that seemed a cheap and obvious charade unworthy of a university environment. I struggled for some time trying to figure out how I could fulfill my commission as a teacher in Zion.

My quest was given some impetus and direction shortly after I was named chair of the Department of Asian and Near Eastern Languages in 1992. It was around the time Elder Henry B. Eyring was appointed Church commissioner of education. I was notified that Elder Eyring wanted to meet for ninety minutes with each department chair and had requested a sample of scholarly writings from faculty in each department. With a bit of anxiety stemming from my newness in the position of chair, I tried to prepare for the interview by reviewing the accomplishments of my colleagues in the department, certain that I would be interrogated about what the department was up to and how we were contributing to the University.

The interview itself came as a total surprise to me and, I think, to Elder Eyring as well. There was no discussion of any kind about the department. For an hour and a half, he plied me with questions about my personal background, extracting from me an oral autobiography, complete with boring details. I suppose near the end of the conversation I must have had a quizzical look on my face, for Elder Eyring smiled a serious smile and answered my unarticulated question by saying, "I'm trying to find out why the Lord is bringing people to BYU."

I cannot pretend to know why the Lord brought me to BYU, whether I attempt to frame the reasons with either humility or pride. What I can affirm, however, is that Elder Eyring's statement has obliged me to ponder the question with great seriousness. In the process of inquiring of the Lord about his purposes — not only in bringing me to BYU but also in leading me on the circuitous and often difficult path through a wilderness that included a great Ivy League school, an institution considered the model of religious schools (that I think has a poorly realized religious mission), and a prestigious public megauniversity — I have very strongly felt the presence of God at BYU. I have come to sense a palpable spirit hovering — and, yes, sometimes brooding — over the place, and a determination on the part of the Lord to bring together people and programs, ideas and initiatives, that will allow BYU to become not just a good university but also a laboratory for lifting souls and a training ground for testimonies, so that those who have the opportunity to study here can be prepared for whatever it is that lies ahead, seen by the Lord but only faintly perceived by any of us here and now.

I have thus seen God at BYU as much in the processes of cultivating our definitions of a BYU education's aims as in the eyes of the individuals — students, faculty colleagues, staff, and administrators — with whom I daily associate and from whom I learn more than I could ever teach. Most of all, it is the students — in who they are and in what potential they embody — who have been open enough and brave enough to afford me glimpses into their spiritual aspirations, however clumsily realized in the present, and have thereby directed my gaze toward a God who so clearly and intensely cares about what they are doing at BYU and what they will do after they leave. I must confess that the priceless opportunity I had to serve for three years as a single-student ward bishop has clarified and deepened my appreciation, not only for the members of my ward but for every student I now encounter, for they all seem connected to me by their hopes, their struggles, and their shared sense of belonging to God.

Alan Jay Lerner expressed this all better than I could in the lyrics for his tender 1974 musical film adaptation of Saint-Exupéry's *The Little Prince*. I somehow cannot help but think of the glowing promise of a BYU student whenever I hear the title song:

Little Prince from who knows where.
Was it a star? Was it a pray'r?—
With ev'ry smile, you clear the air
  so I can see.
Oh, Little Prince, don't take your
  smile away from me.
When you came, my day was
  done,
And then your laugh turned
  on the sun.
Oh, Little Prince, now to my wonder
  and surprise,
all the hopes and dreams I lived
  among
when this heart of mine was wise
  and young,
shine for me again, Little Prince,
  in your eyes.[1]

This particular frog, still croaking away at BYU, no longer yearns to see the ocean, when he can see the image of God and the skies stretching to eternity in the eyes of his students.

Note

1. Alan Jay Lerner, "Little Prince," *A Hymn to Him: The Lyrics of Alan Jay Lerner,* Benny Green, ed. (New York: Limelight Editions, 1987), 212.

And ye shall know that it is by me that ye are led
(1 Nephi 17:13).

I Am Known

Kate L. Kirkham

Kate L. Kirkham is an associate professor of organizational leadership and strategy in the Marriott School of Management at Brigham Young University and a senior associate with Elsie Y. Cross Associates of Philadelphia, Pennsylvania. She was born and reared in Salt Lake City. She has a B.A. in sociology from the University of Utah, an M.A. in human resource development from George Washington University, and a Ph.D. in organizational behavior from the Union Graduate School. She worked in training and development for the National Education Association and for her own consulting firm, Resources for Change, Inc., in Washington, D.C. She joined the BYU faculty in 1978. She has served as the associate director of BYU's MBA program and BYU's Women's Research Institute. Her professional interests are focused on race and gender diversity in organizations and on organizational change strategies. She has also worked with community and volunteer organizations, particularly with local and national councils of the Girl Scouts. Professor Kirkham lives in Springville, Utah.

As soon as I hung up the phone, I knew I was going back to Utah. I was not sure why, but I would accept the invitation to teach one semester at BYU as a visiting faculty member. Since I had an undergraduate degree from the University of Utah and had been in Washington, D.C., for over a decade — living, working, and completing graduate degrees — I wondered how the chair of BYU's organizational behavior department had even noticed me. I doubted that anyone at BYU had discovered my doctoral work. I was completing what is called a nontraditional program. Moreover, my program had focused on a potentially controversial subject for any academic community, including BYU: organizational changes that confront institutionalized forms of discrimination. That is to say, my background was in how organizations could identify and eliminate discrimination from the workplace.

I had arrived in Washington, D.C., as a young, naive, optimistic "girl" from Utah. Most of the time I actually lived in the city itself, determined not to live as a commuter from Virginia or Maryland. But my most distinctive identity was being a Latter-day Saint, often the only one in my work group, graduate classes, or apartment building. However, each Sunday I was one of the many single members of the Washington Ward, on 16th Street, N.W. I developed a range of coping responses for those two very different situations: being viewed negatively in my professional interactions because I was a Mormon and being seen as too different a Mormon by many Mormons because of my professional interests. Sometimes among non–Latter-day Saints I avoided the subject of race and religion; sometimes among Church members I avoided conversations about discrimination, although occasionally I did try to integrate statements about racism into Church lesson discussions. In addition, I learned how to defend a Church position on black men and the priesthood even though I worked as an antiracist trainer. But going to BYU, I thought, would allow me to integrate my professional and Church identities. I saw the invitation from BYU as an opportunity to experience the combination of being employed at a Mormon institution and being a Latter-day Saint at the same time and in the same community. Surely, it would be a journey toward Zion.

In fact, I had felt summoned by the Lord to return to Utah and believed that there was something I was to contribute. So I was not really surprised when I was encouraged to apply for a full-time faculty position after my visiting faculty appointment expired. As a nontraditional academic, one who concentrated on applying knowledge to practical issues in organizations, I did not expect to be valued for research skills or even for work experience. Further, I did not think that I was being called to BYU as a career move; it was more than that. There was no doubt in my mind that I could contribute to the college program and curriculum as a practitioner, a nontraditional researcher, and a skilled teacher. Moreover, I fully expected to be accepted as a Mormon among Mormons in a Mormon work environment. Being LDS would no longer be my most distinct identity either in the workplace or the shopping mall.

From my first semester, I underestimated how much colleagues would shape my experience at BYU when they consistently defined me as a different Mormon. Wanted: older, single, female, seeking professional colleagues. Regrettably, for some colleagues these aspects of my identity seemed to be sufficient for defining what kind of Mormon I *really* was. No direct contact with me was required. In my school days and in my profession I had studied how individuals with a common identity in a workplace can treat others who are, or are perceived to be, different or outside of their group. Now it was my turn to be perceived as different.

For me, the discussions of real or perceived treatment were familiar. They had arisen in uncounted interviews, personal observations, and informal conversations. In the late 1970s and early 1980s, few of us who worked with differences among employees believed that working in the same organization offered employees a strong enough motivation for them to examine their behavior toward fellow workers. It was a challenge to ask employees to eliminate prejudice and stereotypes and to reexamine their own perceptions of "the other."

But I had been raised as a daughter of God. For me, the salutation of "sister" or "brother" was an acknowledgment of a shared bond with all other Church members. The commandment to love our neighbor as ourselves was a constant reminder that we were all in this together. Moreover, it was a togetherness based on eternal principles. In this light, I had anticipated working in an environment where those shared principles would guide daily interactions with colleagues and students and would shape our aspirations toward progress both as employees and as a people. I was surprised.

Gradually the realization dawned on me that many of my colleagues perceived me as truly different. I am still sorting through my perceptions about the behavior of others toward me (of course, I know that one cannot be fully certain about the motivation of others). The sorting process has been further complicated because even though BYU required me to teach, research, and be a good citizen, for me the university also offered a unique "field site." Here I could study and apply my research findings about the dynamics of difference and organizational change.

My journey of being one among many and yet being different can be summarized in three stages. I arrived at BYU believing that I knew what God would have me do. In time, I became discouraged among those with whom I thought I would find most similarity. I then went through a period of asking whether my experience mattered to God, which he answered in the affirmative. Now I know I am found, affirmed, and refined.

In the initial stage, I assumed that similarities would form the strongest bond between my colleagues and me since they rested on a shared gospel foundation that shaped how we approached both service and professional competency. My differences in experience and preparation as a single woman with a nontraditional degree, I thought, would be seen as a unique resource. I assumed that I had arrived "whole" in Zion — that who I was would be a valued part of what I could contribute as a sister and a professional colleague.

I arrived feeling that I was on an errand for the Lord. As a result, a number of comments and actions really did not bother me. For example, one faculty member told me that my degree must have come from a "mail-order" program; I heard others say that I was hired only because I was a woman; my leaders assigned me to serve on multiple committees — department, college, and university. These elements were above and beyond the normal difficulties that a new faculty member faces of preparing for classes that one has never taught. Further, as a nontraditional academic, I did not notice what I did not have: conference money, research assistants, and a network of professional colleagues who knew my work and would promote my work among other colleagues. I simply wanted to be competent as a faculty member; I failed to see the enormity of having a different academic preparation for a very traditional profession and organization. Instead, I focused on my intention to serve an organization that now housed both my work and spiritual communities.

I came fortified. And in the early years, I was nourished by some key relationships with male colleagues in the former organizational behavior department that other women on campus told me were better than in their departments. I had assumed that as an LDS people, we were to constantly seek both personal and organizational development. Therefore, I thought that my skills could help. I did not focus on being accepted or rewarded; my primary criterion was, "Is my contribution useful?"

Of course, my goals were not unique. My associates also viewed service as a common feature of working at BYU. I had thus anticipated that I would work with others on projects of service within both the university and the LDS community. In addition, I believed that we could find ways of valuing and integrating the different others at the university: women, people of color, nontraditional students, and so on. It was with this view in mind that I accepted invitations to serve on and chair numerous university committees, seeing them as vehicles for change. But the behaviors that I encountered seemed to say: It's not that we don't know how to change; we don't see the necessity for change that you do.

Because of my background, I had assumed that I would contribute to the university's ability to change. But what if the real issue was that leaders did not see a need to change and/or individuals did not desire change? What if I was not being useful but being used?

My personal optimism and my desire to be a helpful part of my department and university sustained me for a long time. I went through the tenure process. Because tenure and advancement in rank are distinct parts of professional progress, it was years later that I applied for and was denied rank advancement, creating a personal challenge for me. To be sure, because of my unique focus and preparation, I had not come to BYU expecting to be supported or rewarded for my research. But the sequence of activities that determine rank advancement offered an opportunity for me to reflect on who I was at the university.

I cannot describe an exact beginning and end to this second stage of my BYU experience. But the experience is as tangible as my first employment experience at a raspberry farm on the Utah–Idaho border. In my teenage years, I spent midsummer weeks picking raspberries, from earliest daylight until the heat of the morning began to melt the ripest berries at our touch, about 9 A.M. Our berry-picker tasks were simple: we were to fill the small cartons (to make up a case), to glean the row, not to bypass ripened berries nor pick unripe berries, to move quickly enough to fill a good number of cases, and, therefore, to be seen as able to pick the next day. I was too trusting.

If I looked at the overall berry field from a distance, it seemed that all pickers had a similar task. Our collective job was to pick the berries in the field. But at the individual level, experiences differed: some individuals stuffed unripe berries in the bottom of a carton, some accused the person on the other side of the row of stealing the best berries through the bush, others left berries hanging because of their haste to finish a bad row and to be assigned a better row, and some diligently completed the basic berry-picker tasks. Some of the more experienced and better pickers told me to "just watch me and you will do okay, since one has to learn by doing." Once in a while I even became aware that someone knew of my efforts. There was an older picker who occasionally would offer to top off my carton with her remaining berries if we both arrived at the main berry stand at the end of the shift.

I still vividly remember a morning that I stopped picking in my row and stood and looked around. I had assumed that through our common experience, I was connected, very connected, to the other pickers. But I was surprised to realize that my perceived connections did not really affect the behavior of the other workers toward me. For example, as we worked there was no indication that the others knew or cared about what I was experiencing, unless my work drew the attention of "Old Man Carson" and he came to check the row. If that happened, their work might also be checked. I am sure that the individual pickers' thoughts of caring both about me and about their jobs varied greatly. But the *outcome* of their common behavior on the job was quite similar. They wanted to stay out of the boss's way. That outcome led to my perception that I did not matter to the accomplishment of their tasks, unless I was a liability.

One day at BYU, I stopped in my "row" and stood to look around. I knew the requirements of my row. The requirements involved research, good teaching, and citizenship. I had heard from colleagues at other universities about the politics as well as the practicality of pretenure, tenure, and rank advancement. And, of course, I cared about meeting the requirements that would shape my professional standing. But I also had believed that my most important contribution would be through working with colleagues (row by row) to improve the whole. While one's professional status and preparation can create different individual experiences, my focus was on a hoped-for common goal: at the end of the row was a better department, college, or university. I believed that my contribution to that goal would shape my soul.

But did my contribution make a difference? Was I correct that we were all simultaneously working not only on our own goals but also working together toward the larger common goals? As I "stood in my row," I felt overwhelmed by the effect of my differences on my experience at BYU. Was I a liability?

The key individuals who had assisted me and whom I had seen in the other rows of my early years were gone. During a week, month, or semester no one stopped by my office to talk over ideas; I was no longer in a campus-based church calling, which had provided connections to some colleagues outside my discipline; my college associates did not invite me to lunch, dinner, or a home evening. Was I alone?

When I stood in my row, I realized that I did not have social ties on campus through my professional activities. My research had been reported mostly in proprietary studies sponsored by this or that organization, though some had appeared in journals or were unpublished. Given my interests and the stage of my publications at the time, there was no apparent interest among colleagues at BYU to coauthor works with me. And there was no one outside BYU, in part because I was at BYU. What was I doing at BYU?

I tried to discern what support should or could be available from my associates at the university. I watched to see what came back to me as a member of the BYU community. If it did not matter to others what I did, as long as I did not create a problem, did it matter to God? If I was on an errand of the Lord, then had he forgotten me? Or had I been distracted by seemingly more pressing matters?

I was mildly surprised to realize that I had come to see myself as a liability. When I had arrived on campus, I felt sustained both from my belief that my choice to be at BYU had divine support and by my own studies about differences within organizations. But I had also wanted the experience of being valued in a Latter-day Saint community. For the most part, it appeared that I had failed.

While trying not to judge the intentions of colleagues, I sensed that my experience was being shaped by their day-to-day responses to my differences. For instance, I was not invited to coauthor, as I have noted; I heard that resources would not be allocated to me for research assistance or for travel to conferences since I wasn't "a scholar." Even though I had good evaluations as an administrator, I perceived that there was a ceiling on administrative roles for women. And, although I was a good teacher, women teachers were not referred to as role models. Moreover, from discussions with male and female colleagues about how to enrich teaching, I learned that women's stories, leadership metaphors, or church experiences were not seen as universal teaching tools, for either male or female students in a business school.

While my research suggested, and my theology demanded, that I not judge another's intent, the combination of certain behaviors of individual colleagues created an impact on me that was greater than any single act toward me, positive or negative. And this contributed to my not seeing the few whose behavior really was different—those who cared about me as a colleague and a sister. I felt invisible to the Lord, isolated among my own people.

Instead of my differences being a means of my contributing to BYU, those differences became my major focus as I internalized feelings about the behavior of some toward me. I became immobilized. In my heart, I did not feel that I had arrived at BYU with a what-is-in-it-for-me attitude that sometimes comes from personal or professional competition. But now I began to focus on the question, "What is happening to me?" The intensity of my experience of being different began to accumulate. This intensity was amplified by my inferences about the behavior of colleagues toward me and the seeming lack of interest in or trust of me, even though I was a sister. All combined in me to produce an uncomfortable preoccupation with my own experience.

Was I being too sensitive? Was I the problem? I tried to understand how the combination of behaviors—common patterns in responses, failure to include me, and so on—accumulated to shape my perceptions and experiences. When I voiced my concerns, it was usually in a conversation with one person and not, obviously, with all the people whose behavior affected me. Since the individual to whom I would confide, let's call him Frank, had not been present when the other incidents occurred that shaped my feelings, he could not see how others had interacted with me. So he would focus only on his behavior or on mine. "But, do *I* do that?" was his usual question. Frank would then compare his own experiences with mine and see more similarities than differences. In his judgment, the intensity of my feelings was greater than any individual behavior warranted. He concluded that *my* perceptions must be the primary factor in what I was experiencing. But I was experiencing behaviors based on difference, more than I was being embraced because of similar beliefs. Responding to one who is different in a community where shared values are also operating is a challenge for many. Their focus usually falls on the few who are different.

Stage three of my BYU experience began with the almost simultaneous occurrence of two events. One is too sacred to write about in full detail, and the other forms a secular yet well-constructed parable from God as a lesson in how much I had internalized my "liability" status in Zion.

The sacred place. Over and over I have been instructed to take my problems to the Lord and to prepare for temple attendance with a concern or desire in mind. After being immobilized by internalizing my liability status, I went to the temple seeking peace, needing a few moments in an incubator of holiness away from a hassled world. I had no self-selected topics in mind. As the session began, I heard a voice so clearly that I turned to see who was behind me. The short message, so attuned to who I was and what I was experiencing, gently but clearly affirmed my worth. From the words, I knew that God knew where I was and who I was. I was stunned, and humbled.

The story of two travelers. Delta Airlines maintains a special customer service line for frequent flyers. Since work assignments have required me to travel since I was twenty, I have flown more than a million miles. The payoff for risking life and limb at multiple take offs and landings comes to me in the form of travel benefits and attention to me as a special customer.

I stood negotiating an upgrade for a flight. The friendly agent knew who I was and had talked with me before. Our light banter and laughter covered a number of topics as we waited for the ticket to be printed. I then looked to my right and saw a faculty colleague being waited on by another agent. My colleague looked at me, looked away, and continued his conversation with his agent. This was a colleague who had never initiated a conversation with me, had never spoken or smiled at me in hallways or elevators in over a decade at BYU. My immediate thought was, "Oh no, my agent doesn't realize that I am not as important. He doesn't know that I am not supposed to be getting all this positive attention." For a moment, I felt embarrassed and actually glanced at the agent waiting on me to see if he had noticed. The behavior of the agent assisting me had not changed. And did not change. I was still an important customer.

It took longer than the trip to unravel the implications of my first response to my colleague. It had not come from thoughtful analysis but was instead a learned reaction. I was not usually in a secular situation with a colleague from my own college. Non-BYU professional colleagues with whom I have worked, consulted, or researched have valued me. In me, they saw similarities in values and differences in experiences as resources. Over time, as business and political climates have changed, organizations have wanted more of my assistance in valuing and managing employee differences. In a flash, this circumstance and the airline agent's attentiveness led me to a freeing realization.

When I saw myself in a situation that illustrated my value to others, as my experience with the agent demonstrated, I realized that the behavior of the BYU colleague, whose pattern of behavior over the years gave no indication that I was valued as a sister, colleague, or administrator, was not the norm. Instead, it was *his* behavior that was different. Not greeting me at the airport did not affect my experience in that setting at all (on campus, of course, his behavior had become one more ingredient in my experience of subordination). I started to laugh, which did get me more attention from the agent helping me, but I was at a loss to explain it to him.

As if someone had rotated the kaleidoscope, the same pieces of my experience now created a new image. I sensed that I mattered — not because of an organizational contribution I could make, or because I am similar to or different from others, but because I am. And even though I am among his people, as a people we have not been perfected. My faith must encompass not only the circumstances of my own existence, but also the crucible of the existence of many others. Fundamentally, it is in our own self-interest to understand the experience of others.

Being at BYU has provided me a wonderful opportunity to be one with others who share my beliefs, to be viewed as different from the many, to see others as different from me, and to struggle with the common goal of creating Zion. Moreover, I have come to know that I am known by God who cares for each one of us, just as he does for our progress as a people.

The tender mercies of the Lord are over all those whom he hath chosen, because of their faith, to make them mighty even unto the power of deliverance (1 Nephi 1:20).

Millersville or BYU

Robert S. Patterson

Robert S. Patterson is dean of the David O. McKay School of Education at Brigham Young University. He was born and raised in Fort Macleod, Alberta, Canada. He received both his bachelor and master of education degrees from the University of Alberta and then pursued his doctorate in the history and philosophy of education at Michigan State University. In 1990 he was awarded an honorary doctorate from the University of Lethbridge. Following a professional career in higher education in Canada, he was persuaded to spend the concluding years of his professional career at BYU. He currently serves as a stake patriarch and has done so for nineteen years. Dean Patterson is married to Belva E. Orr. They have four children and seventeen grandchildren and currently live in Orem, Utah.

Finding God at BYU is not the title I would have chosen. At first this title seemed a little presumptuous. I recognize that God can be found in any locale or circumstance in which he is earnestly sought—though some may be more conducive than others. As I thought of contexts in which I have both experienced and observed the development of testimony, I began to wonder whether the unique intellectual-spiritual-emotional climate of BYU would be more or less favorable to finding God than circumstances that might be quieter, less stressful, or less encumbered with demands on the individuals' time, talents, and strengths. Is seeking God at BYU like seeking him in the whirlwind rather than in places where the still small voice is easier to hear?

Another reservation interrupted me: If I were to give public voice to ways in which my BYU experience has enhanced and developed my relationship with God, might this be misinterpreted as a form of pride? Could I do justice to my testimony and my blessings without seeming to exalt myself? Even Ammon was chided by his brothers for boasting when he rejoiced in the way the Lord had magnified his efforts and blessed his work.

Finding God at BYU. As I wrestled with the challenge of writing this chapter, I walked casually through a favorite used-book store, rummaging through stacks of old books, pamphlets, and tracts. *Finding God in Millersville;*[1] the small brown pamphlet would have been easy to overlook, but the similarity in the titles seemed more than coincidence. In 1932 President Heber J. Grant had this story printed to give to friends and family at Christmastime. Eagerly I scanned the simple narrative. I had no idea where Millersville might be, but someone had found God there — and President Grant had thought highly enough of the experience to share it with his loved ones. I wanted to know how this author had treated my assigned subject of finding God.

The story in the pamphlet is related by a businessman who was raised by his grandmother, a God-fearing woman who in her narrow-minded zeal to turn her grandson unto God had turned him away from God altogether. He left her home as soon as he could get away and found work in a cutlery factory in Millersville; soon thereafter he stopped attending Church. As years passed, this young man — "Mr. Thornton" — rose to become manager and principal stockholder of the factory. One day his secretary told him with urgency that "Jimmy" was dying and was asking for him. Mr. Thornton did not know who Jimmy was; he had scarcely noticed the small office boy who waited on him faithfully from day to day. His reaction was to send flowers and some perfunctory note of sympathy to the family, but the secretary insisted that it was important that he see the boy. So, grudgingly Mr. Thornton went to the poverty-stricken home and knelt by the bedside of the dying child. The boy's final words were, "I wanted to tell you I done the best I could, Mr. Thornton." It was the doctor's words that placed the blame: "Do you know what killed that kid? No air; no sunshine; long hours in a dirty hole of a factory. How many days did your people lose last year on account of bad health?"[2]

Jimmy's death was the beginning of Mr. Thornton's search for God in Millersville. As he grew concerned about the health of his three hundred employees, Mr. Thornton took money he had saved to remodel his home and began to remodel his factory to let in more light and sunshine. He shortened the workday and the workweek. He sought to know his workers personally, to show an interest in their lives and their needs. "Gradually, as I got nearer to my people, they began to move in close to me," he wrote.[3] "The closer I got to them, the more I admired them."[4] As he became closer to his fellow man, he began to think more of God: "What kind of a God is he? How does he act?"[5] Reflecting on the fatherly feelings he experienced for his workers, he began to reflect on the fatherhood of God.

Finally, as Mr. Thornton sat in his factory in Millersville he began to realize that "the human personality is greater than the world" and concluded: "The happiest times in my life are when I find someone among my folks who really appreciates what I'm trying to do, and who turns in and tries to help. Having that in mind, I am ready to believe that [God] must have smiled for a second on that Saturday afternoon when I found him in my office. . . . My life really is as valuable, as important, as worthwhile in the world as I have always wanted to believe it. He needs me; that's importance enough."[6]

My office at BYU is far removed in time, and probably in space, from Mr. Thornton's office in the cutlery factory in Millersville. Yet it too has been a vantage point from which God can be discerned in the lives of his children and better understood through the joy of serving them and serving with them.

Mr. Thornton's quest to find God began when he recognized the value in his workers and dedicated his efforts to meeting their needs. As I read his story I thought of a recently retired colleague who seemed to have a knack for learning the needs of his students and quietly, modestly setting out to help them. It has been his practice to petition the Lord to lead him to people who need help; and the Lord's response has been evident as people in need have just kept showing up in his classes and in other aspects of his life.

During one semester this professor noticed that one of his students had missed several class periods. Sensing that this young man's problem went beyond the laziness that sometimes sets in about midsemester, the teacher went by the student's home and found him caring for his wife, who was seriously ill. Two very young and very disheveled children ran about the disordered house. A brief conversation revealed that food was scarce and many bills were unpaid. Quickly calculating how much would be needed to rescue the young family, this professor wrote a personal check for the required amount. While caring for his wife and children, this student had fallen behind in several of his classes. Over the next few weeks the professor spent much personal time in coaching and tutoring so the young man would be able to catch up. An ironic twist on the situation occurred as this student did not have the attributes and abilities necessary to succeed as a teacher, and it was the professor who had given him so much help who was required to make the judgment that he should not be certified to enter the teaching profession. Because of the love and consideration that the professor continually showed him, the young man was able to accept the judgment gracefully and to make the necessary changes in his professional plans.

As this professor continued to pray for opportunities to help others, opportunities continued appearing in his classrooms. An older woman, poorly dressed and poorly groomed, attracted his attention not only through her appearance but through her struggle to attend classes and keep up with her work. Visiting her at home, he found a very dirty environment and three neglected children. The professor hurried to his own home and picked up wash buckets, scrubbing utensils, and other cleaning supplies. Dishes were washed, floors were scrubbed, bathroom fixtures were scoured. On his next visit, he brought a Christmas tree and decorations. Years have passed, and this woman, now confined to a wheel chair, still calls the professor every few weeks to receive the comfort and encouragement that he has consistently and cheerfully given.

Through this professor's influence, encouragement, and help, many young people have become missionaries. One rather unpromising prospective missionary came to the professor's office asking to add a class that was already more than full. The young man refused to remove the hat covering a head of hair that was definitely out of harmony with the University's dress and grooming code. Quickly sizing up the situation, the professor asked, "Do you want it badly enough to go and get your hair cut?" The boy agreed to the haircut, and the professor signed the add card. Some time later the young man withdrew from the University when he spent his tuition money on a marijuana party. Despite this rather inauspicious beginning, he later realized his error, repented of his attitude and his mistakes, and finally entered the mission field. He was effective in his work and found joy in his missionary service. Partway through his mission he wrote to the professor, thanking him for his positive influence and expressing love for the gospel and his mission. The young missionary mentioned in his letter that his mission might be cut short because his father had recently lost his job and his family could not afford to keep him in the field. The professor immediately called the mission president and committed to send the money necessary for the young man to complete his mission.

This professor is one of many who daily go about their business — quietly, modestly, unobtrusively doing good. As I associate with such people, I find God, for these are servants who do God's work as a natural, integral part of their daily lives.

Some of my colleagues and associates at BYU teach us of God through what they are as well as through what they do. One of my former associate deans is such an individual. Through years of close daily association, I have never heard her speak negatively of another person — something which can be said of very few individuals. Widowed at an early age with a number of children, she has faced challenging circumstances with remarkable courage and unwavering faith. If you ask her how she has managed to raise those perfect children alone — working more than full time, teaching, mentoring, and inspiring innumerable university students as well — she'll answer simply, "I've been blessed."

Several years ago we had an opportunity for eight of our BYU students to do their student teaching at a private boarding school in China. I asked this associate dean to accompany the group, help them to settle into their new situation, and generally mentor, supervise, and assist them as they began this cross-cultural living and teaching experience. The culture shock for this group was a shock indeed. In the cramped dormitory in which they were housed there were no mattresses on the beds, and there was only a hose for showering and washing dishes. Many of the children at the school were not as obedient or respectful to the American teachers as they were to the more experienced Chinese and Canadians; and teaching Chinese speakers English — even in English — was more difficult than they had expected. Satan took advantage of the young women's vulnerability: they were homesick and discouraged, some were angry with the University for sending them into such uncomfortable conditions, and a couple spoke of wanting to go home right away.

In this highly volatile situation, my associate dean was the source of stability and optimism. She remained cheerful and positive, taking the students out for special dinners, sightseeing, and shopping expeditions. Through her example she taught them to laugh at inconveniences, find blessings in their experiences, and focus on loving the Chinese children. One of the student teachers wrote in her journal that this dear sister was one of the most Christlike people she had ever known. The student explained the attitude she had developed under this influence. "I know Heavenly Father has a purpose for me and for each of the people I meet, however different or similar we may be. I am grateful to be here and would not wish myself anywhere different — even if given the opportunity." Another went from initial dismay at the living conditions to a strong personal focus on service. "I think King Benjamin was right when he said that when you are in the service of your fellowmen you are only in the service of your God. Service is the key. If you do things for those around you, they will more likely help you. If you are good to them, they will be good to you."

Perhaps the greatest strength in the leadership of this associate dean was her vision of the student-teaching experience as having an important purpose in the lives of those students as individuals and in the work of the Lord in the country of China. This vision infused her personal words and actions — the counsel she gave and the sacrifices she made. The young women caught onto her vision and began to transform their own attitudes and behavior. Some of their communications reveal this change. "Because I am here, I have to remember that I am here because this is where the Lord wanted me to go. Although I still miss my life back at home, keeping my greater purpose in mind has given me the strength to be here and work hard. The Lord's mission and our education are not two separate things but one and the same. I know the Lord has much in mind by leading me and the other girls here. I don't understand all that he has in mind, but I am willing to do my best to represent him."

Though her responsibilities as associate dean prevented her from remaining in China throughout the student-teaching experience, my friend continued to offer encouragement and love through weekly communication. The students confided their joys, their victories, their needs, their trials, and their frustrations. Mattresses were obtained, but the water was still cold. Teaching never became easy, but it became meaningful for the young women who followed the example of their mentor. Love was the wellspring of all that she did, and many of the students followed her beautiful example. Several of them used love in defining their experience. "I'm sure a great love and lasting friendship will develop between me and [the Chinese] people." "We must . . . use love in action to portray our feelings." "It is amazing how fast the heart can love."

This remarkable woman served as associate dean until she was called on a mission—her third in about a dozen years. We sometimes referred to her behind her back as "the Mother Teresa of BYU." As I see her love, along with faith, integrity, and determination to serve, I find even more of God at BYU. Our Savior exemplified unselfish love as he taught, healed, forgave, and ultimately atoned for the sins of his people. Daily I see colleagues who are doing their best to follow his example. And I learn from them.

I learn from my students as well as from the faculty and administration. I am continually renewed by the faith of those young people and moved by the sacrifices that many of them make.

Shortly after arriving at BYU, I requested and was privileged to teach a class on the Doctrine and Covenants. In this class I was to encounter a young man from Honduras who would teach me a great deal about goal setting and persistence, as well as about the early scholar-leaders of the Church.

In class, I was first attracted to this young man through the brightness and enthusiasm that shone in his face. He made few comments, due to his struggle with the English language, but when he did speak he bore a strong testimony of how the Holy Spirit provides insight to those who seek its guidance. The third of ten children raised by a single mother, this student had come to the United States to study at BYU with only ten dollars in his pocket and his determination to succeed. His English language skills were very poor. He took the TOEFL test nearly fifteen times before he could score high enough to be accepted as a student; he took the test so many times he was no longer asked to pay the fee for it. I learned to love this young man, particularly to appreciate the ways in which he depended on the Holy Ghost to guide the course of his life.

About a year after taking my class, this student called to ask my advice about finding employment. He was discouraged because his poor English skills were making it difficult for him to obtain the kind of job he needed to finance the remainder of his education. I had been planning to undertake research on two Latter-day Saint scholar-teacher-apostles, John A. Widtsoe and James E. Talmage. I found myself asking my former student if he would like to become my research assistant on this project. As he agreed enthusiastically, I did not quite anticipate the extent of participation that would come from a third member of our research team. Whenever my assistant would encounter a stumbling block in his work, he would humbly petition the help of the Lord through the Holy Ghost. Whether the obstacle was difficulty in finding particular materials or the refusal of his request to examine documents in a particular collection, he would pray, and without exception the barrier would be removed. I looked forward to our reporting sessions when he would report on these spiritual experiences as well as on the information he was finding to expand my research. After three years of working with me (five years at BYU), this student finally graduated with a degree in computer science. He had completed his degree and had managed to send one hundred dollars home to his mother every month after taking care of his own needs and obligations. And I had gained an enviable pile of research on Elder Widtsoe and Elder Talmage, in addition to a renewed testimony of the presence and influence of the Holy Ghost in the lives of those who humbly request it.

In addition to my teaching, I have felt the influence of many students through my calling as a patriarch in a campus stake. One young man had prepared throughout his life to play football for a major university. With the enthusiastic support of his father, he had trained until he had achieved a high degree of skill. As a successful high school player, he was offered full-ride scholarships at a number of institutions; however, for a reason not understood by his family, he decided to attend BYU, although no scholarship had been committed for him and he would be trying out for the team as a walk-on. During his first few months on campus, a concerned and loving bishop talked to him about a mission. When he came to me for a blessing, he had received his call and was excited over the prospect of entering the mission field. He realized then the reason he had felt drawn to BYU. He had found something more important to him than football, something that would not have happened if he had accepted a football scholarship at a secular institution. His father did not understand his choice and made no attempt to conceal the disappointment and alienation that he felt. But the young man still approached his mission with thankfulness and joy. He knew that his choice was correct, and he hoped that in the near future members of his family would accept and appreciate the decision he had made.

When a young woman from Singapore came into my office, I relived events that had been pivotal in my own life many years before. She told me of her choice to come to America to study and of her decision to attend BYU. Her superior academic record and her family's wealth made it possible for her to attend almost any institution. But when she heard of BYU, she was unable to dismiss the thought that she should come here. When she arrived on campus, her roommates quickly accepted her into their circle of friends and began including her in their activities. Before long she began taking the missionary discussions, accepted the truth of the gospel, and was baptized into the Church. When she came to me she was facing a serious confrontation. Her family embraced a non-Christian religion which had little tolerance for those who challenged its teachings. She feared that the love and acceptance that had sustained her from infancy would be withdrawn, that she would no longer be welcome in her parents' home. But she knew that she had found the truth, and she was determined to follow the gospel's teachings, wherever she should be led. I was at her age and period of life when I joined the Church. As I spoke with her, my mind ranged back to the time when I discovered the gospel, studied it, converted, and entered the waters of baptism. I recalled the reaction of my own family as I shared her anxiety over the reaction she might receive. I was blessed to be able to reassure her that her decision to be baptized had been correct and to affirm that I had not for one moment regretted making that same decision so many years ago. Together we bore testimony that the Lord sustains his people in their time of need.

So I have found God in my office at BYU through the students who have visited me, bringing with them accounts of their ambitions, their sacrifices, their joys, and their faith. Thus, faculty, administrators, and students have shown me by their activities, their faith, and their sacrifices that God is indeed a part of daily life at Brigham Young University. Like Mr. Thornton at the cutlery factory in Millersville, I find God in the lives of those who love him, follow him, and obey his commandments. And I understand more of his nature as I serve and grow to love those who serve and love him.

Mr. Thornton's quest to find God began with a death and with a desire to alleviate suffering in others. The dying words of little Jimmy, the office boy, were an assurance that he had done the best he could. There is something particularly sacred in the service of those who continue to work for others when there is very little strength, energy, or time left for them to give. As I've watched those around me struggle with life-changing and life-threatening illnesses, I've seen faith that continually inspires and strengthens my own.

Daily I see colleagues who smile with faith and courage though they know their illnesses will soon take their lives. In the hall near my office I often pass a professor who has been through several bouts of chemotherapy to eke out a little more time from an incurable form of cancer. Determined to serve as long as he can in as many ways as he can, he teaches religion courses in addition to classes in his own field of specialization, works at the temple, and teaches Sunday School as well. He is the first to notice when someone else seems tired or ill, the first to express concern. He is also the first to offer help when someone needs to relocate a desk, adjust a shelf, or bring a new filing cabinet into an office. He recently returned from his vacation more tired than he was when he left; he had spent his "rest" time helping others to remodel and repair their home.

I remember another gifted and dedicated professor who came to my office near the beginning of a fall semester. Characteristic of her unselfish concern for her students, she had come to explain that she might not be able to adequately teach the classes for which she was scheduled. She told me that she had been diagnosed with a particularly lethal form of cancer and had been advised that she had only a short time to live.

This visit took place two years ago. In a priesthood blessing, this sister was told that she had additional work to accomplish on this earth. With unquestioning faith she has sought and received the blessings of the Lord. Though few people have long survived the form of cancer from which she suffers, she is determined to complete her work. A year after her diagnosis, she invited me to her bedside. Despite discouraging messages from her own body and from the doctors who were caring for it, she committed to attend the annual fall conference of the faculty and staff of the McKay School of Education. We then committed to each other that between the meetings we would walk together in the sunshine. Leaning heavily on the arm of her husband, she met with her colleagues — and then we had our walk.

Trusting in the power of the Lord, this sister taught another course — though others in her condition would not think of leaving their homes. Another year passed, with new tumors and more surgery. Finally, the end came for the mortal existence of this brave sister. Her life was truly a testament of the existence of God.

At our most recent fall meetings, another sister who suffers from terminal cancer was asked how she was feeling. "Really well," she responded. "I'm glad to be able to be back." On close questioning, she was forced to admit that her cancer is not operable, but she is grateful for what she can do and does not complain about what she cannot. Another courageous sister suffers from a serious lung condition, but she conducts workshops to educate teachers with her portable oxygen tank beside her.

I feel the power of the plan of salvation as I watch these brothers and sisters serve with their remaining energy and face their coming transition with confidence and hope. They know that the success of their mortal probation lies in what they contribute to God's work and to his children — and they are going to contribute in every way that they can. Theirs is a consecrated service. As I see it, I see God at BYU.

Elijah found God, not in the whirlwind, but in the still small voice. As I seek for God at BYU, I find him, not in the whirlwind of activity, debate, reputation, or super achievement — though I suspect he exerts a definite influence in some of those areas. But I find him in the still small voices of the people: students, professors, and other colleagues who quietly, modestly, and very naturally dedicate themselves to his service.

Finding God at BYU? It's not so difficult after all.

Notes

1. *Finding God in Millersville* (Salt Lake City: Stevens & Wallis, 1932).

2. Ibid., 21.

3. Ibid., 23.

4. Ibid., 26.

5. Ibid., 35.

6. Ibid., 37.

7. Ibid., 38–49.

Transitions

For he that diligently seeketh shall find; and the mysteries of God shall be unfolded unto them, by the power of the Holy Ghost, as well in these times as in times of old, and as well in times of old as in times to come; wherefore, the course of the Lord is one eternal round (1 Nephi 10:19).

A Matter of Choice

Bruce L. Christensen

*Bruce L. Christensen, formerly dean of the College of Fine Arts
and Communications at Brigham Young University, is now a
senior vice president of Bonneville International. He was born in
Ogden, Utah. He is a graduate of the University of Utah and
received an M.S.J. from Northwestern University. While pursuing
his education, he worked as a reporter, first for KSL, then for WGN
News in Chicago, and then again for KSL. Later he was general
manager of KBYU and then KUED and KUER FM at the University of Utah. He became president of the National Association of
Public Television Stations in 1982 and was named president and
CEO of the Public Broadcasting Service in 1984, serving in that
capacity until 1993, when he accepted the deanship at BYU. He has
served on a number of business and civic boards, but in his heart,
he considers himself a journalist. Mr. Christensen and his wife,
Barbara, are the parents of four children and the grandparents of
four. They live in Orem, Utah.*

Faith looks forward, but its consequences are most clearly
understood by looking backward. The space in-between, the
present—described by C. S. Lewis as the point at which time
touches eternity—is where faith influences action. Faith, at least
for me, has never been the blinding flash of the obvious. The
evidence of faith—which Paul says is of things hoped for but
unseen—is hard for me to comprehend, except by looking backward. So, the opportunity to describe the role Brigham Young
University has played in building my faith and giving me the
opportunity to practice it permits that backward vision. It deep-
ens my appreciation for all that this institution has meant to the
development of my belief in a living and loving Father in Heaven.

I didn't plan to come to BYU as an undergraduate. I applied
and was accepted at Weber State College and intended to live at

home my freshman year. I then planned to serve a mission. A high school friend, Grant Taylor, convinced me that I would be better off living away from home and persuaded me to at least apply for admission. I did, feeling that I might indeed be better off attending a larger, more academically challenging school. I was accepted and began my freshman year at BYU in the fall of 1961.

No one in our family had ever gone to college, so I was unprepared for what I faced. It was a tough year for me. I was homesick. I had few friends on campus. Most of my high school buddies were still in Clearfield (then about a two-hour drive from Provo), so I went home almost every weekend to see them and to spend time with my girlfriend, who was a senior in high school. My classes were large, difficult, and not particularly engaging. I found myself struggling to do the reading and to keep up with my homework. I regretted my decision to attend BYU.

My roommates, on the other hand, seemed to be having a pretty good time. They were getting by with their studies, and their social life seemed a lot more exciting than mine did. At the beginning of the second semester, three of us enrolled in an astronomy class. It met every Wednesday night. On our way home from the first class, we stopped by Heritage Halls, where I was introduced to an apartment of girls. From that point on, my BYU experience changed dramatically.

That night I met a tall, attractive freshman from Mesa, Arizona. Her father was a college professor. Her mother and father met at and graduated from BYU. Her three older sisters and their husbands similarly had met at and graduated from BYU. Her aunt, Dr. Glenna Wood, had been my English professor my first semester. "BYU blue" ran through their veins. She was a person of deep faith, instilled by her family's religious tradition that went back to the earliest days of the Church. Barbara Lucelle Decker changed my life and for thirty-seven years has added immeasurably to my faith.

We began dating that spring (1962), and I spent less time going home on weekends. She coached me through my second semester of English, proofreading my papers. Most of what we did, however, was talk. We talked about anything and everything—long conversations. I never knew that I had so much to say. For the first time in my life, I felt entirely free to talk about anything that came into my mind. She felt the same, and we shared the deepest feelings of our hearts with each other.

Her family and background were intimidating. I teased her that she was a princess and I a lowly frog, waiting for a transformational kiss. Her gifts were more than a kiss; they were a transformational presence in my life.

Before BYU, my faith had consisted of what I believed was a witness that the Book of Mormon was true. I had read it during my senior year in high school and followed Moroni's injunction—asking if it was true. I felt that it was, and if so, then Joseph Smith was a prophet, and the Church was true as well. But my faith wasn't grounded. It often seemed hard to remember that one night's witness, kneeling at the side of my bed, when so many questions about the veracity of my testimony kept coming into my mind.

I realized that a part of my problem was personal worthiness. Those matters were resolved as I received my mission call to the Brazilian Mission. I went into the Mission Home in Salt Lake City (a brief, weeklong occurrence that doesn't compare with today's extensive MTC experience) wondering whether I should go to Brazil for two and a half years. My faith faltered. I talked with my mother (my father having died of cancer when I was fourteen). I talked to my bishop and stake president. I called Barbara and talked to her. She said that her father had some advice. Smith Decker took the phone and told me that there were two reasons why I might be feeling the way I was. One possibility was that I had been called to the wrong mission. I didn't think that was too likely, since President David O. McKay signed my mission papers. The other was that Satan didn't want me in the mission field because I would be a threat to his kingdom.

I had never thought of myself as a threat to anyone's kingdom, but I knew the reality of Satan and his influence. A worthy mission in life would be to weaken his kingdom. So, I went to Brazil, faint of heart but resolved in spirit.

My BYU connections deepened further during those two and a half years. Barbara continued to write to me, keeping me posted on her progress through school. She even took a Portuguese class from the famed Gerrit de Jong. I shared my mission experiences, and together we got through a mission for me and all but one semester of a BYU baccalaureate degree for her. I returned from my mission just before Christmas of 1964. Barbara's graduation took place the following May, and we were married on 17 June 1965 in the Mesa Arizona Temple. We were launched on the next great adventure of our lives—one that we hope will be eternal.

Our problem was similar to that faced by most young couples—money. With the help of Arch Madsen, whom I had met while on my mission, I secured a job as a news reporter for KSL radio and television in Salt Lake City. Barbara found work at the Mountain Bell telephone company. Our workplaces were half a block away from each other, but she worked days and I worked nights—arranged this way so I could go to school at the University of Utah during the day.

The world that I entered as a reporter was new, challenging, and fascinating to me. As a reporter, I found myself on the inside of stories that were among the biggest of the decade. Catastrophic airplane crashes, Vietnam War protests, political infighting, debates over capital punishment, floods, mine explosions, serial murders, venality, greed, sloth, stupidity, mendacity, and plain old-fashioned foolishness made up the stuff of which I was to report over the next six years of my life.

I was introduced to a worldview foreign and different from any I had ever known. I began to wonder about the reality of the one that I had come from. Because I was a returned missionary (the only one in the newsroom at the time I was hired), I was given the LDS Church Office Building as one of my beat assignments. Seeing the Brethren with the eyes of a journalist, rather than those of a faithful missionary and Church member, was a jarring experience. Their humanity was evident. The deification that had taken place in my mind (as it does regularly in the Church) had not actually occurred. They were not perfect. The bureaucracy that they presided over made some of the same mistakes that were so evident in the city, county, state, and national institutions that I had been reporting on. How was it possible for the true and living Church to have failings? Above all else, journalism trains the reporter to question everything and everyone. In the journalist's world there are no eternal verities. Everything is challenged and everyone's motives are suspect. Journalists are trained skeptics. They seek truth by asking who, what, where, why, when, and how. This became my mantra. I made journalism my professional world. I accepted its intellectual grounding. It became my education, my work, and my life.

After earning my bachelor's degree from the University of Utah, I took a nine-month leave of absence from KSL, where I had worked full time while going to school full time. Barbara, our new baby daughter Jennifer, and I went off to Chicago. Nine months later, I had earned my M.S.J. from the Medill School of Journalism at Northwestern University.

This was a time of immense turmoil in American public life. The Democratic Convention had turned Chicago politics on its head. Many of my classmates had received no prior journalism training. They came three months early to start their program at Medill and were assigned to cover the Chicago Convention and reported on the despotic use of political and police power. They were hardened by and bitter toward what they witnessed. Their reporting experience hardened professional skepticism into cynicism. The Vietnam War was at its height. We learned daily of the lies and stupidity of politicians who made authority their truth, rather than truth their authority.

During this time I came to understand that the world of a journalist is unlike any other. If compared to the planets in our solar system, I believe that Pluto would be the planet whose physical properties would most closely represent the worldview of a journalist. It's a cold, dark, tiny, miserable place, where everything is suspect; where everybody lies; where graft, corruption, malfeasance, self-interest, and greed reign supreme; and where the journalist's job is to find out about and tell people about all of these horrible happenings. Some wag said that if journalists had a Thirteenth Article of Faith, it would read: "If there is anything hateful, despicable, shameful, or rotten, we seek after these things."

The democratic assumption is that if people know about such things, they can at least protect themselves from it or vote the rascals out of office. I began to see the conflict and difficulty society has with the press. It comes from a failure of both sides to understand differences between their frames. The cultural assumptions held by society at large and those held by journalists differ. Journalists believe it is their duty to deliver bad news. Society finds an easy and ready scapegoat in the messenger.

The journalist's worldview is democratic. In America, the press enjoys an explicit, constitutionally defined and protected role written by the Founding Fathers. When asked what form of government the Constitutional Convention had agreed upon, Benjamin Franklin replied, "A republic, the worst of all political systems save all others." The Founding Fathers believed Lord Acton's statement, "Absolute power corrupts absolutely." Their antidote to such social malaise was freedom of the press. The press plays a potent role in American democracy because it was intended to do so. The press is one of the forces that the Founding Fathers balanced against the powers of government. The duty of the press is to tell about graft, corruption, greed, and malfeasance in our society. Journalists are trained to be society's equivalent of junkyard watchdogs. They bark at every opportunity, justified or not. It's the best way that the Founding Fathers could find to keep us alert to what is described in D&C 121:39: "We have learned by sad experience that it is the nature and disposition of almost all men, as soon as they get a little authority, as they suppose, they will immediately begin to exercise unrighteous dominion."

The Church's worldview, on the other hand, comes from the planet Kolob. The Church's worldview doesn't flow from democratic principles (as much as we admire the Constitution for the freedoms it provides). Our religious worldview comes from our belief that the best possible government is a theocracy—a righteous King making righteous judgments, ruling a righteous people who live righteous lives. Such a society needs no watchdogs. In a theocracy the media (whatever it is in that state) will be used to disseminate pure knowledge, light, and truth! The entire society will seek that which is virtuous, lovely, or of good report.

Can you imagine how strange that world is to a journalist? Can you understand how difficult it is for these two worldviews to understand each other? For me, at the age of twenty-five, my worldviews were at war. What I was learning in my professional training instantly conflicted with my faith. I struggled, trying to reconcile the two worldviews.

I remember coming home from the newsroom one Saturday morning after covering the opening session of a general conference. Disgustedly, I threw my coat and tape recorder on the couch of our newly purchased home and said in frustration to Barbara, "Why do the Brethren always talk about the same thing—the first principles? I've heard this stuff since I was in Primary. I want more. They should give us more. I'm sick and tired of the same old thing." I went on raging against the credulity of those who accepted this "pabulum" as real spiritual food. I wondered out loud and at great volume about the truthfulness of a religion that purports to be led by revelation but never reveals anything new. "All we get," I told my patient, loving wife, "is the same old, same old, and I am sick of it!"

As I heard myself talking out loud in this manner, doing what I had covenanted not to do, I realized that my faith was in crisis. The faith of my childhood, teenage, and missionary experiences had eroded to the point that I was asking questions to which the answers should have been self-evident. But for me they were not. I was doing what my profession said I should do: ask the hard questions, and unflinchingly report the results. How could I possibly remain faithful, seeing the obvious distance between the semiannual pronouncements of Church leaders from the Tabernacle pulpit and their imperfection? Rationally, faith made no sense, but I wanted it to make sense. I yearned for it to do so. Even in my seasons of waning belief, I felt that there was something to the Church. There had to be. What else could explain the sacrifices people made at the request of the Church leaders (paying tithing, accepting missions to the far ends of the earth, and surrendering brilliant professional careers to render full-time service in Church leadership)? There had to be a reason why people kept struggling, seeking to make their lives more closely fit the instruction that came from Church headquarters. Reason said that such faithfulness was folly, an abandonment of intellectual rigor, and a denial of irrefutable facts. Reason was at war with my faith, and reason had the upper hand.

During this struggle, an unexpected invitation came from Heber Wolsey to work with him at BYU in his public communications effort there. I initially turned down the opportunity, but a few months later, circumstances inside the KSL newsroom changed. We decided to accept Heber's offer and moved our little family (having added Heather) to Provo. I started a new job at BYU in the fall of 1970. We followed another road back to BYU!

I hadn't resolved fully my struggles between reason and faith, and BYU seemed like a pretty safe place to undertake that resolution. For me, it turned out to be exactly the right place. I quickly found colleagues who were working on the same issues as I was. Their professions were different, but their struggles were no less real than my own.

We had an astonishing environment in which to wrestle with those questions — an environment in which it was acceptable (some would say required) to believe. In this atmosphere, not only did I have the benefit of being able to share my feelings with my peers — Bruce Olsen, Pete Peterson, Terry Olson, Mac Boyter, John Kinnear, Claudia Wright, and others — but I began to benefit from other BYU sources as well.

What I learned by coming back to BYU was that my professional education — knowledge, skill, and expertise — had outstripped my education in faith. This built slowly. It was never as clear to me then as it is today. It came "line upon line," experience upon experience, as my faith was built in the nurturing, accepting environment of BYU.

An unexpected aspect of strengthening my faith came from my responsibility to cover each of the Devotionals and Forums for the broadcast media. I found myself again, as I had while I was a freshman, educated in a manner that was quite unexpected. The testimonies — the confessions of faith — of those who spoke touched my heart. Spiritual food midweek came from those experiences, and I realized how much I needed that nourishment. I recalled the richness of the Devotionals my freshman year. The messages of Truman Madsen, President Hugh B. Brown, Elder Spencer W. Kimball, Elder Harold B. Lee, and a host of others came flooding back to me. In some cases I recalled specific parts of their addresses. I remembered the powerful testimony of the Savior and the story of the currant bush given by President Brown. He began his speech by joking that he didn't mind the loss of hair, or diminished eyesight, or reduced hearing. "But," he said, "oh, how I miss my mind."

The advice given by Brother Madsen came vividly to mind. He explained that Church leaders were called to strengthen our testimonies. Some did it by faithful example and others by trial of our patience. "Either way," he said, "your testimonies will be strengthened if you will let them be." His explanation elicited a laugh of recognition from the audience. Who hadn't had a leader or teacher about whom they asked, "What inspiration led to his or her call?" This recollection, prompted by the spiritual experiences of again attending BYU Devotionals, led me to think carefully about why I had such a hang-up about the human failures I had witnessed as a reporter.

Other BYU experiences opened doors of faithful understanding beyond what I had thought possible. I was asked to serve as bishop of the BYU 46th Ward. I was twenty-eight years old, and the ward members joked that they could trust their bishop because he was under thirty. This was near the end of the Vietnam War, and the counter culture told young people to never trust anyone over thirty.

I succeeded Gordon M. Low, who had been called to be president of the BYU Fifth Stake. Darrell Monson and John Covey were his counselors. These wise, seasoned, and able Church leaders poured their knowledge and experience into us as they led a stake of students who themselves were remarkable because of their faithfulness. My counselors and I willingly followed their instruction and for four years we enjoyed the richest blessings imaginable.

The BYU 46th Ward was made up mostly of freshman. Our numbers included women on three floors and men on two floors of Deseret Towers. Our most visible sin was that of pride. We had our own ward fight song ("Fighting 46th"), our own motto ("One for Another"), and our own ward hymn ("To Some 'Tis Given," written by a former ward member and President Low while he was bishop of the ward). We had a ward flag. We won first place in the all-stake road show competitions because we had original music performed by our ward orchestra, and every member of the ward was involved in the show. We considered ourselves "the only true ward on campus." We even had our own section of the Doctrine and Covenants — the forty-sixth section — it explained that all of our gifts were to be used for the benefit of each other!

In spite of our pride, we did learn important lessons. We learned about living for something greater than self. Service was the heart of all that we did. Our stake leadership helped us to see that knowing the gospel meant little if it did not translate into the application of its principles in our daily living. The way that we interact with each other mattered. The gospel needed to inform the way we treated our classmates and our roommates, our faithfulness in home teaching and visiting teaching, our consideration of those who were in our Sunday School, Relief Society, and priesthood classes. Ours was a practical laboratory of gospel action. Such was the faithfulness of those wonderful freshmen that it can be said of them, "There truly was not a happier people!"

Time seemed to evaporate from one year to the next. Gospel lessons learned and applied proved the importance of faith in action. During six years of service in the BYU Fifth Stake, I gained gospel insight that could have been obtained in no other way. Perhaps the most important single lesson for me is summarized in the forty-sixth section of the Doctrine and Covenants: "To some it is given by the Holy Ghost to know that Jesus Christ is the Son of God, and that he was crucified for the sins of the world. To others it is given to believe on their words, that they also might have eternal life" (D&C 46:13–14).

I learned that I didn't have to have knowledge. Faith is sufficient to achieve the desired end of eternal life. What a stunning realization! How foolish I had been to believe that I had to reason it all out in my mind and come to know for myself. Faith achieved the same end. I discovered that through faith, Alma's simple metaphor (Alma 32:28–43) and Isaiah's counsel (Isa. 28:10; see also 2 Ne. 28:30; D&C 98:12; 128:21) worked. "Line upon line, and precept upon precept," seeds of faith were planted. They grew, and the fruit was "most precious" and "sweet above all that is sweet" (Alma 32:42). I could choose and did choose faith, because I was in an environment that invited that choice as the only option.

My BYU faithful education expanded into my professional life. Not long after I was called to be a bishop, I was asked to become the director of Broadcast Services and general manager of BYU's noncommercial, educational radio and television stations — KBYU FM and TV. At the time, I felt that I just happened to be in the right place at the right time (which was true). As events have unfolded in my life, this was to be a time of education in a professional field that I could have obtained nowhere else but at BYU.

I knew broadcasting in general from my reporting experience, but I came from the news side of broadcasting and not from experience in the business or advertising side, which was the most common avenue to top management in commercial media. The world of public (noncommercial, educational) broadcasting was new.

Colleagues who were passed over, who were more knowledgeable about public broadcasting and who were better trained than I to assume the duties of director and general manager, stepped forward to help me succeed. They did not hold back, they were not bitter at someone else being given preference over their years of service, and they willingly shared knowledge, skill, and expertise with me. Those were the best of times — heady times — for those of us who wanted to prove that broadcasting could be used for higher purposes than making money. Our collective goal was to fulfill E. B. White's vision of excellence — television used as our society's "Lyceum, our Chautauqua, our Minsky's, and our Camelot."[1]

Armed with the optimism of youth and inexperience (we often said we were simply too dumb to know that something couldn't be done, so we did it), we transformed the stations into our image of White's ideal. The work was enormously satisfying. Refining our management skills, we had the help of Bill Dyer and his talented group of faculty and students in organizational behavior. The Marriott School of Management offered accounting classes and project management training that were desperately needed. Ben Lewis, Darrell Monson, and Bill Farnsworth provided administrative oversight that was at once encouraging of our collective vision for the stations while requiring fiscal and management accountability of the highest order. Over the next ten years I received the most important and unique professional training one could imagine. Central to it all was the participation and leadership of the University's new president, Dallin H. Oaks.

While the tactical management issues were handled with thorough attention to detail, the strategic vision for the stations ultimately came from President Oaks, who joined the Board of Directors of the Public Broadcasting Service — the television network that supplied much of our daily programming. President Oaks had worked his way through school as a radio announcer and engineer, so he knew the field, but the insight he brought to the PBS Board was much more. It came from his BYU undergraduate financial training, his legal scholarship and experience, and his practical administrative style. His immense skill and integrity earned him the board's deepest admiration and respect. He chaired several important board committees, including a crucial committee on organizational restructuring, and ultimately he became vice-chair and then chairman of the PBS Board.

During this time, President Oaks nurtured KBYU's development with insight that came from his work at the national level. He saw what could be done with the stations and encouraged us to make the possibilities reality. We couldn't have asked for better direction or support.

After nearly ten years of exhilarating experience managing BYU's Division of Broadcast Services, the University of Utah asked that I join their staff to direct the work of their public television and radio stations as well as their university press and instructional media operations. It was a promotion of extraordinary opportunity. We accepted.

So, I went back to my alma mater with an opportunity to practice what I had learned at BYU on a much larger scale, with a larger staff and budget. I found that I was to carry both my professional and my faithful education into a setting that was largely interested in only one set of those qualifications, while unappreciative of the value of the other. I was back on a campus where the choice of faith was defined as the irrational act. My BYU experience, however, had solidified my confidence in the value of faith and its application to a daily routine. The profession and exercise of one's faith was not readily accepted by many faculty colleagues, who were as bright, inquisitive, and competent in their fields as any faculty to be found anywhere in the nation.

My two and a half years at the U of U passed quickly. My public television work expanded from a regional to the national level when I was invited to be a member of the PBS Board. I again found myself working with President Oaks, who continued on the board after his appointment to the Utah State Supreme Court. It was an exhilarating time. I felt blessed beyond measure. I had the perfect job. Our family had grown to three daughters and a new son. I could not have asked for a better or more perfect circumstance in which to live and work.

Then came a telephone call from the chairman of the Board of Trustees of the National Association for Public Television Stations (NAPTS). This was an organization created by the restructuring of public television undertaken by a PBS committee chaired by President Oaks. Its duties included the representation work before Congress, the administration, and the regulators that had been part of PBS (FCC, NTIA, etc.). NAPTS was public television's lobbying organization.

NAPTS Chairman Homer Babbage, president of the Hartford Graduate Institute and former president of the University of Connecticut, asked me on behalf of the board if I would come to Washington, D.C., to direct the activities of the association. Ronald Reagan had just been elected, and there had been deep cuts into the appropriations for public radio and television. Homer insisted that the association needed leadership that was station-based, that had experience managing and operating a local television station. I told Homer that I didn't think that I was the one to do this job. "It's the job of the board to decide whether you can do the job," he said. "We've concluded that you can, and now it's up to you to decide whether you want to do it."

In discussing the opportunity with Justice Oaks, his view was a bit different. "The question is not whether you can do the job," he explained, "but whether you are willing to take the risk."

We took the risk and accepted the offer. In January of 1982, the morning after a huge snowstorm in Salt Lake City, we moved into a brand new world for us. It was a world full of turmoil, contention, wonder, power, and extraordinary beauty. Most of all, it was a world full of opportunity. The choice turned out not to be terribly risky for us, although the move to D.C. was as traumatic as any that our family has ever had. We did it on faith—on the feeling that after prayerfully considering the options, D.C. was the next stop for us.

The work, however, was daunting. Twelve-hour days were routine, fourteen- and fifteen-hour days common, and weekend work inevitable. There was so much to do and so little resource with which to do it that we had to burn the candle at both ends. I quickly learned just how bucolic had been my time at BYU and the University of Utah. Everyone I met in Washington had an agenda. People were smart, ambitious, well connected, and hardworking—the very antithesis of the bloated, lazy bureaucracy condemned by political rhetoric.

The city was in revolution—the Reagan Revolution. Public programs in education, social services, and the arts and humanities were being deeply cut or, when possible, eliminated. Public television was among those suffering deep cuts to its current appropriation. There was no time to lose. My work as a reporter on Utah's Capitol Hill served me well. We organized visits by local station managers to key authorizing and appropriations committee members. These visits were quickly expanded by co-ordinated visits of local station supporters who were also key campaign contributors to members of Congress. There were 535 members and every one of them received dozens of visits from local constituents and national celebrities talking about the value and importance of noncommercial, educational television in the lives of their families — their children and their grandchildren.

Our success was spectacular. We restored the cuts to public broadcasting and even increased our authorization and appro-priations in the face of the full opposition of the Reagan Admini-stration. No Republican or Democrat in Congress wanted to be painted in his or her reelection campaign as the representative or senator who killed Big Bird.

My professional activities were so demanding that little time was left to attend to things spiritual. Barbara cared for the family's needs. I was off crusading. The inattention took its toll. Alma's warning clearly came true for me. "If ye neglect the tree, and take no thought for its nourishment, behold it will not get any root" (Alma 32:38). I chose not to care for the weightier matters, and it was taking its toll on my faith.

About this time I began reading a book published by the Brigham Young University Press (another example of BYU strengthening my faith). It was the first volume of a biography of President J. Reuben Clark by Frank W. Fox. I was mesmerized by the life of a man of intellect who came to Washington and drank from its alluring waters. He ultimately chose a life of faith over reason. To my mind it was an act of heroic proportions — an act that I had never considered was possible in the way that he did it. At the end of his book *J. Reuben Clark: The Public Years,* Fox wrote about the extraordinary intellectual powers of this man and the duality of his nature — one part realistic and the other idealis-tic. "One pointed toward hardheadedness, practical-mindedness, and ultimately a doctrinaire conservatism, while the other pointed toward open-endedness and possibility."[2] This duality of Clark's nature and his disagreements with Senator and Apostle Reed Smoot mirrored some of what had gone on in my own mind during my early days as a reporter. I understood his need to reconcile these conflicting parts of his nature. The full extent of that struggle and the ultimate outcome were made much clearer in the next volume of his biography (also published by the BYU Press). This book, written by D. Michael Quinn, was entitled *J. Reuben Clark: The Church Years.* President Clark described his dilemma to Cloyd H. Marvin, the non-LDS president of George Washington University: "For my own part I early came to recognize that for me personally I must either quit rationalizing . . . or I must follow the line of my own thinking which would lead me I know not where."

Then Quinn describes the rest of the dialogue between President Clark and his "non-Mormon friend."

But J. Reuben Clark soon recognized where an uncompromising commitment to rational theology *would* lead him, and he shrank from the abyss. "I came early to appreciate that I could not rationalize a religion for myself, and that to attempt to do so would destroy my faith in God," later he wrote to his non-Mormon friend. "I have always rather worshipped *facts*," he continued, "and while I thought and read for a while, many of the incidents of life, experiences and circumstances led, unaided by the spirit of faith, to the position of the atheist, yet the faith of my fathers led me to abandon all that and to refrain from following it. . . . For me there seemed to be no alternative. I could only build up a doubt. — If I were to attempt to rationalize about my life here, and the life to come, I would be drowned in a sea of doubt."[3]

What an astonishing statement! As I read this, I began to realize that someone else had wrestled with the same issues that I struggled with. President Clark's long and tempestuous relationship with Apostle Reed Smoot, his questions of authority and orthodoxy — which included a letter written to the First Presidency questioning the wearing of temple garments in the insufferable heat of Washington, D.C., before air conditioning, and his pleading missive that his brother Frank not be sent on a mission — spoke to some of my own feelings and concerns.

I came to the realization during this time that faith is a matter of choice — not something that "happens to you." I could choose faith or not, but the choice was mine. I'm not sure why this crystallization of options suddenly meant so much to me. I had carried with me the impression that faith was something that you either had or didn't have, that it was a gift from God, not a conscious selection to be made and then exercised. What a revelation! How little I had really understood of Alma's teaching on faith. I never considered faith a matter of choice because it is not rational. Of course it's not. I was so connected professionally to facts that choosing faith never would occur to me. President Clark's example, however, gave me the answer I needed. Having made the choice, a new world opened to me. Not only did I have a new and successful career as a Washingtonian, but also my faith was renewed in a fashion that I never had expected.

I felt fully and completely at peace with my choice of faith for perhaps the first time in my life. I was not compelled to exercise it. It was a true and free choice, strengthened and shaped through my BYU experience and associations, and by the publication of a set of books on a remarkable life that changed my view of how one accepts and acts on faith.

In May of 1984, I became the president and chief executive officer of the Public Broadcasting Service. The pace of my life, which was already hectic, seemed to double. My travel schedule took me to every state and to many foreign countries. I had an office in New York City in addition to my principal office in Washington, D.C. Being the head of America's public-service television network was heady stuff. I had just turned forty years old, and I did not fully grasp just how unique my position was. Every week there were receptions to attend and speeches to give. There were almost daily interviews with the media.

Gradually I began to understand that these folks were not interested in meeting Bruce Christensen; they wanted to meet the president of PBS. They didn't care what Bruce Christensen thought or said, but they would listen to the chief executive officer of PBS. I had a "bully pulpit," and I used it to explain the value and importance of noncommercial, educational television to a society in which everything has its price. Our hope was to create a "national park" for a small part of the public's airwaves – a reservation of television spectrum to "enrich the human experience and build a better world." Our driving force was public service (PBS Vision Statement, 19 February 1992).

Everywhere I went, the Church was known and the fact that I was a member added a unique dimension to my very public life. My faith and the manner in which I lived it were almost always a matter of curiosity to those whom I met. I don't think that I wore my religion on my sleeve, but we are a peculiar people. If nothing else, living the Word of Wisdom is always a distinguishing characteristic.

An unrelenting schedule of travel, speeches, program screenings, fund-raising calls, and board activities left little time for family. My Church involvement was focused on scouting, which gave me some time with our son, Jesse. On Sundays, I taught the Gospel Doctrine class in the Arlington Ward. This assignment required careful and consistent study. Over a period of eight years, I read and reread the standard works. My weekly study kept me spiritually fed and allowed me to share what I had gained with others.

After almost ten years at PBS, I was restless, feeling that I had done what I could do in this assignment. I felt that my family needed more of my time and that Jesse, in particular, needed a different social environment. Job offers of various sorts had come during my tenure at PBS, but none had felt right for us. Barbara and I talked about what might be ahead. It seemed like a return to the academy could be a wise choice. We loved the East Coast and our home and friends in Arlington, so we had thought that there might be something that would keep us in the area.

In the spring of 1993, Robert Webb, a colleague at BYU, called and said that he was chairing the search committee for a new dean for the College of Fine Arts and Communications. My name had been recommended as a potential candidate. He wondered if I would be interested in applying. Barbara and I talked about it, and I sent my resume to Bob. That led to an interview with the search committee and a phone call from Rex Lee, whom I had known in Washington during his several tours of duty there.

Rex offered me the position of dean. I accepted, and BYU was again at the center of our lives. I couldn't have asked for a better opportunity. I welcomed the chance to give a measure of my professional experience and faith back to the institution that had given so much to me. I quickly felt that mine was the best job on campus. The college was a collection of my most ardent passions — art, design, music, theatre, film, journalism, broadcasting, and a host of related activities — all taught and practiced in an atmosphere of faith. I was soon engaged with all of my loves. My time away made it possible for me to see BYU with "green" eyes. The value of the institution is clear to me now. I know and understand the importance of a venue in which to learn and practice the arts and communications from the perspective of faithful adherence to the gospel of Jesus Christ.

Philosophers describe five different ways of discovering truth. Truth can be obtained through our senses, through reason, from authority, through revelation, and from intuition. Science and our tradition of intellectual enlightenment during the past three hundred years recognize only two of these means. Sensory and rational processes are supreme in the academy. BYU, however, gives full access to the other three means of discovering truth, while still honoring sensory and rational experience.

Here's a simple example of BYU's uniqueness. Meetings, performances, and classes open with prayer, inviting divine influence on such activities. Returning to BYU, I found that this practice gave me great comfort. I hadn't realized how much I had missed it. Those for whom BYU has been their only professional experience, however, sometimes take these experiences for granted. One of my BYU colleagues called the practice of opening our performances with prayer a folk tradition. It has a much deeper meaning for me.

Soon I was asking, "What can I contribute to the faithful education of those who study and work in our college? How can we follow Commissioner Eyring's admonition to create a learning environment that nurtures faith? How do we encourage the development of *great learners*?"[4] We daily wrestled with questions central to the application of faith to fields of discipline in higher education. This gave new meaning to the term *higher education*. We struggled with some particularly thorny issues in our college. How should our beliefs affect the content of our artistic performances and inform our communications practices? How do we prepare students to compete in the world, while schooling the applications of their talents from the perspective of faith in the restored gospel? How can we honor agency, while requiring behavioral conformity? These issues include nudity in art, studying and viewing R-rated films, profanity and sexual innuendo on stage, investigative reporting in journalism, integrity in marketing and public relations, composition and performance of categories and classes of music, and the list goes on. The application of faith reached into every discipline studied and taught in that college.

The answers aren't easy or simple, but at BYU the questions can be asked and tested. BYU faculty and staff have the intellectual stature to do the research and the creative work that will inform their disciplines from a position of a belief in Jesus Christ. The faithful foundation upon which BYU stands provides access to truth that is rarely available to scholars. BYU offers a road less traveled, and that has made all the difference in the world for me.

Notes

1. Carnegie Commission on Educational Television, *Public Television: A Program for Action* (New York: Bantam Books, 1967), 13. E. B. White, in a letter to the Commission, "Noncommercial television should address itself to the ideal of excellence, not the idea of acceptability—which is what keeps commercial television from climbing the staircase. I think television should be the visual counterpart of the literary essay, should arouse our dreams, satisfy our hunger for beauty, take us on journeys, enable us to participate in events, present great drama and music, explore the sea and the sky and the woods and the hills. It should be our Lyceum, our Chautauqua, our Minsky's, and our Camelot. It should restate and clarify the social dilemma and the political pickle. Once in a while it does, and you get a quick glimpse of its potential."

2. Frank W. Fox, *J. Reuben Clark: The Public Years* (Provo, Utah: Brigham Young University Press and Deseret Book, 1980), 604.

3. D. Michael Quinn, *J. Reuben Clark: The Church Years* (Provo, Utah: Brigham Young University Press, 1983), 25.

4. Henry B. Eyring, "A Child of God," *Brigham Young University 1997–98 Speeches* (Provo, Utah: Brigham Young University Publications & Graphics, 1998), 47.

Having then gifts differing according to the grace that is given to us, whether prophecy, let us prophesy according to the proportion of faith (Romans 12:6).

Stages

Charles Metten

Charles Metten retired from BYU in 1996 after completing thirty-five years in the Department of Theater and Media Arts. He now serves as dean of the College of Performing and Visual Arts at Southern Utah University in Cedar City, home of the yearly Utah Shakespearian Festival. Professor Metten was born and reared in California, where he received his B.A. and M.A. from UCLA and met his wife, Patricia, who introduced him to the Church. He completed his Ph.D. at the University of Iowa and joined the faculty at BYU, where he was an insightful teacher, actor, mentor, and friend. He developed the first film courses at BYU, which have proven to be highly popular and enriching in the lives of thousands of students. The Mettens are the parents of five children and the grandparents of fifteen.

In the visual and performing arts, realities are portrayed by visible symbols. Because of the sanctity of the subject, however, rarely does anyone try to portray God in modern theater. As a consequence, in my career I have not found God in some sort of representation or performance. Further, as a teacher I have not found him in the mechanisms of Brigham Young University, whether its buildings or its committees. Where I have found him is in the most precious resources of the University, in its students, in my students.

My students have helped me to understand God, to appreciate God, to know him better, because I found in them and through them the qualities of patience, courage, understanding, compassion, love, caring, sacrifice, and discipline. For me, these qualities — qualities that the Savior teaches and exemplifies — represent God in my students. The following includes two examples of what I mean. They represent many other, similar experiences. A third story offers a glimpse into the joy that I have felt as a teacher of young people. On occasion, that joy has been full, even inexpressible. The source of such joy, as I have learned, is God himself.

I remember a young woman who came to BYU in the early 1960s. She was a vivacious, energetic, loving-of-life young woman with a terrific sense of humor. Over time, she took acting lessons from me, and we worked together in productions. She found that the University opened up the world for her. She buried herself in learning by studying dramatic literature and by acting in plays. I directed her and also saw her in productions directed by my colleagues. She was young, and her BYU experiences began to shape her maturity and her curiosity. As she worked with others in the classroom or in a play, she always had a positive word to say, she always had a nurturing thought, and she always had a laugh that was warm and wonderful.

The summer after she graduated from BYU, when her friends were getting jobs and starting families, she quietly accepted a mission call. In those days, not so many women went on missions, and I was impressed with her decision to go. Her decision was a lesson for me because it involved sacrifice on her part. She went to Europe. She came to love the people. I am sure they loved her. By the time she came home, she had fallen in love with a young man who also served his mission there. She was beside herself in love with this young man. A sparkle and a light came from her. They were married partway through her study for her master's degree in theater history. After her graduation, they left the BYU community so that he could go to school elsewhere, and I lost track of her.

Over ten years later as a participant in the Know Your Religion lecture series, I was assigned to speak in a town in California. While sitting on the stand as I waited my turn on the program, I looked down and saw this young woman in the audience. I was delighted to see her again. She now had two children, and her husband had a wonderful job. She invited me to their home after the meeting, where we talked and renewed old acquaintances and relived some memories.

When I went back to BYU, I lost track of her again. A few months later, I received a letter from her asking if it would be possible for her to receive a teaching assistantship if she were to return to the University for further graduate work. I responded that I was sure she could earn an assistantship and didn't think more about it. Another few months passed. Then, to my surprise, she appeared in my office. She and her husband had separated, and it looked like they would be getting a divorce. I was stunned.

While she didn't show me the anguish or tears she had been through, I could sense that her pain was inexpressibly deep. She only told me that her husband had "made some decisions" that she couldn't live with and that she now needed the assistantship she had inquired about. She had her children with her, and she was going to raise them in Provo while she was going to school. I wondered if she knew the size of the mountain in front of her. She now had the burden of raising these children alone, of creating a profession of her own, and of forming a new home. In addition, there was tremendous anguish, pressure, and disappointment from the separation and the pending divorce, all while she was helping her children adjust to the changes in their lives.

Here's where I became aware of the power of God in her life. Never once when she came to my office — as we worked on her program, as we worked on her classes, as we discussed the writing of her papers — did she ever present a negative attitude or express a mean, vengeful kind of feeling toward her husband, or anyone else for that matter. The life she had prepared for and planned on was gone. Yet, instead of displaying bitterness and anger, she turned to the Lord. She told me that she was sure that bitterness only hurt the person who felt it and that she, like Joseph Smith, hoped to learn that "all these things shall give thee experience" (D&C 122:7). Her testimony of Jesus Christ and the importance of his teachings grew. She was determined to raise her children with love and peace, and she knew she had to prepare to support them at the same time.

We worked together. Her graduate committee was organized as well as her classes. Because she was proficient in German, her study focused on Georg II, the duke of Saxe-Meiningen. He is often referred to as the father of modern theater directing. His community, Saxe-Meiningen, was then in East Germany, a place that at that time was under Soviet control and for which it was extremely difficult to obtain a visa and permission to visit. But this did not stop her. She said she needed to see his theater, his library, and the museum that is housed in his former castle. She wanted her dissertation to be a real contribution to the field of knowledge, and she wanted it to be complete.

Somehow she got her passport and her visas, and all of the red tape worked out for her to go into East Germany. (I became aware of the near impossibility of obtaining visas when we discovered a recent dissertation written by a scholar at another university who explained how the Soviets refused to let him in.) She took her children with her and went to that remote place. She was able to visit Georg's theater and interview several people there who explained his importance in their own work. Her travel was adventurous for her, and she completed the primary research which added to her dissertation and filled out the period of theater history that she was writing about. It was a real contribution.

She came back and completed her degree and found work at a university. Never, never did the words "I quit, I can't do it, I am just too tired" come from her. She continued to have her sense of humor. She continued to have her encouraging attitude. She expressed her faith to me and told me of the Lord's blessings in her life. We talked often in my office about our families, and we shared ideas about the raising of our children — I still had two sons at home myself.

Over the years, I find that I think of her often. Whenever the pressures of life become too much for me, I think about her. Her example has inspired me to work at being less critical, less impatient, less angry with an inexperienced actor or an opinionated colleague, and less frustrated at the competing demands of work, family, and church. In expressing her faith and testimony, she actually gave me advice as well as understanding and patience. For this I will be forever grateful. She was an example of a student who will live in my memory and in my heart forever, because in this student I was able to see God working positively in the life of a person torn by heartache.

The second student was a young man who was very much a part of our film program. He was one of the hardest workers whom I have ever met. He was always willing to bear his testimony — I even asked him to do that in class in either Japanese or English, and he did. His was an obedient spirit with a smile and with a positive attitude.

He started out in theater because he thought he wanted to be an actor. He performed as an actor in some of my productions, and then he became my assistant director for the play *A Tale of Two Cities*. He gradually learned the mechanics of directing and stagecraft. But then his main love, his great passion emerged — and oh, he had a passion. He wanted to become a writer and a director in the film industry. He began to work in the film program and took the basic courses. Finally, it came time for him to create a student film. His script had to be approved by several faculty members in the film program. Every time he submitted it, they sent it back to be rewritten. He rewrote and rewrote. But he couldn't win the approval of the committee. At one point they even suggested that he change the subject matter or the theme. But no, he would not give up on his project. He had a great belief in this film concept. He was determined that it was the film he wanted to do.

Eventually he came to my office, and he presented the script to me. I read it, and we talked about it. I tried to point out the various weaknesses in it. He listened. Then big tears came to his eyes, and he said, "Will I ever make the film that I believe in? I know it can touch people's hearts. What am I going to do, Brother Metten? What am I going to do?" I suggested that he sleep on it for a while and then try again.

He did try again. And again after that. Each time he rewrote his script after it had been to the committee, it became stronger. Each time the clarity they were looking for became more evident, and eventually, working together, they approved his script. He could now begin filming the story that he cared so much about.

I should explain that all student films are a real test of fortitude, strength, courage, and belief in oneself and one's talents and skills. Getting the script approved, no matter how difficult, is only one part of the project. Student filmmakers have to raise their own money. Then they have to obtain equipment — heavy cameras, lights, dollies, carts — from the motion picture studio. They have to create a crew from their fellow students. His film took place in sheep-herding country, so they had to go on location. When films are done on location, the director has to provide food, housing, and warmth — the weather was bad. The mud and the cold made working conditions almost impossible. One experienced actor told me it was the worst experience on location he had ever undergone.

Yet this young man did not lose his passion. That's the lesson I learned from him. When we believe in something, know something is right, we must defend it without giving up. We must look for ways to solve the problems and overcome difficulties that appear. Then we learn. Eventually this young man overcame every obstacle, met every requirement, and completed the film. It was a good film and, naturally, he learned a great deal.

When he graduated from BYU, he applied for graduate school at UCLA. He was turned down. He applied a second time. This time he was able to coax a faculty member into looking at his film. The faculty member saw this young man's passion for his work, and he was accepted to the UCLA film directing program. While there, he made some student films, one of which won a prestigious award and was shown on French television. When it came time to make his major M.F.A. (Master of Fine Arts) film — a substantial requirement in completing the program — he applied for several grants and won one. The grant was based on his experience of working in theater, learning stage directing and stagecraft skills, and then applying his knowledge of stage direct- ing and stagecraft to create a story on film. In short, it was based on the discipline and understanding that began to develop as he wrestled with that little undergraduate film.

I sent him to a major producer at Universal Studios, whom I knew, to see if he could give him some advice on raising money for commercial films and how to get a major studio to back him. The producer interviewed him and was impressed with his en- ergy, and above all his spirit — his spirit of calmness, his spirit of joy, his spirit of life. The producer helped him, and the young man was able to get the camera equipment that he needed. He also helped him to get film stock — a very expensive ingredient — to go to a remote area in Utah during the winter to film and complete the project necessary for his graduate degree.

I am firmly convinced that without the gospel, this young man would have been just like every other young filmmaker who was in competition with him. But his testimony, his experience on his mission, his willingness to work, all sustained him when seemingly insurmountable barriers were put in his way. The gospel of Jesus Christ was paramount in this young man's life. He lived it everywhere he was. Whatever I asked him to do for me when we were working on *A Tale of Two Cities* he enthusiastically completed. On occasion, for example, I asked him what he would suggest to make a crowd scene better. He would study it out. Then he would talk to me about the actors in the crowd — that is, the supernumeraries, the spear carriers, the ones in the fifth row away from the audience. He would point out a few to me, three or four of them, and tell me what a great job they were doing. His comments were always positive. He always had an uplifting comment. I always felt better after working at a rehearsal with this young man.

In my own life, I have pursued projects that I believed in. For instance, when we were developing the film program at BYU, I struggled hard to get it off the ground. In some ways it seemed so silly. Here we were, hundreds of miles from filmmaking centers, isolated from talent and opportunity. Yet I dreamed that young members of the Church, with dreams of their own, might learn to make film at BYU and lead happy, productive lives doing something that they really wanted to do. During those years I thought a lot about my young friend and his love for film. His courage increased my own as we developed our program. Now our young graduates are getting jobs — I can think of three executives at major film studios who are graduates of our program. Again a student at BYU let me know who God is and what God stood for in his life so I could understand better who God was in my own life. I will be forever grateful to that student.

Now let me share a story about the joy of being a teacher of young people at BYU. The young woman in this experience helped me solidify something in my own mind that I have now come to believe is truth. Teaching, *real* teaching, occurs only when the student is the focus, and the process of working together helps her accomplish something that is within her.

This young woman came to BYU from an Italian family living in California. Her family was a large one, although she was the only girl. She had come to BYU, where I first met her in one of my beginning speech classes. My, but she was shy. She wanted to drop the class because she was so frightened at having to get up in front of the other students to speak. I discovered that all her brothers were football players, basketball players, or track stars. She told me that she couldn't do anything. I kept talking to her — I wouldn't let her drop the class — I kept telling her to just stay with it and watch the other students.

Finally, the day came when I asked her if she would complete an assignment of telling us something she did well. She cried. After class she came up to me and sobbed, "Oh, Brother Metten, Brother Metten, I can't do anything well. I don't know anything well." So we talked. For several days I had her come to my office, where we talked about her life on the farm and life with her brothers, life with her mom and dad. Finally in our discussions I found out that she loved to make pizza. So I said, "Show me." Right there in my office she showed me with nothing — she just pantomimed — how she made pizza with all the ingredients. She went through all of the motions. She stirred, and beat, and rolled the dough, and threw it in the air, thinning it out. She did the whole thing — laid out the olives and the salami, the pepperoni, then the cheese, and then she baked it. I said, "Would you do that in class?" "Oh," she said, "no, I can't. No. I'm scared, I'm frightened." She said, "I'd faint." (Many of the students say they will faint, but they never do. It's always an exciting experience to think about, though.)

Finally she agreed to do it, and one day she stood in front of that class. Only this time she brought her ingredients and her bowls and she started from scratch and made that pizza. The class was fascinated. They watched, they laughed, and they cheered as she went through making the pizza. And then, as she was finishing her talk, she said, "I put it in the oven and bake it. And now I would like you to taste some of my pizza." She had brought a big pizza that she had cut up into twenty-one slices, and we all sat there and ate some of her pizza. When we were done, the class stood up and applauded and whistled and stomped their feet. They knew how difficult this presentation had been for her. She just stood there with flour on her face and hands and cried.

I went up to her and put my arms around her and said, "What is the matter? Why are you crying? You have done so well. Everybody loved what you did." She said to the class, and this stays in my heart, "I have never been applauded in my life."

Well, from that point on she began to gain some courage. She made friends, got an A in the class, and on the day she graduated she made it a point to introduce her family to me — her mom and her dad and her brothers.

About a year later she became engaged and married her young man in the Salt Lake Temple. I was invited to the wedding reception, and when I started through the wedding reception line, there she was, a beautiful bride, my pizza girl who had just blossomed in that class. And in turn, she had become a mentor and guide and teacher to other shy frightened students, both men and women, in other classes. As I greeted her and shook her hand, she pulled me to her and whispered in my ear, "Thank you, Brother Metten, for being my *teacher*."

My working in classrooms and projects with young people improved after that. I looked for ways to connect with students and ways to increase their own gifts and talents. This young woman reminded me that God himself represents understanding and love, and that God lets people know that he loves them. He lets us know that we are important. He lets us know that we can do things well. This young woman—my pizza girl—certainly made me feel so.

These three are only a few of the students who have helped bring God into my life. Through them—and others—I found God in many interactions during my office hours, in my classes, in play rehearsals, and on student films where I worked with young people. They made a difference in my life. I know that they have moved on from BYU to make a difference in other lives. I thank the students whom I taught for thirty-five years at BYU for teaching me and for bringing God into my life. And I thank the mothers and the fathers of those students, who were so willing to share, sacrifice, and let them come to BYU so I could benefit from their sons' and daughters' spirits and learn the meaningful things they taught me.

Trust in the Lord with all thine heart; and lean not unto thine own understanding. In all thy ways acknowledge him, and he shall direct thy paths (Proverbs 3:5–6).

Put to the Test

Vivian K. Mushahwar

Vivian K. Mushahwar was born in Jerusalem. She attended Brigham Young University, graduating with a bachelor of science in electrical engineering in 1991. She then pursued a doctorate in bioengineering and neuroscience at the University of Utah. Currently, she is doing postdoctoral work at the University of Alberta on improving and restoring function and mobility after spinal cord injury. Earlier, she did postdoctoral work in rehabilitative medicine at Emory University in Atlanta, Georgia. She is fluent in three languages, speaking, reading, and writing Arabic, Hebrew, and English. Dr. Mushahwar lives in Edmonton, Alberta, Canada.

I was born in East Jerusalem thirty-two years ago to a young Palestinian couple. I was the second of three children. I came to BYU not knowing anything about the University other than that it was listed among competitive universities in the U.S. My knowledge of the people and their religion was limited to the Honor Code I was asked to abide by as a future BYU student. I was very impressed by the Honor Code, and so were my parents. My family believed that I was going to be part of a community that preached Arab values and standards, because aside from not allowing the drinking of coffee, the Honor Code resembles very much the Arab way of living. My Palestinian upbringing instilled in me a strong sense of honesty and generosity. Within my frame of values, education and a belief in Christ were deeply engraved. Familial, cultural, and religious edicts compelled me to accept graciously the friendship of upright individuals regardless of their ethnic or religious backgrounds.

Yet, as a non-LDS student, adapting to the unique environment of BYU proved to be difficult. Part of the difficulty stemmed from the notion that acceptance at the University was based primarily on religious beliefs — beliefs perceived by many cultures as personal and private. It appeared as though LDS students were continually attempting to convert their peers of other religions. Little time and effort were spent on getting to *know* non-LDS friends, and interest in them dwindled when no conversion was in sight. Overcoming these impressions and adapting to the seemingly difficult environment of BYU required personal growth and reaffirmation of what I held to be true.

For all students, Brigham Young University presents a distinct environment to which they must adjust. LDS teachings govern numerous aspects of students' daily lives, beginning with the Honor Code and encompassing the majority of social activities on campus. While some students take exception to the defined structure of the University and set out to beat the system (after all, for youngsters, rules are made to be broken), the majority of students accept this unique environment and joyfully participate in what it has to offer. For LDS Church members, BYU provides an exceptional opportunity for enjoying an all-encompassing, Church-influenced life not easily available in their home states or countries. For students of other faiths, BYU is a puzzle that quickly turns into a challenge.

While all societies expect their members to live an honest life upholding the laws of the land, a person's sense of morality is shaped by a more personal set of experiences intimately affected by family interactions and religious teachings. It is this set of personal beliefs that was frequently put to the test for me at BYU. In the BYU context, religion becomes an ongoing daily activity rather than a weekly confession of beliefs. Thus, a person's lack of acceptance due to differences in religious affiliation poses a remarkable challenge to that person's values. In attempting to deal with such a challenge, I have found that individuals respond in one of four ways: first, a feeling of rejection can promote resentment toward the University and LDS culture. The expression of resentment may, however, occur at the expense of one's own personal values. Along this path, an obsession with beating the system by compromising one's own morality and integrity often leads to the loss of one's own values and, ultimately, oneself.

Second, the need for acceptance may encourage conversion without the precursory faithful admission of these beliefs. By converting without really believing, one is compromising one's morality in return for social acceptance. By knowingly abandoning what is true, one is again at risk of losing oneself.

Third, one may faithfully accept the new beliefs and values. A conversion to these beliefs provides the individual with an honest and enlightening sense of morality necessary for a complete transformation of one's life and value system. Within this transformation, one can discover oneself and establish a new covenant with God. A fresh, unblemished beginning follows.

Finally, the most difficult and frightening path one may pursue in dealing with a perceived lack of acceptance is an honest reassessment and recommitment to one's own beliefs. In this case, one is allowing oneself to candidly look deep within and rigorously affirm what one's core beliefs are based on. Intimate religious beliefs and personal values are put to the test— not even the slightest slack or diversion is allowed. The emergence from this honest assessment reaffirms one's beliefs, and the fear of having them challenged by others disappears. Moreover, the notion of lack of acceptance diminishes as one realizes that acceptance should be mutual: one cannot demand what one is not willing to offer. Though such a path may very well lead to the loss of a few friends, it enhances one's internal light and renews one's contract with God. It further embellishes self-confidence and provides the strength one needs to maintain one's values. More importantly, it grants the strength needed to allow one to understand that the truthfulness of one's religion does not preclude nor supersede the truthfulness of other religions. In fact, it grants a person the strength to accept and learn from all religious and moral teachings. It allows for an openness to all truth. Indeed, it allows for the reaffirmation of the presence of God, an experience I gratefully acquired at BYU.

Soon after I arrived at BYU I realized that I was at a university where church and religion dominated every aspect of a student's daily life. I found people discussing religion every minute of the day. Everyone seemed to be so wrapped up in religion that there was no chance for a non-LDS student to participate in any discussions. All opinions and stands were based on religion. There appeared to be no controversies; things were understood in one set way, and all other ways were considered wrong. I saw no chance for critical thinking and felt my brain was going to burst from boredom. I came from a place where controversy is a way of life, where active and heated discussions are social activities, and where individuals struggle hard with concepts prior to accepting them. Yet, once accepted they become solid, unshaken values implemented on a daily basis with sincere conviction. I was taught that faith does not mean submitting and following without truly believing. Inquisitions of one's own religion were accepted and even encouraged. Therefore, the common "it has not been revealed to us yet" answer that I received from fellow students to my questions regarding LDS beliefs was completely unsatisfying. In discussing general issues spanning euthanasia, abortion, and the rights of all people regardless of gender and ethnic background, answers such as "I only believe this because the Church tells me to" were equally ungratifying.

I came to resent the new atmosphere of BYU as well as the cultural differences I encountered. In addition to what I saw as a lack of critical inquiry at BYU, I was irritated with the frequent question of what religion I belonged to. I could not see what difference it made whether I was a member of the LDS Church or not; nor could I understand why I should be treated differently being one or the other. In my mind and heart, religion was a private matter with its principles upheld and practiced in daily interactions. I started responding to persons who mentioned anything about religion with open animosity. I took every explanation about Mormonism as a personal attack on my church and myself. I became extremely sensitive and intolerant of any comments made about "people from another faith." Sitting in a religion class became psychological torture. I read the assigned scriptures, studied diligently for my tests, wrote my papers, and got A's in my religion classes. But this did not come easily. I used to literally force myself to sit down and do the reading and writing. My religion assignments were constantly on my mind. They affected all my other classes. By forcing myself to get my religion homework done, I was expending so much time and energy that I was totally drained when it came to attending to my other classes.

"But why did you let those religion classes affect you so much?" you might ask. After struggling with this question myself, I realized that it was because I was very interested in learning about the LDS Church and religion, but at the same time I had a closed mind and an intolerant spirit. While I was very interested in learning about people through their religion, I was not interested in the constant pressure I felt pushing me toward converting to Mormonism without anyone even attempting to discover what my beliefs were about. Without realizing it, I had become as intolerant as I thought those around me were. The situation continued until the fall semester of 1987.

At that time, I enrolled in a course covering the first part of the Book of Mormon, taught by Professor Donna Lee Bowen, a political science professor with whom I had a prior acquaintance and whom I highly admired. Professor Bowen was very tolerant of other religions and very understanding of the cultural and religious differences I encountered at BYU. She did not push me but treated me like the rest of the LDS students in class. Unfortunately, I had been pushed to the edge in a course covering the second part of the Book of Mormon. The previous spring term I had taken the course from a professor who seemed to have made vows to convert me to Mormonism before the end of the course. He was exceptionally nice and answered my questions. He explained all the doctrines in the first part of the Book of Mormon that I had not yet studied, but he pushed me hard to believe and convert when I did not need to be pushed. This experience sharply increased my feelings of resentment.

Because I had known Professor Bowen before I started taking the first part of the Book of Mormon, I hoped that things were going to be all right and that the feelings of frustration I had developed during the previous spring would have all been washed away during the summer. I was mistaken. By the second or third week of the semester I realized that all of the frustration was still there, and the inner struggle over doing homework for the class began anew. During the next few weeks, the frustration intensified until it came to a point where I could handle it no more. I hated everything around me, and I knew that things could not continue as they were. Grades in other classes suffered, and it was time for me to rid myself of this "religion syndrome" that had captured me.

I went to Professor Bowen's office determined to tell her that I had had it, and that I was simply not going to write the last religion paper. (I had already written a large number of short papers in the course, but the fact that it was nearing the end of the semester or that I had done all of the work to date did not matter — I was not going to do another thing in a religion class.) I walked into her office and bluntly announced that I was not going to write that last paper. I can still remember how shocked she was. Apparently, I had managed to hide my frustration quite well throughout the semester. The only time I had expressed some anger in one of my papers, she followed me after class and told me that it was all right. Unfortunately, I was beyond the stage of believing that.

She asked me to sit down and with great concern asked, "Vivian, what happened?" I had very little to say in response. So she presented me with my alternatives: "If you don't write that paper," she said, "you'll drop your grade to an A minus. But let's talk about it." She tried to ask me about what was bothering me. But she was not very successful because I gave an "I don't know" answer. It did not take her long to realize that she was not going to get me to talk. Still, she continued to ask questions, basic questions, such as whether I believed in God and Christ. As I gave affirmative answers she repeated the question of "what's bothering you then?" For the first time I realized that it was not Mormonism itself that bothered me.

I had grown up among practicing Muslims and Jews. Therefore, it was not LDS religious principles that disturbed me but the way I was received at BYU. I was not made to feel that I belonged. Certainly, I made things worse by adopting a reciprocal attitude of intolerance. I explained to Professor Bowen that I resented the way I was received. I hated feeling that the way the Book of Mormon was taught became the root of discrimination against me and that it was providing grounds for people around me to do the same. I complained that people were not open enough, were very narrow-minded, and would not deal with anything out of their norm. I complained about being judged because of what religion I belonged to rather than the kind of person I truly was. I resented being looked upon as an inferior who had not yet seen the light. Professor Bowen just listened. It seemed as though she understood what I was going through and limited her comments to gestures of disapproval of the ways I felt I was mistreated. She let me talk. By this, she let me hear myself complaining about things that I was not applying to myself. And in doing so, it became clear to me that I was not open enough, that I was extremely intolerant of people around me, and that I was not about to deal with them on their terms. I realized that I was as rigid as I thought the BYU community was.

It clearly was time for me to change. I had to change my attitude, and I had to reintroduce myself in the BYU community. I started opening up gradually and was able to communicate with people around me. I realized that I could find some individuals with whom I could carry on fruitful intellectual discussions based on logic and mutual understanding. By opening up, I realized that I could be the person I was no matter where I was. It was I who formed my image and not the people around me. I was the only one who could make myself into the person I wanted the people to know. I learned that my values could not and should not be compromised because of people's attitudes toward me. To compromise them meant to live in misery, for I could not find happiness when I was myself intolerant and resentful. I had to change my way of thinking and doing things.

I then came to see that understanding Mormonism and its different doctrines was my means of understanding the majority of the students and faculty at BYU, their culture, and their way of thinking. This understanding helped me relate to others and to communicate with them. I found that members of my BYU community were approachable, but that there was a particular way of approaching them. My peers could not deal with ideas that were not familiar to them. Introducing different ideas by using examples from the Book of Mormon that held significance for them proved to be very successful.

Washing away my intolerance reaffirmed my belief in God and gave me the strength to face the community I was living in rather than to shut myself out. After I opened up, life became brighter in that I saw that there were many opportunities for advancement and growth. I found that not everyone was against me and that I could accomplish many things. I started getting involved with the different activities held on campus, and I began initiating my own activities. I found out that there was a way for me to express myself and to influence people's thinking. I realized that I was much better serving my people by going out, getting in touch with others, and teaching them about my country, my history, my culture, and my traditions. I started accepting people the way they were. We were different, but that did not mean that one of us was wrong while the other was right. I realized that we could both be right and that we could both advocate upright and righteous living.

I eventually wrote the last religion paper and did get an A in the class. That last paper was the one paper that I truly enjoyed writing. I did not have to struggle or force myself to write it. I was relaxed, and the writing went very smoothly. I attribute that smoothness to the change in my approach to the LDS religion. I was able to acknowledge that this was a class about a religion that was very interesting to me and that I wanted to learn as much about it as I could. Understanding this religion or having others talk about it no longer seemed to be a personal affront. I felt comfortable with most of the doctrines presented and could extract many principles that helped me evaluate my own behavior and become a better person.

The situation I was in before my change was very painful and did not lead anywhere. I seemed to be stuck in a deep, dark hole. To me, nothing could have been worse. I could have dropped out of school and gone home. But then I would have had to deal with a sense of failure that would have accompanied me for a long time. I could not allow myself to quit without trying to resolve my difficulties. I had to take responsibility and change my own life. Furthermore, I had a golden opportunity that I could not have wasted: I had a scholarship and was going to school, when my friends in Palestine were denied the right to do that. In short, I had to make things work out for me, and nothing could have been worse than where I already was.

By listening to me, Professor Bowen made me hear things that I ought to have been doing myself before demanding them from other people. I have great admiration for Professor Bowen. I have great respect for her strong faith, diligence, and patience. Her honesty and straightforwardness allowed me to trust her and hold her in the highest regard. My interest in initiating different activities, following them through, and having them succeed would not have been possible had I not changed. I feel that by stepping out of the hole I had dug for myself, I have contributed a lot to my people and my country. I was able to reach out and educate some BYU students about myself, my nation, and my plight. I was able to communicate my aspirations, hopes, needs, and feelings. Knowing that a few people now realize that I exist as a Palestinian with the need to be free is yet another reward.

The vividness of this experience has been with me for the last ten years and will stay with me for many years to come. I can never forget that it was at BYU where I developed and grew. My experience there, as difficult as it was, made me a better person. While I urge people to carry an open and tolerant mind now, I exert a lot of effort to do the same myself. When the Book of Mormon and the Doctrine and Covenants call for honesty, charity, and righteousness, I try my best to comply. These books are no longer my enemies, but they and other religious books have become providers of upright principles.

As I pondered over these things which are written, the eyes of my understanding were opened and the Spirit of the Lord rested upon me (D&C 138:11).

Lessons Learned

Michael K. Young

Michael K. Young was reared as a Latter-day Saint. When he enrolled at BYU he carried only modest expectations for his future. But one professor changed forever his outlook on the value of education. As a result, he graduated from BYU with highest honors and went on to a distinguished graduate career at the Harvard University law school. After serving two clerkships – one for Chief Justice William H. Rehnquist of the United States Supreme Court – he taught at the school of law of Columbia University, where he was the Director of the Center for Japanese Legal Studies. While on leave from Columbia University, he also served as Deputy Undersecretary of State for Economic Affairs and Ambassador for Trade and Environmental Affairs. Currently he serves as dean of the George Washington University Law School. He has been a visiting professor at the law faculties of the University of Tokyo, Waseda University, and Nihon University. He is also a member and vice-chair of the U.S. Commission on International Religious Freedom, established by the International Religious Freedom Act of 1988. Dean Young and his wife, Suzan, are the parents of three children.

When Professor Jim Kearl asked me to contribute to a book of essays on the topic of finding God at BYU, my first response was typically flippant: I did not know that he was lost, and lost at BYU of all places. However, I have enormous respect for Professor Kearl, great affection for BYU, and a deep and abiding testimony of the existence of God. The combination of all those sentiments persuaded me that the topic deserved more serious reflection and consideration.

As is often true, moreover, my lame joke provided a useful starting point. After all, just how pervasive was the concept of God at BYU? How much did that idea of God shape and inform my studies? How central to the enterprise — at least my enterprise — at BYU was the thought of God or the quest to discover his reality in my studies and work? All these questions suddenly seemed important. I am, after all, of an age when fundamental questions emerge after long suppression and demand serious attention. And at this time in my life I have the experience and background at least to understand their importance, if not necessarily to provide any better answers than I did when I was twenty-one. But most important, I have three college-age children. I thought I could use this essay to tell them something about my college experiences, especially as those experiences related to the development of my testimony. Perhaps that would help them avoid some of my mistakes and maybe even help them develop stronger testimonies than I had at their age. Perhaps my experiences would give them some small additional help as they attempt to answer those critical questions for themselves. Professor Kearl's request seemed timely and useful. I agreed to try.

Not surprisingly, the answer to the questions I posed for myself did not come easily. It may not even have come at all. Nevertheless, the inquiry has been useful, and I hope my reflections may be of some small utility to others.

A number of negative conclusions occurred to me. First, I realized that I did not secure my testimony at BYU. Rather, I first learned of the gospel and felt the quiet whisperings of the Spirit at the feet of my family, especially my mother and her parents. For those who knew my mother's family, this is not surprising. My grandfather, who passed away in his late nineties and worked at his small corner grocery store serving countless BYU students until just a few days before he died, served three missions for the Church, two in the deep South, including two after he was married. To give you some idea of just how far back into the Church's past his life reached, when he served his missions, missionaries still lived in genuine fear of lynching. Indeed, in Kentucky, he replaced a missionary who had suffered just that unfortunate fate. A few years later, while on another mission, he and his companion opened up the city of San Diego for missionary work. Upon his return, he was called as bishop of a ward in Provo where he served for thirty-two years. That was when men were men, and bishops really were bishops, often for life!

I spent many days and evenings literally sitting at his feet, listening to him tell of his missionary experiences, of his close brushes with death, and of the Lord's intervention and protection. Those were dramatic stories for a young boy, full of high adventure, of close calls, of too many rescues to count. But in the midst of the excitement, I learned of my grandfather's deep and abiding conviction of the truthfulness of the gospel, of the Atonement of the Savior, of the reality of God, and of his place in the heavens. I learned that the Lord could truly be counted on to save and protect those who were on his errand. And I learned that in the end, his errands were all that mattered in life; indeed, they were life itself.

Second, I concluded that contrary to the experience of some, my sense of the Holy came not from religion classes but from secular classes. That is, my religion classes at BYU did not play much of a role in expanding my understanding of God or strengthening my testimony. For the most part, they were perfectly acceptable classes. They did not light me on fire, but they were adequately instructive. That they were not more might well have been my fault, of course, but, too frequently, I felt that perhaps the priesthood lessons in my local ward were better than anything I heard in my religion classes. (Of course, in all fairness to my instructors, Hugh Nibley was in my ward and generally taught those priesthood classes.) Still, when I think of finding God at BYU, I do not think of my religion classes.

What then do I think of? What did shape and influence me? What really made a difference at BYU in terms of my relationship and understanding of God? Indeed, did *anything* happen at BYU that made a difference in this regard? The truth is that I now strongly believe that I had experiences at BYU that influenced me deeply, pervasively, profoundly, and permanently. But to understand how and why requires a bit of background.

I need to confess at the outset that, for the most part, I engaged my undergraduate studies rather too casually. I found that if I took the right classes, I could get by largely with some last minute study. This initially seemed to suit me well. I had a pretty good short-term memory and could generally remember most of what I read, at least for the few hours necessary to repeat it back on the examination. More important, this approach to education left time for my real passions, skiing and girls (probably in that order, as my wife will attest). I am not proud of this, of course. Indeed, I have spent much of the remainder of my life trying to secure the undergraduate education I so casually avoided. I did not understand what I was missing and continued to work assiduously to ensure that I continued to miss it as much as possible.

A few professors were unwilling to let me off the hook quite so easily, however. They taught classes in which I could not do as well—indeed, could not do well at all—through mere memorization. To my initial annoyance, those classes required real thought and effort. I not only had to memorize the material, but I had to think about it and understand it as well. Those professors were not satisfied with anything less than a genuine attempt to wrestle with the broad implications of the material they were presenting, and they never neatly packaged those conclusions or served them up in a finished manner. For the first time in my life, I encountered educators who forced me to think, really think.

My initial reaction was, of course, high irritation. After all, I thought I understood the game pretty well, and I had certainly mastered it, at least as I understood it: the teacher would present me with prepackaged material, and I would memorize it quickly and repeat it back on the examination. The teacher would then give me a good grade, and we would both pretend that I was smart, even though we both knew that all I had done was demonstrate a good short-term memory, rather than produce any real evidence of intelligence or even effort. But then I met professors who departed from the accepted pattern. They were even prepared to give me a low grade if all I did was repeat back to them the materials in the textbook. They seemed to want something more. They wanted me to think.

This was a remarkable turn of events, and it took me some time to come to grips with it. Having always done relatively well in school, however, I thought I would at least give this startling new form of education a chance, at least during one fall semester, before the snow fell. Perhaps I could find an easy way out of this as well.

In the end, I never did find an easy way out. Rather, the experience was exhilarating, indeed, life changing. The whole enterprise was so extraordinary that now, three decades later, I am still at it. This exercise was so exciting, so novel, and, in the end, so meaningful that it became the focus of my entire professional life. I so fell in love with the academy, with the life of the mind, that I have never been quite able to leave it. Thirty years later I am still trying to learn how to think carefully, critically, and with insight.

What was unusual about virtually all those classes, however, at least for purposes of this essay, was something quite different. It was the way each one of those classes started. I am relatively sure the professors never consulted with each other on this matter; I suspect some of them did not even know the others. Nevertheless, each started their class in much the same manner. Sometime during the first class or two, virtually every one of those particularly demanding professors would pause and bear a testimony. They would go to great lengths to ensure that we understood that the inquiry upon which we were about to embark did not diminish or threaten their belief in God or the gospel and that the questioning and analysis we would undertake was not intended to, nor, if done correctly, would destroy our faith. Interestingly, it seemed very important to those professors that we understand this central tenet, that we understand that study, thought, and analysis were not antithetical to a life of faith. Indeed, to the contrary, for them at least, such an approach was almost essential to their faith. What was particularly noticeable about this phenomenon, moreover, was that these were the only classes that started this way. In my more conventional classes, no one seemed to feel it necessary to profess their faith or defend their approach.

This contrast was striking, and I was initially a bit offended. As a nineteen year old, moreover, I felt completely entitled to be offended by both groups of professors, those who confessed their faith and those who did not seem to think it necessary. Why, after all, I reasoned, should someone have to defend his own personal orthodoxy just because he intended to make us think for ourselves about some matter of legitimate academic inquiry? This seemed to suggest rather bad things at various levels about the degree of intolerance or lack of free inquiry at BYU. At the same time, if the whole purpose of my education at BYU was to strengthen my testimony, then why didn't every professor intersperse professions of faith throughout lectures and classes? The answers to both of these questions were revealing and taught me a great deal about testimony and about God, who wasn't, it seemed, lost at BYU after all.

Turning first to those professors who felt compelled to defend their faith, I learned from them something that has been extraordinarily important to me throughout my life. I learned the exhilaration and thrill of discovery. I learned how deeply exciting it can be to use one's mind to discover more about the world and how it actually works. I learned that a better understanding of the world was not only extraordinarily exciting in and of itself, but that such understanding was essential to my efforts to make that world a better place. I learned that thought and analysis could, and should, shape my behavior, and shape it for the better. In this regard, I discovered that I was actually moved to action by understanding, and the better the understanding, the better the action. I learned that mere exhortations to excellence, to do good, were not enough for me. I need to understand not only what to do but why and how I should do it. I found that ideas and thoughts truly shape my behavior, and the better the thoughts and ideas, the better my behavior and the greater my contribution to the world which I study and in which I live.

But I learned from those professors an even more profound lesson. Over time, I eventually began to understand that most of them were not starting their classes with a testimony as a defensive gesture; nor did their actions derive out of a perceived need to protect their jobs. Rather, they were engaged in teaching of the highest order. Their testimonies were profound and, at least for me, extraordinary teaching moments, though the full impact of those moments wasn't realized until many years later. What I have finally concluded is that those professors were trying to teach me the most important lesson in their subject matter: they were making clear by their statements and by their example that rigorous and demanding intellectual inquiry was not incompatible with faith.

Those professors were demonstrating through their own life experiences that a life of the mind — of deeply engaged analytical and empirical inquiry, of intellectual rigor, of academic pursuit — was completely consistent with a life of faith. Indeed, I believe some of them may have been going even farther; they may have been testifying that a life of intellectual inquiry just might be essential to faith, at least for some people. For some people — I am one — testimonies start with a deeply engaged intellectual analysis. We study it out in our minds first. Then we seek confirmation through fervent prayer and fasting. Each of those professors taught me that this approach was entirely acceptable to the Lord. They showed me that I could study the world and things in it, and that I could learn from great works, and that I could even take seriously the gospel as an intellectual discipline.

They also taught me the most important component of that approach. In order to understand genuinely the world and all the things that we learn from secular sources, we should start the inquiry first from the perspective of the gospel and its basic truths. The rest of the world then begins to make much more sense. It isn't so much that secular learning necessarily confirms the truth of the gospel in every instance, though I am frequently surprised with just how often it does exactly that, but rather that we much better understand the world and everything in it when we put the secular learning in a gospel context. In other words, if one first seeks the light of Christ and inspiration from the Lord, then inquiries about matters of science, politics, economics, history, indeed, society in general, are not only entirely acceptable, but likely to lead to a better understanding of the gospel and a stronger, not weaker, testimony. If we seek first the kingdom of God, then indeed all things will be added unto it.

That lesson has been perhaps among the most important that I took away from BYU. I have a deep and abiding testimony of the gospel. But, I must confess, I am not always entirely sure of everything that comprises the gospel. I think I know what the essentials are. But even those occasionally elude me. After years of study, for example, I understand the importance of the Atonement, and I think I have at least some rudimentary understanding of what I must do to take advantage of its tremendous blessing in my life. But I certainly do not understand the Atonement itself, how it came about, how it works, or even quite how it fits into the broad, eternal scheme of things. I have learned that I can have a testimony of it, even though based on incomplete understanding. I have also learned that I can have that testimony while I continue to study and learn more about its essential components. I have learned that it is entirely acceptable to have a strong testimony of the gospel, and I do, even if I am not entirely sure of the precise meaning or content of the gospel. I have learned that I can remain an active, deeply committed Latter-day Saint, even while I continue my inquiry into exactly what that means. I can have a testimony even as I continue to inquire about exactly what the gospel means and how the gospel is consistent with things I learn and observe from more secular sources. That lesson has been a source of tremendous comfort and support throughout my life, and I can hardly express my gratitude for it. Nor do I imagine that I would have learned it anywhere else but at BYU.

At the same time, I also learned an important and useful lesson from those professors whose classes comprised more rote learning and who did not feel compelled to defend their faith in class. From those professors I learned that not everyone is wired like me. For some, a testimony does not derive from a deepening intellectual understanding of the world and things in it. It has an entirely different wellspring. Theirs is truly an otherworldly understanding. For them, the life of the mind is not the center of their being and is not necessarily an essential component of their testimony or their life of good works. By reflecting on their contribution to my education, I have come to understand that while each of us may have quite different approaches to the gospel, to the development of a testimony, and to a life of faith, this is perfectly acceptable. Just as different people may have different gifts of the Spirit, different people may obtain the Spirit in quite different ways.

The importance of this lesson became clearest to me when I had the opportunity to serve as a stake president. In that capacity, I found myself constantly urging others, as well as myself, to higher degrees of effort, to deeper levels of engagement in the gospel and in the Church. But not everyone responded equally well to identical types of encouragement. It became very important for me to understand and tolerate all sorts of different approaches to the development and retention of a testimony. As a church leader—and as a father and even simply as a Church member—it is imperative for me to understand, tolerate, and love those who approach the Church and the gospel quite differently than I do.

Indeed, I do not think the words *tolerance* or *acceptance* even quite capture the essential attribute or behavior that the Lord expects of us. Rather, I believe that he expects us to embrace these differences in our community, to welcome them, to revel in them, to love them every bit as much as we love and embrace our own peculiar approaches to developing a testimony.

So, after all, if I didn't quite find God at BYU, I certainly learned better how to live more devotedly a life of faith and dedication in his kingdom. I learned a profession, a profession in both senses of that word. I learned to love the life of the mind. I learned that a life of the mind and a life of faith and practice are entirely compatible. And I learned that the gospel is constructed to allow many different paths to faith, and all are to be welcomed and embraced.

Y

Crossings

Look not on his countenance, or on the height of his stature; . . . for the Lord seeth not as man seeth; for man looketh on the outward appearance, but the Lord looketh on the heart (1 Samuel 16:7).

Leaving Room for Holy Envy

David Rosen

Rabbi David Rosen taught at the BYU Jerusalem Center for Near Eastern Studies from 1988 to 1997, serving as professor of Jewish studies and enriching the perspectives of more than four thousand students. Born and educated in Britain, Rabbi Rosen received his rabbinic education and ordination in Israel. Since then he has worked to promote Jewish interests as rabbi of the largest Jewish congregation in South Africa and as the chief rabbi of Ireland. He now holds the post of director of the Anti-Defamation League in Israel. Both before and after moving with his wife and three daughters to Israel, Rabbi Rosen has been one of the most influential voices in interfaith organizations for seeking ways to understand people of other faiths, believing that such understanding leads to genuine peace. It was in this spirit that he served on the Israeli team that normalized relations with the Vatican in 1995. He is president of the International Council of Christians and Jews and of the World Conference on Religion and Peace.

I cannot say that I discovered God at BYU. But I did come to understand aspects of the Divine in ways that I might not otherwise have. How this understanding developed is closely tied to the reasons for my association with BYU's Jerusalem Center for Near Eastern Studies.

I like to describe myself as a willing victim of creeping annexation at BYU's Jerusalem Center. When I started, I never envisaged the extent of my involvement. It began like this:

I returned to Israel in 1985, having studied there earlier in my life. Prior to returning, I had been involved in interfaith relations when I was a rabbi in South Africa and then as chief rabbi of Ireland. My involvement in interfaith relations in South Africa came out of a commitment to social justice. In Ireland it came from a unique position where, as I jokingly put it, 95 percent of the population is Catholic, 5 percent are Protestant, and I was chief rabbi of the rest. That of course is something of an exaggeration, but I couldn't do my job very well in the Irish setting if I were not involved in interfaith relations. Whatever the initial reasons for becoming involved, I really took to it, loved it, and found it spiritually enriching. I therefore naturally got involved in it when I came back to Israel.

About one year after we arrived, the Anti-Defamation League said, "We'd like to pay you for what you do, and then you'll do it under our masthead. It will be, therefore, mutually beneficial." This sounded like a very nice proposition, and I became the ADL's director of interfaith relations in Israel. This was about the time that the BYU Jerusalem Center was being constructed, and the controversy over the presence of Mormons and a Mormon school in Jerusalem was at its height. The ADL came out very firmly and squarely in favor of the construction of the Center, supporting Mayor Teddy Kollek's commitment to the principle that Jerusalem should be a city in which those who have spiritual and religious attachments should be able to find their home and place. As a result of this active support for the Center, I developed a close rapport with the leaders of the LDS Church, and I was invited to Salt Lake City to help the Church to get some kind of insight into the issues at the heart of the controversy over the construction of the Center. I went with a colleague from the U.S. to meet with the late President Howard W. Hunter and Elder James E. Faust. This meeting took place at Church headquarters in Salt Lake City, opposite the temple, at a lovely restaurant where I was looked after with all care and consideration for my religious dietary requirements. It was a very lovely meeting, at which I sought to clarify for those men who was who and what was what in Jerusalem, and why people reacted in the way that they did to the construction and to the Mormon presence in the city. At the end of our meeting, they said, "Well, this is the sort of thing that all our students should hear. When they come to Jerusalem, you could meet with them and orient them." I said, "With pleasure." So the beginning of my relationship with the Center was an invitation to give some kind of orientation presentation to the students.

Some time later, I was invited to expand this orientation to a class. Because of my various commitments, I was reluctant to take this on. Yet I enjoyed very much the contact with the Center, with the people, with the staff, and with the students. As a result I succumbed, and the brief orientation became a full semester's class. Initially, I was to offer to the students an elective class in Jewish history, culture, and religion. Because of concerns about balance in the curriculum, the orientation that became an elective class then became a core class, required of all students. Over time, we added a field trip component and yet another class as an elective as well.

At the same time that my class evolved, students had been visiting homes for Sabbath; but that became problematic. Therefore, my family and I agreed to come over and share with the staff and students a Shabbat experience. Later we added simulated Passover Seders. So now I had a core class and an elective and a field trip and a Sabbath meal and a simulated Passover Seder each semester. Recently my wife was also brought in to teach a class. I'm sure many people around are saying, "See, we knew this was going to happen all along."

From the very beginning, it was a great pleasure to be associated with the Center and its students. What I gave up for teaching at the Center was a teaching position I held at the time at the School for Overseas Students at the Hebrew University. After dealing with those students, teaching at the Jerusalem Center was just sheer pleasure and delight. For all the problems at the Center—especially during the summer program, some of the students could be quite bubbly and active and even a little bit noisy—they were still far better behaved, far better disciplined, and far more respectful than the kind of students I had encountered at the Hebrew University School for Overseas Students. From that point of view, it was a pleasure.

More importantly, the whole core of my own professional, vocational being is the encounter with people of other faiths and in other communities. Meaningful encounters are a two-way process. From one direction, I feel very privileged to be able to present my faith and commitments to other people so they can learn to respect and appreciate them, notwithstanding the obvious fact that not all my commitments are going to be theirs. Being able to communicate to other people of religious commitment the beauty of one's traditions is, I think, a very important thing. It is especially important for me in terms of Judaism's relationship with Christianity. Therefore, what the Center was offering was not merely a teaching position, it was also something that was responding to my own vocational being and aspirations.

From the other side, the encounter with people of faith not within my tradition is a very enriching experience. I would call it a religious experience in its own way, and I would describe it as follows: God is more than any of us can grasp. If God relates to his children in all their diversity, then there must be diverse ways of being able to relate to him. Above all, it is obvious to me that no one religious tradition can encapsulate the totality of the Divine. Therefore, in encountering other people created in the divine image, one is in fact encountering the divine presence, God's presence, to a greater extent in one's own world, which must be greater than simply any one tradition in itself. This understanding is even richer when one encounters people of faith who bring their own spirituality with them. Therefore, for me the encounter with people of faith, and especially when that faith is close to certain values and sources and texts that are holy to me, is an immensely rich experience. Each experience and encounter with people of faith is for me, therefore, a religious experience.

In the beginning, however, my involvement in interfaith dialogue was basically just enlightened self-protection. It was my perception that if people understood me, they would be less likely to be hostile to me and, hence, that through greater acquaintance, one can combat prejudice and bigotry. So what initially led me to this kind of dialogue was a kind of self-defense. But then as I got involved in it, it became much more. It became an appreciation of shared values and a recognition that working together, we can become greater than the sum of our different parts. And as I have already said, above and beyond all this, the actual encounter with another person of faith is an experience of the divine presence in the life and community of the other. I believe that the interfaith encounter is of the utmost value for Israeli society and indeed our region at large. If we don't learn to appreciate and to respect one another in our deepest attachments—which are our religious attachments here in this land—then no peace process of any description is going to hold together for very long.

For all of these reasons, it should be obvious that there was nothing that made me feel uncomfortable about teaching young Mormons. There were times when I was conscious that I was an outsider and not part of the group. It was not uncomfortable, but I had a strong awareness of it. For example, my awareness arose in faculty meetings, when a prayer was said at the beginning, or in other settings where a prayer might be made and the language of the prayer was Christological. It makes me aware that I am not part of that prayer, even if those who are praying might have intended to incorporate me in it. In this regard, there was once a person on an assignment at the Center who spoke to me about this. He had listened to me talk with the students and understood the difference in terms of the Messianic concept in Judaism. For in Judaism the Messiah is not the Redeemer, God is the Redeemer. He said, "If I said a prayer in the name of the Redeemer, I would be saying what I mean and you could understand it your way." I acknowledged that was the case. I was very touched that when he said prayers in my presence, he said, "We ask this in the name of the Redeemer." But again, even the fact that he had gone to those lengths to accommodate me, which I felt very moved by, still reminded me of my difference. So there were moments. Obviously it couldn't have been otherwise, and I wouldn't really have wanted it to be otherwise.

There were also times when students would ask questions that made me very conscious of the differences between us. We used the same terms but we meant different things, both in a general Christian sense and sometimes also in a particular LDS sense. These differences needed to be clarified. But because our religious systems, for lack of a better term, were different, I was aware of occasional frustrations on the part of the students. In fact, if anything, they might have felt a little uncomfortable with me. That circumstance arose when, for example, I was emphasizing how diverse Judaism is theologically and doctrinally, and how the major aspects of traditional religious conformity relate to conduct. They asked me, "Well, doesn't it bother you not to know what is exactly the case or what isn't? Doesn't it bother you not to know exactly what's going to happen to you?" I could see that they were sometimes a bit frustrated, if not exasperated, with me. I didn't find that uncomfortable; in fact, sometimes I found it amusing. But it is an interesting awareness on my part that there is that big difference in terms of our religious systems in the way we approach certain things.

I think that as students tried to understand my concept of the Messiah, which is different from their own concept, we connected; we were not alienated. Indeed, as I said to my students, when the Messiah comes we will go up to him hand in hand and say, "Excuse me, Sir, have you been here before?" And if he says yes, I will know you were right all along.

What has happened to me at the Jerusalem Center is almost like what's happened to me in my life. It is sort of a conglomerate topsy. It just grew. I had no anticipations or expectations, for better or for worse, that were in any way different. In other words, nothing negative, nothing positive in that regard. It was just a growing, learning experience, and a very lovely one. And I continued to enjoy the discovery of the people who work and study at the Center. My only regret is — and I do have one great regret — that I didn't do the students justice. I'm not saying that I didn't do a good job in terms of what I actually did. But I don't think I did enough because of my lifestyle and my commitments, which are so substantial that I didn't have enough hours in the day, let alone days in the week, let alone months in the year, to be able to do all the things I wanted with the students. But I was moved by their commitment to me and to their own integrity. On two occasions — one was a little more inadvertent than the other — but in two cases students came to me and confessed that they had given answers in an exam in an illegitimate manner, either through having looked over someone else's shoulder or whatever. The sincerity, the contrition, and the integrity of those students who came up to me to tell me about this — I don't think necessarily to ask for forgiveness but simply to confront their own misdemeanor and not to run away from it — that religious integrity has deeply moved me. It is something of a paradox that I speak of those two who erred, because what it emphasizes is that the vast majority of these students would not have dreamed of doing such a thing. That integrity is a superb tribute to the faith and community that these young people have been raised in.

For me, the overall experience with BYU's Center was enormously enriching. Where there were difficulties, the difficulties were not in relation to the people in the Center. The difficulties were difficulties within my own community here in Israel born out of the complexity, the diversity, and the enormous burden of an overwhelming, tragic historical experience. That means that there are many who didn't understand what I was doing in the Center and may even have been hostile to my involvement with the Center. That, of course, was a challenge for me. But I suppose that President Hunter and Elder Faust may have had some intention, even insight and vision beyond my ability to have anticipated. Obviously what they succeeded in doing was to get, I think, a pretty good PR agent for their own community, church, and institution, who is trying to give his own community a more true understanding of who these people are and what they are doing. This can only contribute positively to the mosaic of Jerusalem and of the Holy Land. Think of what one saw when I conducted a simulated Passover meal: Nasser (the Center's chef), a devout Muslim who is a *hajj* (one who has been on a pilgrimage to Mecca), caters for Christian students and then specifically for the dietary requirements of a Jewish rabbi at a simulated Passover meal. That's a wonderful image. But I can't deny that the process is not without its difficulties.

Many of the interreligious encounters that take place, especially in a very open society like the United States, tend to be encounters at the lowest common denominator. Often those involved in such encounters are only superficially rooted in their faith and its religious knowledge. This kind of encounter has its value but also contains real dangers. In my opinion, the most valuable and constructive interreligious encounter is between people deeply rooted in their own faith and religious tradition. Such encounters, I believe, not only do not threaten our own religious commitments but on the contrary can deepen them. In effect, my involvement with BYU's Jerusalem Center only strengthened my own Jewish religious commitment and accordingly helped me to be even more aware of God's presence within me, within my neighbors, and within the whole world around us.

Bishop Krister Stendahl (former presiding Lutheran bishop of Sweden and formerly of Harvard Divinity School) proposes certain ground rules for interfaith dialogue. One of them is, "Leave room for holy envy." That is a beautiful idea. The fact that I can see something beautiful in another's religious tradition should not make me feel disloyal in any way to my own tradition. On the contrary, as I suggested above, it seems obvious to me that no one tradition can encapsulate the Divine totality. At the BYU Jerusalem Center, I saw some very special, beautiful things in LDS religious life that testify to God's presence, which it has been a privilege and pleasure for me to witness.

And he gathereth his children from the four quarters of the earth; and he numbereth his sheep, and they know him; and there shall be one fold and one shepherd; and he shall feed his sheep, and in him they shall find pasture (1 Nephi 22:25).

Transplanted

Benoy Tamang, a son of Nepalese parents, was reared in a home where his father was a British Army officer. Respect and propriety were simply a part of life. Benoy was born in Singapore, graduated from high school in Hong Kong, and because of his father's assignments traveled extensively throughout the world. However, it was not until he accepted a scholarship to BYU-Hawaii that he faced a most serious challenge to his background from a most unexpected source, a young woman. Mr. Tamang received his M.B.A. degree from BYU in 1989. He and his wife, Angela Dawn Adams, are the parents of four children and live in Alpine, Utah, where he works for a computer software firm.

It's amazing how powerful the impact of mothers is on their children. With my own family, I can see how my wife impacts the language, thoughts, school and skill levels, and confidence of our children. It is also wonderful to see the tight bond of love that my children share with their mother. I, too, felt the same for my mother, and there is still no better mother in the world for me than she. My mother, who had given birth to me, had raised me as her first and precious son, and had endured the difficult role of motherhood on my behalf, experienced the most difficult time accepting my new lifestyle as a Latter-day Saint. She could not understand that this decision, though seemingly innocent at first, would lead her eldest son (the eldest son, in my culture, has the first responsibility to look after his birth family) to marry a Caucasian at a ridiculously young age, to marry in a temple that my parents could not enter (they stayed outside in the grounds of the Hawaii Temple), and then to live thousands of miles away among Latter-day Saints rather than be close to her at home. And though she saw the wonderful attributes and love that Angela has for our children, along with the gospel in action at our home when she

once came to visit us, sadly my mother died without understanding fully the meaning of my decision. That decision, though
right, hurts a little when it comes to the memory of my relationship with my mother during the last years of her life.

My family is from Kathmandu, Nepal, and Darjeeling, in
northern India. At some time in the past, with the influence of
British rule, my family became Protestant Christians. My parents'
families were large, and both their parents died while my parents
were very young. My father joined the British army as a Gurkha
soldier in his seventeenth year, and over the years he rose in rank
to become a British commissioned Gurkha officer. On an extended
leave, he was fortunate enough to return to Darjeeling and to
marry a pretty, intelligent, nontraditional, opinionated young
lady — my mother. Because of the military lifestyle, our family
moved between countries every two years. I was born in Singapore, and we lived in India, England, Hong Kong, Singapore
(again), Brunei, and Nepal. Life was based on acquiring and losing
friends regularly throughout our growing years. Because of the
constant moving, we had to learn to rely on each other. We were
a very happy family. Although we children grew up with a British
education, our parents brought their own strong culture of tradition, hard work, education, and family devotion to us children.

Looking back, religion in our family was more tradition than
anything else. We would try to go to church every Sunday. We
were taught that God and Jesus exist. We learned the Lord's
Prayer and repeated it nightly. I followed and did not understand,
or did not try to understand. As a teenager, I distinctly remember
using the excuse of homework to miss Sunday church at 11 A.M.
My teenage years were too busy with school, friends, sports, and
family to allow space for other thoughts. But I had heard of
Mormons — they were people that I occasionally heard mentioned
on television when cowboys made their way through a western
town.

My life started to change during my senior year of high
school. My cousin, Subas Subba, came back to Hong Kong from
BYU-Hawaii as a graduate and a new member of The Church of
Jesus Christ of Latter-day Saints. He started talking to me about
where I wanted to go to college. Of course, I mentioned Hawaii,
where I knew there was plenty of sun, surf, and bikinis. He told
me that he had just come back from a tremendous college where

I wouldn't be lost because of its modest size, where the location was right next to the beach. And yes, there were lots of pretty girls. And, oh yes, it was a Mormon institution. I don't believe I heard the last part, and I enthusiastically agreed that it sounded like the place for me. Incidentally (but now I know it was not incidental), Charles Goo, a dean at BYU-Hawaii, *happened* to be in town, and Subas arranged for Brother Goo to meet me at our house. Looking back, I am embarrassed now because I greeted him in our home dressed only in shorts and flip-flops (Hong Kong can be unbearably hot in the summer). Although it seemed miraculous then (but not so when I look back and see the hand of the Lord in action), Brother Goo extended a scholarship to me to attend BYU-Hawaii the fall semester after my graduation from high school.

In Hawaii, I fell in love with the climate, the beaches, and the warm and friendly people. There were lots of huge Americans and Polynesians with bone-crushing handshakes and beaming smiles. I learned that "What's up?" was more of a "Hello" than an inquiry into my health and well-being, and that it did not take a long response to answer. People genuinely approached each other and were sufficiently personal that, like home, they were willing to greet each other with hugs and kisses. While I was determined to succeed on the academic side of BYU-Hawaii, I was equally determined to adamantly refuse any approach to learn about the LDS Church, even though I had to take some Bible courses as a required portion of my degree. I remember making a personal commitment to go through the program without letting the religion affect me.

Right after the September enrollment, at one of the dances where I was stunned to find out that no alcohol was served (I remember asking, "And they have fun here?"), I saw a lovely, tall, blonde young lady, and I asked her to dance. I found out her name was Angela. She politely avoided pronouncing my name until she could clearly hear it. We became intrigued by our opposite characteristics. Angela Adams had beauty, brains, and a great spirit. Over time, she gently introduced me to her beliefs and values. I found them astonishing. I could not believe that students on campus did not drink alcohol, smoke cigarettes, or use foul language. I found it amazing that people believed in being chaste. My world was so different, and all those new concepts seemed unnecessarily harsh and restrictive. Listening to Angela, it sounded like one was to live as a monk! I repeatedly used the argument that since I had not killed anyone, since I was not out to intentionally harm others through words or actions, and since I was a fairly likeable guy who no one in the past seemed to think needed changing, why would I need to pay any attention to such a severe form of religion? Wasn't one hour of church enough? Other friends and members of the Church also supported Angela, but I saw no need to change. So I vigorously stood my ground when anyone tried to convince me otherwise. I particularly remember relishing moments when I walked through Sunday crowds, dressed and lined up to go to church, with my surfboard or boogey board, and dressed just in shorts and flip-flops. I was sure that I received lots of nasty looks, and that was fine with me.

On Sundays, with her heart full of tenderness and with the spirit of love, Angela would try to explain her love for Jesus Christ and his gospel. For my part, I made her cry every Sunday, right after she bore her testimony (even now, she says that bringing this "one soul" was all the missionary work she could do for a life time). I would ridicule her beliefs, her faith in such trivial topics like abstaining from tea and coffee, and keeping the Sabbath day holy by not studying, shopping, or boogey boarding. I kept strongly recommending that she keep her testimony to herself, but she wouldn't stop. Some of her friends shared their testimonies with me, and after a while I knew that they were all ganging up on me. I thought they were being friends only to try to baptize me. I did not like meeting them, particularly with the full-time missionaries. Those missionaries, with their perpetual smiles and ulterior motives, were to be shunned. I always looked away if I saw them coming. If they extended their hands to shake hands, I would look down at their hands, scowl, turn around, and walk back the way I came without any hesitation or embarrassment. I was very focused on not letting them get close to me in any way. After a while, I believe I succeeded in scaring Elder Schmidt and Elder Barker away.

But I did recognize some amazing things that BYU-Hawaii and its student population exhibited. Almost without my noticing it, the general atmosphere of the campus began to seep into my heart. In time, it would help to bring about a most important change for my life. For example, there seemed to be an air of peace and tranquility. The people were happy and continuously smiling. Teachers and students seemed to be interested in each other. I rarely heard any swearing and, of course, saw no drunken brawls. People seemed to be modestly dressed. While I thought that was prudish, it seemed fitting within that overall atmosphere. Or was their conduct causing that atmosphere? Angela seemed unaffected by stress, and most things did not fluster her. I was amazed that when a dorm-mate borrowed something from her and went back to the mainland without returning it, Angela dismissed it as "just a material thing." I was ready to strangle the other girl! I couldn't believe that the social occasions and dances could be so fun without drinks or drugs. And most amazing, when I did sneak looks into church meetings, I would find big, hulking men, who previously were ripping each other up in a game of touch rugby, shedding tears as they addressed the congregation. What would make these guys openly cry in front of girls? Why would they allow themselves to repeat this scene regularly?

Then, one day, while the missionaries were still interested in seeing me, Angela gave me a challenge that changed my life. She said, "If you think you are so smart, then why don't you use your head and see if our church is really true, instead of just ridiculing my faith and beliefs. How can you tell if you haven't tried to find out whether it's true?" It was a "How can you tell something doesn't taste good if you haven't tried it?" question. After about seven months on campus, enjoying the people, I was intellectually intrigued by her question and agreed that her logic was right. So, to the missionaries' amazement, I went up to them and asked if I could take the lessons. I'm sure that they didn't know whether to laugh, cry, or run.

By this time, I had moved off campus. It was my second semester, around March. I had moved in with a family that worked on campus. The mother, who worked in the administration office, was actually very much against the Church (I didn't know that at first, although I knew they were all non-LDS in that house). They put posters up on palm trees advertising their Monday prayer nights, and I remember holding hands with them in a circle and praying aloud in turn. I didn't join the circle after the first time. When the mother of the house found out that I was going to take the missionary discussions, she did everything she could to dissuade me, even crying. So, I felt a lot of doubt and opposition. As for the missionary discussions, I took them in quick succession (I think we finished in two weeks). After the last discussion, I thanked the missionaries for the nice "story" and promptly left. By this time, summer break had started, and Angela had left for home in Los Angeles. I was sad to see her leave.

Now I was left without my conscience, living off campus with anti-Mormons, and had time to think and ponder about my future. One portion of my thoughts lingered on the fact that I was not necessarily an evil person—I hadn't killed anyone, stolen anything much. I lied only occasionally, swore infrequently, didn't smoke or really drink, and was too intelligent to take drugs. BYU's environment was, though a little alien, not too bad to be living in, and the people certainly were good, safe, wholesome, and nice. This was a comfortable environment that had little need for change. Or was I just being lazy? Didn't I have a goal to be better than my parents? Isn't there more to success than earning more, living in a higher lifestyle, and having a better name? And at what point is a name important? How will I honor the Tamang name in the future? Where do children enter the picture? Didn't I want children earlier than my father's thirty-something, so I could play with them and be active? Wasn't there an eternal family concept that the missionaries and Angela talked about that I wanted? I certainly wanted a family and would not want to lose my children, or my parents, just because I died. The concept of eternal families was a very comforting and pivotal point of doctrine that started to grow on me. Certainly, I had come to value my own family growing up; moving from country to country made us a tight-knit family. Wouldn't I want that, and more, for my own family?

I continued to think more about God and what his plan was for us, his children. I started to think about ideas that the missionaries and Angela had shared with me, and it felt somehow comfortable as I really started to focus on my spiritual goals. Though I did not know what was truly happening, looking back I can see that I had planted a seed, as Alma had said, and the seed was starting to grow its root structure. I was starting to dwell on concepts, and they were starting to become familiar. During the missionary discussions, I had read the scriptures very casually and superficially, looking for drama and action. And though I had now learned to pray as the missionaries had taught me, rather than merely repeating the Lord's Prayer, it felt uncomfortable to speak my mind and to address him in more familiar terms. Yet, I found that I rather preferred that to an impersonal, sterile prayer that anyone could say, and yet not really mean anything. The more I started thinking about God and his plan, the more regret I had for taking the missionary discussions so casually. I regretted not praying or reading the scriptures as intently and as sincerely as I had been asked by the missionaries. In fact, I had not followed through on my first commitment—I had not really tried to find out whether the Church was true before dismissing it.

To their amazement, Elders Schmidt and Barker were once again asked to teach me the discussions. This time, I was intent on following through with the full spirit of the discussions. I apologized for my previous behavior, and I asked them if we could go over the missionary discussions again. I was motivated to find out if I liked the "food" by "tasting" it first. I now also had deeper, unspoken reasons for taking the discussions again. So, living where I did, knowing the lady of the house would not like to see me read or pray, I started reading the scriptures and praying, somewhat awkwardly at first, but not missing an opportunity to read the scriptures and pray. The missionaries also spread out the time between lessons, giving me more time to ponder the key points of doctrine. A few weeks into the discussions, I rang up Los Angeles and told Angela that I was taking the missionary discussions again. I couldn't tell whether she was excited or deliberately calm.

After about six weeks of this, I was reading the Bible and came across the passage in Matthew where Jesus was looking over Jerusalem. With a swollen heart, he hoped that the people would come to him for what he was about to do, "even as a hen gathereth her chickens under her wings" (Matt. 23:37). And he cried out of love and compassion. As I read that verse, all of a sudden I received goose bumps. My whole body started heating up, starting from my heart, and I couldn't see the scriptures any more because tears obstructed my vision. I felt an overwhelming sense of gratitude. I felt so sad and happy at the same time—sad that my Savior felt pain because of my personal unworthiness and hardheartedness and that he had been there all the time, and happy that he would still love me enough to break through my crusty layers and tell me that his gospel was true. Of course, I can explain it now, but all I felt then was an incredible warmth, love, gratitude, goose bumps (in the middle of a warm day), and confusion as to why I was crying. I was bewildered and also scared because I sensed that this was some form of an answer to prayer. Though it was incredible, I had not really expected such a miracle, nor did I really want it! The truth that I wanted was for purposes of satisfying an intellectual theory on the surface, and hopefully some meaningful questions below; but it certainly should not have led to anything this dramatic or deeply moving.

I immediately called the missionaries and told them that I had to see them right away. When I saw them, I almost shuffled to them in embarrassment. With the feelings still so fresh, I asked them what I was feeling and what was generally going on. Of course, the missionaries didn't know why I had called them and were probably expecting the worst again. But when I told them what I had just experienced, they broke out in huge smiles that radiated out from their faces. I'm sure they were relieved beyond measure, happy to see their prayers and hard work had paid off, and probably also thought, "Gotcha!" They patiently explained that I had received my own testimony of the gospel of Jesus Christ and that the goose bumps, although new to me, were one of the ways that I became alerted to the presence of the Holy Ghost. They also reiterated the scriptural reference about the burning in the bosom and how it signified the truthfulness of the gospel. I walked away dazed, happy, and scared about the ramifications of this new experience, with a growing understanding that my life was going to change. But most of all, I could not shake off the feeling of deep love that I was continuing to receive from my Savior, a personal and caring Savior, who took the time to answer such a temporal person as myself. To that end, I have never forgotten his love, and I still treasure that burning sensation, feelings of gratitude, and the unexpected warm tears that streamed down my face that summer day in Hawaii.

I called Angela on Father's Day, 1984, and told her that I was going to be baptized the next week. Angela did not doubt the reasons for why I was being baptized, nor did she quiz me, because, as she told me later, I would not make such a commitment without deep conviction. She also knew that this decision was my own since she was too far away to influence it. It was a wonderful day for both of us. She said later that she cried with joy, and probably relief. I remember telling my landlady (she starting crying in despair), and then I quickly moved out. I called and asked my parents for permission to join the Church. My mother said, "Fine, as long as you don't bother us with it." Though my faith was just growing, I knew that I could not doubt what I had experienced and what I continued to feel as I read the scriptures and started hearing testimonies from other people. I could not turn back. I had "tasted the food," and it was absolutely delicious. It meant that I could no longer go across campus on Sundays in shorts and flip-flops and with a surfboard just to make the Saints angry or jealous, and that I had to improve my many different weaknesses. And I had to do them not because of Angela, the missionaries, or the intellectual knowledge that I had gained during this period, but because I sincerely found out that Jesus lived and that I loved him, and he had been there for me all this time. I could not turn my back on my Savior and Creator. If he was willing to stick it out for me, then the least I could do was acknowledge his love and presence by joining his Church, understanding his requirements, and living so I could see him without shame. Even though I was terrified about public speaking, I now understood why all those Saints stood up in front of their peers and openly shed tears of testimony. I gradually started to understand.

About a week and a half later, I was baptized in the ocean by my faithful missionaries, Elder Schmidt and Elder Barker. And though I did not go on a mission, I made a promise to Heavenly Father that I would make my life a mission on his behalf and serve in whatever capacity I could as if I were a full-time missionary. And as with all good things, there were trials, including Satan's attempts to thwart my baptism by sowing seeds of doubt. But due to the great counsel and intervention of friends and ecclesiastical leaders, I was able to make that promise to be baptized and to be one of the newest members of his true Church. That baptism morning was a glorious morning, and one that I will always cherish. The only person missing from that special occasion was Angela.

Angela has now been my best friend and wife for almost twelve years. I still remember the phone call to her Dad three years after my baptism. I called Claude Adams on the phone and point blank offered him fourteen cows in exchange for his daughter's hand in marriage. Without hesitation, Brother Adams said, and I remember this clearly, "Fine. As long as it's in the temple." We have four lovely children, who, thanks to the temple, are sealed to us under the covenant of eternal marriage and family. We serve, we love, we pray, and we continue to grow in the gospel together.

The gospel of Jesus Christ is so true that it cannot be pushed onto any individual. It's precious message can only be received with love, example, and gentle guidance. The gospel requires personal testimony and understanding before it can be preached. For that, I will ever be grateful to my wife. The love that Jesus has for all of us is incomprehensible, magnificent, and readily available to those who wish to receive it. Growth comes from some pain, a lot of effort, and self-mastery over the natural instincts of this world. The goal of this life is to be self-correcting every day, and to seek for guidance from him on high. Even within the Church, I have realized that if there is no continual growth, then we are moving toward Satan rather than Jesus and Heavenly Father. As much as I passionately love the gospel, I know that every member of this Church must also find that self-propelling testimony that fuels daily evaluation and growth. I no longer become bitterly disappointed at members who have erred or gone astray. I feel compassion for them and rekindle my own sense of urgency in doing that which is right for myself and my family.

Hopefully, my mother can now better understand what we are trying to do.

For I am not ashamed of the gospel of Christ: for it is the power of God unto salvation to every one that believeth. . . . For therein is the righteousness of God revealed from faith to faith: as it is written, The just shall live by faith (Romans 1:16–17).

Just a Closer Walk with Thee

Eula Ewing Monroe

Eula Monroe is a Southerner by birth and by culture, having been born in western Kentucky where she has lived most of her life. Her high school was in Clifty, Kentucky, and she spent her college years at Western Kentucky University in Bowling Green. Her doctorate is from the George Peabody College for Teachers of Vanderbilt University. Dr. Monroe accepted an appointment at BYU in 1992 where she helps prepare teachers. She is a member of the First Baptist Church in Provo and serves on campus as advisor to the Baptist Student Union. A deeply religious woman, she has found her faith strengthened by being at BYU. Dr. Monroe and her husband, James M. (Matt) Monroe, are the parents of one married daughter.

Just a closer walk with thee,
Grant it, Jesus, is my plea.
Daily walking close to thee,
Let it be, dear Lord, let it be!
Author unknown

My story of finding God at Brigham Young University is singularly different, I feel sure, from that of most writers of this volume. As a Southern Baptist whose colleagues and students are almost all of the LDS faith, my story of finding God is not one of conversion to Mormonism. To the contrary, it is the story of how my own faith has been strengthened during my years on the faculty at BYU. It fits within the context of a journey—one that transcends miles and years. Let me share with you some experiences along the way that have brought me to this time and place.

Hitler and his followers were on the rampage in Europe and the world was in turmoil in the early 1940s, but the influence of these events was not of recognizable impact on the Ewing family.

Of more eminent significance to the remote rural community of Britmart, in north Todd County, Kentucky, were the lingering effects of the Great Depression. The young Ewing couple struggled for daily survival amid a culture that had limited their educational opportunities and inhibited active hope for upward mobility.

John and Bonnie Ewing were able to provide only the barest of necessities for themselves and their two children, Mary and William, ages five and two, when on 20 July 1940 another child was born to them. This daughter, named Eula Mae after a family friend, was quickly inducted into the life of the sharecropper family who raised tobacco and corn in the small, rocky fields of the hilly terrain. As soon as Bonnie gained a bit of strength she returned to the field, and Mary and William watched over baby Eula as she lay on a quilt in a zinc washtub under the shade of a nearby oak or maple.

Eula's interests during her preschool years centered on the farm activities of her parents and the school pursuits of her older sister and brother. She spent much of her time following in her father's footsteps as he guided the mule-drawn plow or harrow. She was a child full of questions. When her father tired of her queries, he sent Eula to be with her mother.

There were no books and few other print materials in the home; the school books and seemingly vast knowledge Eula's sister and brother shared with her held special mystery and intrigue. Much of the year prior to her fifth birthday was spent with her brother and sister teaching her what they had learned in school. She entered first grade in 1945 in a one-room schoolhouse about a mile's walking distance along the dirt, later gravel, road leading from her home. Within this mecca of learning, the teacher unveiled the secrets of reading and mathematics and started Eula on an academic journey that proved to be life-shaping and eminently fulfilling. As a young child Eula felt the tug and calling to become a teacher herself, to spend her life helping to open doors of opportunity for others as her teachers were doing for her.

Within this seemingly austere home and school environment, dedication to duty was modeled and expected of the three (later four) children. John was a hard and willing worker, always in the fields early and late, and he expected the same level of commitment from his family. There was no allowance for shirking responsibility. Bonnie was equally committed, if not more so; she worked all day on the farm to help make a living, then returned to the house in the late afternoon to the work to be done there. Miss Willie Sue, the teacher of all eight grades in the one-room schoolhouse, also modeled hard work and expected the best effort from students, as did other teachers along the way. Discipline at home and at school was strict, and immediate measures were taken at any breach of respect for authority or resources. During Eula's growing-up years, the family usually moved every two or three years from one farm to another in north Todd County, always in search of a better livelihood. Her parents were not churchgoing, but they made right and wrong both visible and concrete in the home; the school and pervasive culture reinforced these principles. In this Bible Belt region the word of God was revered, and children became aware of the need for a personal relationship with God at an early age. Because the Ewings did not own a car until Eula was a senior in high school, transportation for any event beyond walking distance was difficult. Kind and caring neighbors from different faiths — Church of Christ, Methodist, or Baptist, depending on where the family lived at the time — took Mary, William, Eula, and younger brother David to church, helped them to learn God's word, and witnessed the love of Jesus to them.

But Eula's nature as a sinner was to resist God; she was prone to being "stiffnecked . . . in heart and ears, . . . resist[ing] the Holy Ghost" (Acts 7:51). For some time she had known that she was lost without God, that "the wages of sin is death" (Rom. 6:23), and that her soul was condemned to hell unless she accepted Jesus Christ as Savior (John 3:18; John 14:6). Even though she had been convinced of her sinful nature (Rom. 3:23), she resisted the promptings of the Holy Spirit to accept Jesus as Lord of her life until she was almost twelve years old.

Eula's parents and siblings had guided her footsteps, and others along the way had also cared enough to direct her path. It was not until 12 July 1952, however, that Eula accepted Christ as the ultimate Guide for her life, both for this world and for all eternity. On this date I was born again (John 3:3); I became a new creation (2 Cor. 5:17), a child of God (John 1:12). During vacation Bible school at Bellview Baptist Church in the little community of Allegre, Kentucky, the pastor gave the altar call, and I responded by faith to the invitation to accept Christ as my personal Savior (Eph. 2:8–9). My conversion experience was not as dramatic as that of Saul on the road to Damascus; rather, it was a quiet and total submission to God's will, accompanied by the assurance of salvation that came with knowing that I had given my heart to the Lord (Rom. 8:1–2; 1 John 5:13). Shortly thereafter I followed the Lord in baptism, an act of obedience to the Lord's command (Rom. 6:4).

After I accepted Christ, my conviction of my call to teach was strengthened. I came to understand that Christ taught us to serve him through helping others (Matt. 25:34–40; Luke 22:26–27), and that my call to service was to become a teacher. This goal, however, seemed not only lofty but essentially unattainable. One had to attend college to be a teacher. To my knowledge, no one in my family had ever gone to college. I knew little about what going to college entailed. I could not envision myself as a college student (it is said that what one cannot envision, one cannot become), and I could not imagine where the finances would come from for such an odyssey.

But when God calls an individual to service, he also provides the means. He placed caring people at every juncture—individuals who believed in me and my potential, some who helped me gain access to resources necessary for pursuing my dream, and a few who provided model footsteps for me to follow before I was secure enough to find the path on my own.

Several wonderful teachers along the way helped to convince me that I could indeed go to college, and my high school English teacher helped to make attending college a feasible goal. She encouraged me to believe in myself and nurtured my dream of becoming a teacher. She helped me develop the oral facility with English usage necessary to enter the mainstream of college life. She shared practical guidance about how to seek scholarships and submit applications. She and her husband transported me to her alma mater, introduced me to college officials who helped with financial arrangements, and lent me, interest-free, the $675 I needed to borrow during my undergraduate degree program.

During my late high school years I fell in love with Matt Monroe, who lived "over the hill and holler" from me and attended the same little country church. We were married in 1959, one year before I graduated from college. We are blessed with one child, our daughter Jamie, and, as of January 1997, her husband Roger. As a family we share virtually congruent religious beliefs, and we continue to sustain each other in whatever endeavors—spiritual, academic, career, or otherwise—each prayerfully chooses.

The early years of my elementary teaching career were busy yet rewarding for our little family, with Matt being very supportive of my career. He and I devoted much of our time and energy to work, church, and home responsibilities. The joy of our life was our daughter, the precious little being that the Lord had placed in our keeping for us to nurture and raise (Eph. 6:4).

During those years I also completed my master's degree and an additional year of graduate work. Although I sensed that eventually I should pursue a doctoral degree, I could not see myself doing so then. As I approached the age of thirty-five, I faced a mid-life crisis (at that time no one I knew in my family had lived past the age of seventy): I doubted that I had done half of all the Lord had set out for me to do. Again I was blessed by God with the support of caring individuals, especially those nearest and dearest to me. As a family, we decided that I should go back to school. Matt and Jamie shared this venture by supporting me wholeheartedly for its duration, and I graduated with my doctorate one week before Jamie graduated from high school.

This degree prepared me to serve in a slightly different way—as a teacher of teachers. The Lord blessed me with colleagues who were good role models and collaborators, and with administrators who helped me to thrive in the university environment. I loved teaching with a fervor, and I loved the research, writing, and service aspects of my assignment nearly as much. After all, having grown up in the circumstances that I did, how could I have access to these marvelous opportunities? Only through the grace of God!

Over the years, however, I allowed myself to be caught up in the many demands of my profession. I worked many hours each day, did much of my writing on weekends, presented frequently at professional conferences, and conducted numerous workshops for teachers. I had allowed myself to become like Martha, "careful and troubled about many things" (Luke 10:41), forgetting that "but one thing is needful" (Luke 10:42), to sit at Jesus' feet and hear his word (Luke 10:39). I continued my church service but often posited it around my life in academia. The amount of time I spent with the Lord diminished. I rationalized my decisions about priorities by telling myself, "After all, the Lord called me to serve him through teaching, and that is what I am trying to do."

But I am a child of God, and "whom the Lord loveth he chasteneth" (Heb. 12:6). He helped me to know that my life was not truly focused on doing his will. As I approached my fiftieth birthday, I asked myself the same kinds of questions that I had asked at each ten-year milestone: What is this decade supposed to count for? In previous years, this question had led to detailed planning. But somehow I knew that the current decade needed to be different. I felt life slipping away and began to wonder if, when the Lord welcomed me into his kingdom, he would say, "Well done, good and faithful servant" (Matt. 25:23). When I faced my own mortality, I questioned whether the epitaph I desired for my life's journey would be accurate or even satisfactory. For many years I had thought I wanted "She made a difference" to be a fitting tribute. Through the influence of the Holy Spirit, I realized that this epitaph needed to be reframed to place the emphasis on God rather than on me: "God made a difference through her." I also came to understand that I did not need to try to see the big picture anymore — I was to accept on faith one day at a time and use each day for the Lord (Ps. 118:24). I knew, most of all, that in my heart I desired a closer walk with him. I prayed that he would grant that closer walk, that I would sit at Jesus' feet and hear his word. Not in my wildest imagination would I have thought that the Lord would answer my prayers by leading me from a career at Western Kentucky University in Bowling Green, where I taught for many years, to Brigham Young University!

During the early months of 1990 I did not feel the Lord leading me to explore professional opportunities at BYU, but later I could see how he had prepared the way. Although a decision to live in Utah would seem preposterous to my extended family and friends, several circumstances contributed to this decision. Jamie had already completed her internship in Salt Lake City and was considering returning for additional training in ophthalmology. We had visited her several times during her internship and were somewhat familiar with the area. Matt was planning to retire soon, making his a more flexible schedule. And I had a friend at BYU.

In May 1990 I attended a national conference for mathematics educators in Salt Lake City. While at the conference, I rented a car and drove to Provo to visit Bob Cooter, then a faculty member in the Department of Elementary Education at BYU and a longtime friend from graduate-school days. In passing and almost in jest, I chatted with Bob about potential opportunities for part-time employment in mathematics education along the Wasatch Front during my retirement years. Shortly after I returned home to Bowling Green, I received a call from Marv Tolman, chair of the faculty search committee for Bob's department. I was amazed that a Southern Baptist would be considered for a position at BYU, and I had serious doubts about whether I would want to work in such an environment if the opportunity arose. Although I frequently felt overwhelmed by my professional commitments, I loved my employing institution, Western Kentucky University. I had earned two degrees there and had been on the faculty for more than two decades; I saw little reason to finish my teaching career elsewhere. For reasons known only to God, I accepted the invitation to return to Provo and meet with the departmental faculty during late fall of that year.

I could not have faced a warmer welcome; it seemed that the faculty wished to share love in abundance. I had never actually interviewed for a position before, and I did not know that I was to have a presentation ready for a faculty meeting. When asked to speak to the group for about thirty minutes, the Lord gave me the words to say. Because they were from him, they were the right ones. But even after investigating the position in some detail and finding it to be attractive professionally, I was not sure that moving across the country at this time in my life was the way the Lord was leading me.

Dr. Tolman assured me that I could consider the position and interview formally the next year. Our family prayed about this issue over the ensuing year, and I revisited the campus during late fall of 1991. At this time I interviewed with Dr. Dennis Thomson, then an associate academic vice president of BYU, who told me of the Baptist Student Union on campus and asked me to serve as its adviser. I know that the Lord speaks to us in many ways; was this a message from him?

In retrospect, I can see that the Lord had prepared me for every step of the employment process, but not all of it seemed easy at the time. My next scheduled interview was with a member of the Second Quorum of the Seventy in Salt Lake City. An LDS General Authority interviews each prospective BYU faculty member. The prospect of this event was intimidating enough, regardless of my level of interest in a faculty position at BYU. As I left the motel in Provo on the morning of the interview, I found that I had misplaced the keys to my rental car. My anxiety level was heightened even further by this complication, and I temporarily forgot the promise that God is with us always. After a frantic search of my belongings, I called AAA, who sent a locksmith. Finding the keys required some persistence, since I had absent-mindedly dropped them into one of my bags in the trunk of the car the evening before. Then I remembered to pray, and I felt the immediate presence of the Holy Spirit. Even though I knew I would be more than an hour late for my appointment, the panic disappeared with a phone call to reschedule the interview.

I had no idea of what to expect or how to prepare for any questions I might be asked; I simply prayed for God to be with me and to direct my responses. I found the interview to be very straightforward and the conversation with the General Authority pleasant, even easy; I felt the Lord actually giving me the words to say during this interview. The Holy Spirit spoke to my heart so powerfully that I knew I could indeed work in the BYU environment and that "this is the place" where I should serve the Lord, at least for the meantime. When I called Matt back in Bowling Green that evening, our decision making was fairly simple. It was not whether to come to BYU, but for how long.

I requested a year's unpaid leave of absence from Western Kentucky University, rented an apartment in Provo, and came to BYU. That one year at BYU has now lengthened to nine, and my husband and I have joined the commuter generation. I do not know how much longer the Lord plans for me to be at BYU; I do know that he guided me there, and if I listen to him, he will let me know when it is time to serve him back in Bowling Green or elsewhere.

Often I have pondered why the Lord led me to BYU; I probably will not have a definitive answer until I meet him face to face. I do know that the events surrounding my coming here were not chance occurrences—he guided me and prepared the way. Stripped of my usual "security blanket" within a familiar cultural setting, I faced a new set of challenges: being in a different culture, learning a different "language," living amid a different religion, and being away from family and lifelong friends. As a result, I learned to trust in and rely on Jesus more than before. And once again at a critical juncture in my life, he surrounded me with caring people. My family, my colleagues at work, and fellow members of my church helped to make my transition more of a joy than a burden.

Any apprehensions I may have felt about coming to BYU have been, for the most part, unfounded. Being a part of the BYU School of Education as the only faculty member of another faith has been a uniquely rewarding experience. I have been welcomed, supported, helped to feel that I belong and have something important to contribute, and loved and accepted for who I am.

Prior to my coming to BYU, several of my friends at other universities shared serious misgivings about such a move. They knew something of the reputation of BYU as a strong academic institution, and they respected that dimension of the university. Nevertheless, they knew me as a born-again Christian whose beliefs are doctrinally distinct. They also knew something of my life history, including my early struggles to achieve under somewhat difficult circumstances. Because of some of the expectations they held regarding the majority culture, they feared that my opportunities to grow professionally might be limited by my being Southern Baptist and female.

In my case, their concerns have proved to be unfounded. The reality is that I have almost more opportunities than I can "say grace over." I have a demanding yet reasonable teaching load, am engaged in more self-selected research and writing projects than I care to count, and serve the University and professional organizations through committee work and in other ways as opportunities arise. In each facet of my work I enjoy the interest and support of my administrators and colleagues. The Lord has called me to this work, and, to the extent that I am faithful to his calling, I walk in the abundance of his joy.

Although the Southern Baptist position is lonely doctrinally, being at BYU has not been a threat to my faith in God and my belief in biblical principles. On the contrary, I have grown spiritually in ways I could not have imagined. My years at BYU have been a time of learning and reflection about my faith and its

Author (Heb. 12:2). As I have encountered differing views regarding issues such as family, marriage, baptism, and salvation, I have prayerfully revisited biblical teachings. My own beliefs have been strengthened; I have been able to sort out what is really central to my faith and to articulate more clearly my belief about and understanding of what being a born-again Christian means. The obvious commitment of my colleagues to their religious beliefs has prompted me to examine daily the consistency of my commitment to my faith and to a closer walk with the Lord.

The conditions of my employment preclude my witnessing for my faith in this environment, yet I have many opportunities to share the love the Lord has placed in my heart. To the extent that I allow my life to be Christ-centered, that love is evident. I also have the opportunity to incorporate biblical principles and examples in my instruction (e.g., the teachings of 1 Corinthians 12 affirm the need for collaborative learning) and to begin each class period or meeting I conduct with public prayer. My work with the Baptist Student Union has helped me to understand the social, emotional, and spiritual needs of students who do not identify with the predominant culture and religion and to serve those students in ways that help make their stay at BYU more meaningful.

I am convinced that had I stayed in Kentucky, the focus of my spiritual life would not have been as clear as it is today. I have come to realize that within academia or any other worthwhile pursuit I can become more like Mary, remembering that the one needful thing is to sit at the feet of Jesus and hear his word, and less like Martha, caught up in the busyness of life that distances me from him.

At this writing I have completed my fortieth year in the teaching profession, with retirement pending according to the Lord's timing, which hasn't been revealed to me yet. Although I do not look forward with eagerness to that part of my life journey—I love my work at BYU and have no desire to leave it—I know he will have other ways for me to serve. I trust that he will surround me with caring, supportive individuals just as he has at every other critical juncture. And whatever God's plan, he will guide me to a closer walk with him.

Y

Have I not commanded thee? Be strong and of a good courage; be not afraid, neither be thou dismayed: for the Lord thy God is with thee whithersoever thou goest (Joshua 1:9).

Translating

Johnny A. Bahbah

Johnny A. Bahbah is a Palestinian Arab born and raised in Jerusalem. His family has been Christian longer than there are memories or historical records. Membership in one of the oldest Christian communities of the Holy Land is a matter of substantial pride to the family. Mr. Bahbah graduated from Fréres High School (a French private school) in Jerusalem in 1979. He followed his brother to study at Brigham Young University in 1982, where he received a bachelor of science degree in travel and tourism in 1985. He then completed his master's degree in geography and began work at the Harold B. Lee Library on the BYU campus as he studied library science. He and his wife, Eija, from Finland, are the parents of three children. They live in Lawrenceville, New Jersey, where Mr. Bahbah is a librarian at Princeton University's Firestone Library.

I am a Palestinian Arab. I was born in the Old City of Jerusalem. My family has been Christian for generations stretching back hundreds of years. When I was a baby, I was baptized into the Greek Orthodox Church. When I started going to school, I attended a Catholic school, like all my brothers before me. I have four brothers and two sisters, and I am the youngest of the family.

My father was a barber and his shop was on Saladin Street, the main street outside of Jerusalem's Old City walls, opposite Herod's Gate. Because of the convenient location of the shop and also because my father and his partner spoke several languages, people from different foreign consulates used to come to my father's shop for haircuts. BYU people also came to his shop. David Galbraith was the first BYU person to have contact with my family.

In 1975, my father told Brother Galbraith that he was looking for a scholarship for my brother Bishara to study abroad. At the time, BYU was offering five privately funded scholarships to

Israeli students. My father asked whether anything would prevent his son from applying to the university. Brother Galbraith told my father that he would ask. Later he informed my father that Bishara could apply if he would like to. When my brother applied, he was accepted and received one of the scholarships offered that year. While Bishara was attending BYU, he became very well known among teachers and families traveling to the Holy Land. Over the course of time, besides hearing news about Bishara and how people in Utah were trying to make him feel at home away from home, my father was impressed by what he saw from BYU people. As a natural consequence, my family and I became increasingly familiar with the traditions and the religion of the LDS Church.

My parents had taught us children to be respectful and considerate of other people's beliefs. When members of the Church were invited to our home, my father and brother refrained from smoking in their presence. My parents did not serve alcohol or any of the traditional beverages of the Middle East, such as coffee or tea.

Another brother, Michel, came to BYU in 1979. Michel had been working two jobs in Jerusalem and came to feel that his life was going nowhere. Bishara convinced Michel to apply to BYU. In time, he was accepted. After my father passed away in 1976, I took upon myself the responsibility of looking after my mother. It was in this role that I came with my mother to visit my two brothers at BYU in 1981. It was my first trip to Provo.

At the time I was working for the Anglican Church in Jerusalem. The job with the Anglican Church was strictly employment. While at BYU, I observed students younger than I was who seemed to be happy going to college. At that point I realized that I was missing something in my life. I said to myself that I needed more out of life than just working as a clerk. While in the U.S., I also visited several friends of the family. As I was listening to them, I was also closely observing their way of living in the U.S. compared to mine in Jerusalem. As a result, I came to feel that my life was empty and that I needed to make some changes. I realized that I had no long- or short-term goals set for the future. I also concluded that I should not delay making changes in my life.

The first thing I did when I went back to Jerusalem was to submit an application to BYU. At the end of 1981 I received a letter admitting me. The letter stated that I could start as early as the spring of 1982. So I did. Because I knew several friends who were having a hard time gaining acceptance to a U.S. university, I felt that I had accomplished a lot already. To me a fresh start felt good. Yet I could not tell what the future held for me.

The first year was rough. I had difficulty trying to adjust to being a full-time student after four years of working. Although I was extremely busy with school, I was also keeping an eye on the Church. Every day, it seemed, I was learning more and more about the gospel. But there was a hitch for me.

I have learned that many people struggle when they approach conversion to the gospel. Very often the issue has little to do with religious matters, such as doctrine or ordinances. Instead, these persons struggle with a social or political question that, because of their backgrounds, attaches itself in their minds to the gospel. For me, it was mainly a political matter. I had grown up a Palestinian Arab in Jerusalem. As a result of my experience and that of family members with representatives of the Israeli government, I had no respect for the State of Israel. Right or wrong, my gospel dilemmas grew out of this background.

I knew that I would be embarrassed to become a member of the Church. If my Arab friends were to hear certain members talk about the Church and glibly connect it to the State of Israel and to the Zionist movement, these friends would automatically look at me and say, "You joined a pro-Israel and pro-Zionist church. You have sold out your people and country!" For me it was a big disappointment that many members of the LDS Church believed that the spiritual "Israel" referred to in the scriptures was the same as the current political State of Israel. One further element that kept me at a distance from the Church was the attitude of some people at BYU toward Arabs. The people were consistently negative, which turned me off. These issues became the main blocks in my coming closer to the Church. At the time I felt that I would be genuinely embarrassed to tell anyone from my country that I had joined the LDS Church. For the longest time, I had thought that Church leaders were teaching these false concepts to Church members until I took a class called "Sharing the Gospel" from Brother John Fugal. This class was the turning point in shaping my views toward Church leaders. It was an important moment.

I took this class for prospective missionaries because I knew Brother Fugal. I believed that he would not be hard on me because he knew my background. Of course, I saw in Brother Fugal's eyes that he wanted me to accept the gospel. But he never pressured me. In his class, I saw other students change during the semester. And I felt that this class brought out the best in everyone, including me.

On many occasions we saw videotapes of talks given by Church leaders, including a tape of President Spencer W. Kimball. Whenever President Kimball talked about the Holy Land he referred to it as the land of Palestine. Further, none of the leaders talked in any way that would offend my people or me. It was very impressive to me that President Kimball, whom Latter-day Saints called a prophet of God, looked and sounded like a very nice and caring human being.

For many years I had lived under occupation, which felt as if someone was sucking the air out of my lungs. I was determined not to let it happen again. I was looking hard for a Church leader from whom I could feel that politics had no place in the Church and that all human beings are equal. In the eyes of President Kimball I saw the love of Christ, and I also saw the caring of God for all the peoples of the earth, yes, even the Palestinians. As I was watching the tape of President Kimball with the rest of the class, I was able to feel that the good spirit in the class grew stronger. Surprisingly to me, I felt that I was floating in the air with nothing under me.

For about a year I did not share my thoughts or feelings about the Church with anybody. But I kept on studying and searching for guidance from God as to what to do. Something deep inside of me said repeatedly that there was something missing in my life. One of the questions that I dared keep asking myself was whether I should join the LDS Church.

During my second year, I became the head resident of the Arabic House, which was located three or four hundred feet from the Provo Temple. I moved in with four returned missionaries who were learning Arabic. I made it very clear to them from the beginning that I was not interested in the Church, and that they should not try to push their views on me. Almost every member of the LDS Church whom I knew had tried in one way or another to convert me. This time I was not going to allow it. Over time, however, one of the students became very close to me. He never pushed his views on me, and he accepted me just as I was. Eventually he became my best friend, and his name is Steve Hawkins. Steve and I talked several times about life. Only a few times in those conversations did he talk to me about the Church. Most of the time when the subject came up it was to answer one of my questions.

Both my roommates and my Arab friends in Provo kept telling me that I had grown more calm. In December of 1983, I went to Jerusalem for Christmas. While there, I realized that I had changed, but I could not pinpoint how. When I came back to BYU in January of 1984, I decided to turn to God for answers.

For two months on a daily basis I walked around the Provo Temple asking God to guide me to do the right thing. I started asking God and myself whether I was supposed to join the Church. For the longest time, I received no answer. Yet I kept having a feeling that something was about to change in my life. I felt confused and distressed.

I had always believed that God would be there when I needed him. I had always turned to God whenever I was going through drastic changes in my life. Then, about the middle of March, Dilworth Parkinson, an Arabic professor at BYU, approached me. He asked me whether I was interested in translating one of the talks for the upcoming LDS general conference into Arabic.

A few days before the general conference, I received a copy of a talk to be given by Elder Neal A. Maxwell. As I started reading the talk, I discovered that I had a hard time understanding the talk in English, let alone being able to translate it into Arabic. After spending many hours, I was able to successfully finish a translation of the talk. Unfortunately, the talk was still missing something because it did not sound right to me. I started praying to God to ask his help in inspiring me to choose the right words so that it would be free of my interpretation. As I was rewriting the Arabic text, I started to feel the Spirit of God in what I was translating. When I had finished the first basic translation of the text from English into Arabic, I had read it in Arabic and it sounded grammatically correct. But it felt like a meal that had been cooked but all the spices were missing. It felt plain, uninspiring. Praying was like opening the cookbook, finding the right ingredient, and adding it to the food. After rewriting it, the text was flavored to God's taste, something that I somehow knew to be true.

Toward the end of March, after working on the translation for few days, I decided to share my thoughts about the Church with Steve. I mentioned to him that I now wanted to join the LDS Church, and that I needed him to help me make all the arrangements for the baptism. I also asked Steve to baptize me. On 1 April 1984 I announced to all my friends that I was going to be baptized on 6 April 1984. It was a shock to many friends because they had no clue about my interest in the Church. Steve was the only one who had not acted surprised at my decision; I felt as if he knew all along that it was going to happen.

At that point, I had no doubt in my mind about the gospel or about President Kimball being a prophet of God. I also knew that people could say whatever they wanted. What they say might change from time to time, but one thing that will never change is the gospel. It is true, and it will continue to be so.

When I made my decision to join the Church I felt as if a mountain had been lifted off my chest and I could breathe again. My family supported me in my decision, especially my mother. From that day on, I became involved in many translation projects for the Church, which included the Book of Mormon, the Doctrine and Covenants, and the Pearl of Great Price, as well as the temple ceremonies. When I did translations for these many projects, I had to study what I was translating. Since I was not allowed to interpret, I had to depend on the Spirit of God to put the right words in my heart and mouth.

In July of 1988 I met my beautiful Finnish wife, Eija. We were sealed in the Manti Temple on 4 October 1988. We have three beautiful children, Filomen, Jessica, and Matthew. My wife is also a convert to the Church, having joined the Church in her homeland of Finland in January of 1984. Her faith in God and the Church has always been strong, and I am glad to have her strong spirit present in our home. It is perhaps unusual that Eija and I both joined the Church the same year. We were in two different countries and knew nothing about each other.

Other people, who were a big influence in my life include President Howard W. Hunter, who took the time to meet with me and listen to what I had to say. We talked about everything. Brother and Sister Robert Taylor and Brother and Sister Stan

Taylor were always there for me before and after I joined the Church. When I needed support, I could always count on them. To me they are the ideal members of the LDS Church. Their love for me did not change when I joined the Church, because they already treated me like a son. The list could go on and on if I were to start listing the names of the people who had a big influence on me in finding the truth while I was at BYU. Nevertheless, the name that I must never fail to mention is that of our Lord, the Savior Jesus Christ.

Yea, and when you do not cry unto the Lord, let your hearts be full, drawn out in prayer unto him continually for your welfare, and also for the welfare of those who are around you (Alma 34:27).

Mirroring Influences

Larry and Terry EchoHawk

Larry EchoHawk is a professor of law at Brigham Young University's J. Reuben Clark Law School. He was born in 1948 and is a member of the Pawnee Indian tribe. He joined the Church when he was fourteen. Recruited to play football at BYU, he graduated in 1970. He earned his juris doctorate from the University of Utah in 1973 and pursued graduate business studies at Stanford University. Professor EchoHawk practiced law in Salt Lake City until he was named chief general counsel to the Shoshone–Bannock Tribes at Fort Hall, Idaho, a position he held for over eight years. From 1990 to 1994 he served as attorney general for the state of Idaho. Terry EchoHawk grew up in Farmington, New Mexico. She was baptized a member of the Church at nineteen by her husband while both were students at BYU. She graduated with an associate degree in nursing, eventually receiving a B.S. in community health. Terry currently works part-time at the BYU Health Center and the Missionary Training Center in Provo. She enjoys family history research and temple work. The EchoHawks are the parents of six children. Both enjoy running and have completed several marathons.

Terry:

Larry and I met in the fourth grade in Farmington, New Mexico. When my family moved from California, Larry and I attended the same elementary school for six months while our home was being built across town. We did not see each other again until junior high, when we once more attended the same school.

Larry:

When Terry and I met, neither one of us were members of the Church. I really didn't have contact with any church. But that soon changed. My father is a full-blood Native American, from the Pawnee tribe, and my mother is of German descent. There are six children in my family. The two oldest are sisters. I am the third youngest of four boys. When I was growing up, there was a lot of turmoil in my family. We never went to church. My father had a drinking problem. When he was drinking, it was terrible at home. I didn't think my parents were going to stay together.

One day a neighbor, who was standing next to my father in a line at a bank, asked him if he would be interested in having the missionaries come over. At the time, my older brother, an excellent student who was close to graduation, was applying for one of the military academies. My dad thought it would be nice if my brother listed some church background on his application. So he was willing to let the missionaries come.

The stake missionaries, Brother Pearson and Brother Camphuysen, came to our home. I was fourteen years old. I don't remember much about the lessons because I didn't pay a lot of attention. When we were asked to commit to baptism, my dad said yes. He was a real disciplinarian in our home. He went down the line from the oldest to the youngest asking, "You want to be baptized?" I remember when he looked at me. After my mom and dad had said yes, it was automatic that the rest of the family would too. Although I had no testimony, I was baptized. Indeed, after joining the Church, my older brothers and I lived as we had before. By the seventh grade I was already doing things I shouldn't. That didn't change immediately for me. Fortunately, my father made us go to church every Sunday, and I got the benefit of listening to Sunday School teachers, priesthood leaders, and sacrament meeting speakers. I paid attention, but it wasn't influencing my life. However, I could see that it was better for our family because the problems associated with my dad's drinking disappeared. Our home was a much better place to be.

Terry:

I came from a home where my mother took my brother and me to a Lutheran church every Sunday. My father would go with us at Christmas and Easter. I was confirmed at the age of twelve, an important event for me. I remember participating in the church Christmas plays and vacation Bible school, singing in the choir, and playing the organ. The church was a part of our lives. Sunday morning was for church, then my family would usually go water skiing or snow skiing with friends.

When I was a sophomore in high school, I started dating an LDS boy, named Brent Packer. This young man had a Book of Mormon in the glove compartment of his car. He asked if I'd like to read it. At about the same time, my friend Tammy asked if I would like to take the missionary lessons at her home. It was then that I met my first missionaries. I will be forever grateful for them.

My family's response to my interest in the Church was not positive. I loved my family, but as I started learning more about the gospel, I wanted to keep the Sabbath day holy in a different way than I had in the past. My friend and classmate Tyra Brown was a very positive influence on my life at this time. I asked to go to the LDS Church with her. My parents didn't like that, but they agreed to let me go to the LDS Church if I also went to the Lutheran Church. Family ski trips would come up on Sundays, and I would say, "I don't want to go skiing on Sunday." I remember vividly my father's response. I can still see him when he said, "What kind of a church would pull families apart like this?" His response really hurt me. Of course, the Church wasn't pulling our family apart. I simply wanted to change some things in my life. Although my father didn't go to church, it was interesting to me that he paid attention and became concerned when I became seriously interested in the LDS Church. Because of his concerns, he would not give permission for me to be baptized. As a consequence, my interest in the LDS Church caused friction with my family.

I remember that Tracy, my best friend from grade school and high school, reacted differently than I did when the gospel was introduced to us. We were sixteen and we started associating with Mormon kids. Both of our boyfriends were LDS. I wanted to take the missionary lessons, so Tracy took them too. Tracy chose not to have anything to do with the Church after the lessons. But after

I took the lessons, I knew that I wanted to join the Church. This decision didn't change my friendship with Tracy or with other non-LDS friends in any way.

Larry:

My achievement in sports is tied very closely to my conversion to the Church—it's one and the same story. A key moment for me occurred between my junior and senior years of high school, after I was a member of the Church and had become a priest. Brother Richard Boren was the quorum advisor. He took a special interest in me. In a real sense, my experiences as a member of that priests quorum prepared me to take advantage of the spiritual and academic opportunities that I found at BYU.

Brother Boren was a very instrumental part of this. My brothers and I all played sports. We loved it. My brother Fred is a year and a half older than I am, but we were in the same grade. He is the better athlete, and as a consequence I was always in his shadow through grade school, junior high, and high school. I didn't excel in football until my senior year.

Brother Boren was a very successful lawyer. He told me repeatedly, "You can do anything you want. You can get a good education and you can do wonderful things in your life." He knew that I loved sports. So he pulled me aside and said, "If you really want to do well in sports, you have to work at it. You have to set goals and you have to develop yourself." At this point I was not a particularly good football player. Although I wasn't a bad athlete, I wasn't anything special.

However, during my junior year I decided that I wanted to be a good, not mediocre, football player. Brother Boren had said, "In order to succeed you have to set goals and work to prepare yourself." He did more than talk; he helped me set up programs for weight lifting and running. He provided constant encouragement.

Physically I was small for my age (my friends called me "Little Larry"). Along with lifting weights and running, I began mixing up a special weight-gaining formula to drink. It consisted of raw eggs, powdered milk, peanut butter, and all the fattening things I could think of. I put a little vanilla in it to help the taste. I drank this daily and worked out hard. With this and Brother

Boren's encouragement, I really started to develop. I probably gained twenty-five pounds in one year.

When I showed up for football practice at the beginning of my senior year, the coaches could hardly believe their eyes. I thought I was going to be a defensive player because I was quick, but when I came to practice I found that they had me listed as a quarterback. This was disappointing because the captain of our football team was already the starting quarterback. But I had prepared. After a few days, I came into the locker room before practice, and my name was listed in the starting position. I had beaten out the captain of the football team! I remember thinking that the coaches were just trying to spur him to do a little better. But I had clearly impressed the coaches because I was bigger and faster and had worked on my skills. I was doing all the things I was supposed to do. I thought, "Man, I've made it!"

Terry:

My first visit to BYU came when I was a high school sopho-more—an experience that helped shape my life. I had begun taking the missionary lessons when I was sixteen years old in the home of my friend Tammy Huntzinger in Farmington, New Mexico. About the same time, her mother drove five girls to Provo to visit. I had never seen the BYU campus. But I remember that it was like coming home. Recalling the trip brings back a flood of memories. Even today, when I drive down University Avenue and see the "Y" on the mountain, I recall that day when we were coming from the southern part of the valley. I remember looking up then and seeing the "Y." I can still recall the unexpected feelings that came over me. From that moment, BYU was special.

I dated Larry for a short time at the beginning of high school, and during my senior year I began dating him again. My parents had plans for me to go to the University of New Mexico when I graduated, but all my friends and Larry were planning to go to BYU. When I told my parents I wanted to go to BYU they were adamantly opposed. My father said, "I will let you be baptized if you go to the University of New Mexico."

While pondering this choice I had a wonderful experience at Mutual. I was the only non–Latter-day Saint that night as I went into a Laurel class taught by Sister Faye Mathews. She taught a lesson about temples. I don't remember exactly what she said, but at the end of her lesson she walked across the circle of girls and laid a set of pale blue pillowcases on my lap. She looked into my eyes and said, "Would you keep these to use after you get married in the temple?"

What I now know to have been feelings prompted by the presence of the Holy Spirit were very powerful and influencing. Each time Larry would invite me to go to Mutual with him and our friends, I became more and more convinced that baptism could wait. I had to be at BYU to be in a place where the Spirit would be too. I chose to go to BYU and postpone baptism for one year.

Larry:

A pivotal moment in my life came during two-a-day practices before the first game of my senior year in high school. Between practice sessions I was out playing with my brother and two friends. Someone threw a ball. I turned around just at the wrong time, and the ball hit me squarely in the eye. It was a serious and painful injury. I was taken to the emergency room at the hospital. My eye was swollen shut. I couldn't see a thing. When the doctor met with my parents, he said that it was too early to tell, but I might lose the sight in my eye. He bandaged both eyes and sent me home.

I had to lie in bed for a week. You can imagine how devastating it was to me because I had pushed myself to a position where I was the starting quarterback and it was just a week until the first game. I kept asking, "How could this happen?" But it was a turning point of my life. As I lay there in bed, for the first time I started to think about other things Brother Boren had told me. I had been listening as he and others had talked about the gospel of Jesus Christ and the power of prayer. As with Enos in the Book of Mormon, those thoughts started coming back to me. But I was still thinking, "How unfair. How could something like this happen to me?"

I remember finally slipping out of bed to my knees. That moment was the first time I had ever prayed intently in my life. There I was with bandages on my eyes, alone in my room, praying. I remember saying, "Heavenly Father, please. If you are there, listen to my prayer and help me not lose the vision in my eye." I later wondered whether I should have made this promise, but I said, "I promise, if I can just keep the vision in my eye, I will read the Book of Mormon as Brother Boren has challenged me to do."

When the bandages came off, I couldn't see. I recall looking toward the light, and if I held my hand in front of my face I could detect something dark in front of me. But gradually, day by day, my sight came back to the point that I had near perfect vision within a week. Of course, I was ecstatic! Then I remembered my promise, and I felt bound to read the Book of Mormon.

The football team had played its first game, and the season was underway. I didn't think I would be able to play, but the doctors cleared me to practice with the team. The captain of the football team was again the starting quarterback.

During the next game, this one in Grand Junction, Colorado, the coach came to me and said, "Do you want to play?" I said, "Sure." Later he said, "I talked to your mother and father and they said it's okay. I talked to the doctor, and you can play." We were already far behind in the game. When we went out for the second half, we didn't do very well. Finally, the coach came and said, "The next time we get the ball, you're going in." I remember going over to the sideline and kneeling down on one knee (football players often kneel down like that to watch the game). I just dropped my head and said a prayer. I whispered that prayer with "real intent" because I was going to face my biggest challenge on an athletic field. This would be my chance.

The coach called me over, gave me the play, and sent me in. It was a play where I faked to a halfback and rolled out. I could either run with the ball, or I could throw it to receivers downfield. Taking the snap, I could tell after just a few strides that I wouldn't be able to run the ball. The other team had the play defensed. At the last minute I saw one of my teammates down the field. I stopped, planted my foot—this was where the weight lifting paid off—and threw that ball as far and as hard as I could. As soon as I turned the ball loose, I was tackled. Then I heard a roar in the stadium. I remember thinking, "I don't know whether they're cheering for my side or the other side." When I could look down field, my teammate had the ball in the end zone! That was the greatest moment of my teenage life. To me, it was as an answer to my prayer.

I had another wonderful high school game in Albuquerque. We played harder against the state championship team than any other team that year. Afterward, one of the coaches from the University of New Mexico came into the dressing room. He introduced himself and said, "We liked what we saw tonight." To me the experience was unreal because I had never been in a position where I had been successful before. He shook my hand and told me that he would be watching me the rest of the year. By the end of the season, I had been selected as the all-star high school quarterback for the state of New Mexico.

After recovering my sight from the accident, I started reading the Book of Mormon. I had not been a good student when going through junior high and high school. I really struggled because my mind was not on school. I loved sports but not school. I'm sure that the Book of Mormon was the first book that I read from cover to cover.

As Brother Boren had suggested, my plan was to read ten pages every night. I never missed a night. When I finished, I knelt down and prayed. At that moment, I had my first very strong, spiritual experience. I knew then the Book of Mormon was true. I had received my first real answer to prayer.

The wonderful thing about the Book of Mormon is that it is about my ancestors. I have come to tie my knowledge and my testimony of the Book of Mormon to my own Pawnee ancestry. The Book of Mormon talks about a people who would be scattered, smitten, driven, and nearly destroyed. But in the end they would be blessed. That's exactly what I saw in my own family history. In fact, I found myself and my family in the pages of the Book of Mormon. When I read the Book of Mormon, it gave me a very positive feeling about who I was and a knowledge that Heavenly Father had something for me to accomplish in life and that I would be an instrument in his hands. It was as if I had always believed those teachings. When I arrived at BYU, I felt those things even more strongly.

Terry:

One weekend just after Larry and I started attending BYU, we returned to Farmington, New Mexico. Bishop Richard Mathews called on Larry and me to bear our testimonies in Larry's home ward. I remember thinking, "I'm not even a member, and this bishop feels I have something to contribute!"

James Baird, who taught in the Education Department, was my first bishop at BYU. He knew I was not LDS. He called me in and got to know who I was. He knew that I was waiting to be baptized. I don't know what prompted him, but he called me to be a visiting teacher. It meant a lot to me that Bishop Baird took an interest in me and gave me many of the benefits of being a member of the Church.

My calling as a visiting teacher at BYU helped give me a sense of belonging. I also loved the feeling in the dorm when we would gather together for family prayer each night and sing a song. This was all a part of what drew me to the Church. I saw and felt these same things in my friends' homes when they would kneel together in prayer. Larry, Tyra Brown, Tammy Huntzinger, the Packer family, Bishop and Sister Mathews, and other good LDS friends and their families were very instrumental in pulling me closer to the Church in Farmington. Many of those friends were now at BYU with me and formed a support system. Friends really made a difference.

At BYU, Bishop Baird encouraged a lot of growth with fasting and prayer. In the spring of 1967, I knew the time for my baptism was approaching, and I needed to have my life in order. Tyra Brown talked to me about fasting and suggested I try it. It was an important experience for me. Living in the dorms where the kitchens only served one meal on Fast Sundays, students were sometimes forced to fast. But to fast with a purpose changed the whole feeling of fasting. Now I love to fast. Fasting has become an anchor for my soul.

Did I receive an answer to my prayers? Definitely. As a Lutheran I said a lot of set prayers, memorized prayers, things that came from the liturgy. Until the age of sixteen my prayers basically consisted of kneeling down and saying the Lord's Prayer. Prayer wasn't ever talking with the Lord and thinking about gratitude or asking for needed help. It wasn't really a two-way communication. Prayer now became something new. Feeling the influence of the Holy Spirit drew me closer to the Lord. I came to love prayer.

Larry:

After the high school football season, I was sitting in a study class one day when a student messenger passed me a note. It said I was to see the coach. I went down to his office. The door was closed. I knocked and he said to come in. I opened the door and looked across the room. The head football coach of the University of New Mexico was sitting there. I remember that moment vividly, because as soon as I saw him, I knew I was going to college. Before that moment, I never thought I would go.

BYU also recruited me because the coaches had seen my athletic achievements. But I wasn't sure whether BYU would offer me a scholarship. I remember the meeting with Tommy Hudspeth, the head coach. He asked me whether I had any other scholarship offers. I said, "Yes. I have a four-year, full ride scholarship to the University of New Mexico." I happened to have the scholarship offer from New Mexico in the notebook I was carrying. I handed him the letter and he read it. He folded it up, handed it back, and said, "You have a full scholarship at BYU if you want it."

Terry:

Did the University somehow make a difference in my life that first year? Absolutely! Recently I have heard President Hinckley and President Monson talk about "the BYU experience." There is something real there. It's tangible. I'm grateful that I came as a young woman. Our whole lives, Larry and I have dreamed of our children going to BYU so they could experience what we did. It's difficult to put into words. I still think I would have embraced the gospel if I had been in a different setting, but BYU really helped to nurture and sustain growth that was just beginning. I remember I loved fast and testimony meetings on campus. Those meetings influenced me the most.

In retrospect, BYU has had an enormous influence on my life, in shaping my goals, my ideals, and my testimony. I can remember distinctly kneeling by my bed in Q Hall in Deseret Towers in the spring of 1967 and pouring out my heart to my Father in Heaven and feeling so surely his presence and his love.

I can state unequivocally that if I had followed my friend Tracy, who took the lessons at the same time I did and attended a different university, I would not be who I am, or where I am today. I would have had to do a lot more alone. I prepared for baptism and became a member of The Church of Jesus Christ of Latter-day Saints on 10 June 1967, when Larry baptized me in my home ward in Albuquerque, New Mexico, where my parents had recently moved.

Larry:

Spencer W. Kimball was one of my greatest mentors. At church in New Mexico everybody talked about the apostle who had a great love for the Indian people. We revered the name Spencer W. Kimball. I met him in high school at a Lamanite youth conference in Kirtland, New Mexico, a largely LDS community about fifteen miles outside of Farmington. I remember sitting out on a softball field with a number of other Indian youth, waiting for this apostle to come. There was a lot of anticipation. A car pulled up. Men in dark suits got out and came walking across the field. All these Indian kids were there waiting for them. As they approached, I was standing there thinking, "Which one is he?" Finally, he stepped forward. My first impression was disappointment because he was short and balding. He started talking to us in a raspy voice. My thought was, "Is this him?" But the wonderful thing about him was that he befriended us all very quickly — this was a real accomplishment because Indian youth are not easy to get close to.

Later, when I was at BYU, I heard him speak several times. Like Brother Boren, he provided a blueprint for my life. To this day in my scriptures or in my journal I carry an excerpt from a speech that he gave when I was a BYU student, entitled "This Is My Vision." In this talk, he tells of a dream: "I woke up and I had this dream about you — about the Lamanites. I wrote it down. It may be a dream. It may be a vision. But this is what I saw you doing." In one part of it he said, "I saw you as lawyers. I saw you looking after your people. I saw you as heads of cities and of states and in elective office." To me that was a patriarchal blessing and a challenge from a prophet of God: "Get an education. Be a lawyer. Use your education to bless your people." That is what I wanted to do. At a certain point in my life, when I read the passage where he said we could become leaders of cities or states, it was as if it was directed to me. Even though I had never envisioned running for elective office, I knew that I could and should do it because of President Kimball's vision for me and those like me.

I loved President Kimball. The day he passed away, I cried. When I heard about his death, I was overcome because I had felt his love. I had seen so much of the good that he had accomplished among Native Americans. I was also a recipient of his vision for us as individuals and as a people.

Others at BYU were also mentors. For example, Floyd Johnson at BYU in the athletic department took a special interest in me. I think most athletes at BYU felt Floyd's love and concern because he took so many young men under his wing. In my case, I really thought so because right away he told me that he had raised several Indian placement students. When I came in—and he probably said this to everybody—he said, "You're special. I'm going to look after you." I thought he was just talking about me. I felt that all the time I was at BYU. If I had any need, he was there to take care of it.

During my years at BYU, my generation of Native Americans heard, "You are a special people. You have a destiny in this Church. The Book of Mormon is about you. You have roots in that book, and you need to do certain things." And I believed every word that was said. There was a purpose for me being at BYU.

Terry:

Life takes us on curious journeys sometimes. In December 1968 we were married by Spencer W. Kimball in the Salt Lake City Temple and moved into Wymount Terrace at BYU. After four years of safekeeping, and my temple marriage, I used the pillow-cases Sister Mathews gave me. Then in December 1995, twenty-seven years later, we returned to live in Wymount Terrace for ten months when Larry was asked to teach at the J. Reuben Clark Law School after his unsuccessful bid in the Idaho gubernatorial race in November 1994. BYU had many things to offer us as eighteen-year-old freshmen in 1966; it still has much to offer today. BYU provides us opportunities to serve and to find ways to increase our faith and testimonies today.

Larry:

I enjoyed my classwork at BYU. I was a much better student in college than I was in high school. It was because I became focused. I knew what I wanted out of life, and I had some self-confidence. Even so, university work was a challenge for me because I wasn't used to doing well in school. When I came to BYU I had to work harder to catch up. I underwent the same experience when I went to law school. Because I didn't have the background that other students had, I needed to work harder. But, with Terry's support, I was successful.

When I graduated from BYU I wanted to be a lawyer for one reason: to help Indian people. Subsequently, I spent nine years as a tribal attorney. I have seen a marvelous awakening under the laws that now help native people to become self-sufficient and economically strong. I have always thought it was no accident that we were able to survive as a separate, identifiable people. I don't know how the Lord is going to use such people in his ultimate plan. But I see many people I went to school with who have been able to go on and do the same kinds of things I have done. I think it has a cumulative impact.

BYU gave me a vision of who I am and what I should do. I think I have effectively—and I hope it is okay to say this—executed that in my life. I think it is exactly what Richard Boren, President Kimball, Floyd Johnson, and other people who cared about me at BYU wanted me to do. It's as if I went to BYU not only to learn to make a living but to do something to impact the lives of other people. Because of where I started, I feel satisfied that I have done that.

There is now a regular flow of Native American students coming to my office. I'm not sure who sends them, but I enjoy visiting with them. I feel that in some small measure I am in a position to inspire them, to lift their sights, and to encourage them to focus on what is important, especially finding God in their lives.

Terry:

Our dreams for our children are coming true. Five of our six children have attended BYU, where their lives are being blessed as ours have been blessed, although perhaps in different and individual ways.

Seek ye diligently and teach one another words of wisdom; yea, seek ye out of the best books words of wisdom; seek learning, even by study and also by faith (D&C 88:118).

Sustaining the Presence

Karandeep Singh

Karandeep Singh is a graduate student in art history and curatorial studies at Brigham Young University. He was born in New Delhi, India, and grew up there. Following completion of high school in India, he enrolled at BYU and completed a degree in anthropology and philosophy in 1995, graduating with honors and as the valedictorian of his class. He enrolled at Brandeis University to pursue graduate work but decided to return to BYU to continue his master's degree. His story was written in two stages. The first part was written shortly after Mr. Singh left BYU for graduate school in the East. The second was written two years later, after he had returned to BYU for additional graduate education. Mr. Singh currently resides in England where he is pursuing a Ph.D. in philosophy at the University of Essex.

God found me four years before I found BYU. He came to the fifteen-year-old New Delhi (India) suburbanite, who was also a newly proclaimed atheist and an aspiring cardiovascular surgeon, in the form of a soft-spoken, retired army officer. Something about this dashing octogenarian Sikh struck me as extraordinary: his radiant forehead, the conviction in his speech, or maybe just his handlebar mustache. Concealed in his understated demeanor, though, was the spark of a revolutionary. Either that, or I was all too combustible on that balmy February day in 1988. The flame was kindled; the contagion contracted. Almost in spite of myself, I began the journey of a Sikh.

Don't misunderstand me. My family has been Sikh for several generations. We have worn our turbans with pride and adorned unshorn hair with fortitude. But all I found growing up was stagnation: an unthinking faith that cared more for the soporific norms of a complacent society than for the dynamic dictates of its prophets. There was no—how shall I say it?—commitment.

Well, there was a *kind* of commitment, but a very superficial one of the kind where a community gangs up against missionaries from another faith but gets lackadaisical as soon as the missionaries leave. Nobody cherished repentance over convenience; not one of these so-called disciples practiced their credo of "service before self." So at fifteen, I was disenchanted with life, with religion, and with God. Then that retired army officer accosted me in his delectable half-British, half-Hindustani accent.

He spoke of *living* the word, of *becoming* scripture, of being *elevated* to Godhood. He talked of *implementing* doctrine, *personifying* charity, and *cultivating* virtue. I had never heard anything like it before. Sure, I had all the usual read-your-scriptures and be-nice-to-others and pay-your-tithing and attend-church-regularly coming out of my ears. Mere preaching, I used to think. The blind leading the blind, as if we all knew where we were going. But when "Bauji" spoke (I have come to call him that — it is Punjabi for "grandpa"), a thunder roared in my insides. It was as if the very pauses between his sentences were pregnant with truth. He had merely to look my way, and I felt as if I had become the locus of the entire Sikh community. Eighteen million Sikhs converged in me when "Bauji" narrated awe-inspiring tales of valor from our shared religious heritage. He had a way of personalizing the impersonal, of rendering the abstract accessible, that foiled all habitual attempts on my part to deflect responsibility. Was this guy for real?

Ever the doubting Cartesian, I probed his life (oh, he has to be another charlatan) but found it unimpeachable. I discovered that he did not let a sermon escape his lips until he had preached it through his actions. He was so large, so brimming with life, so utterly simple in his faith that I found myself more and more in his company. I hungered for his words, craved his wisdom, sought after his simplicity. He seemed to eat, drink, and sleep the Guru Granth Sahib (Sikh scriptures). What struck me most was his intuitive capacity for the spiritual realm; in fact, it was precisely his mastery of the spiritual secrets of everyday life that won over my unruly intellect. Even his stern discipline—he was an army man after all—had an inexplicable attraction. In short, he became my ideal of a disciple, which perhaps is the best way of describing a mentor. I was given a mentor; God had found me!

Interestingly, the entire time I was being initiated into the rigors of discipleship, I had no idea that twelve thousand miles away, across a continent and an ocean, fellow adolescents in another community were experiencing similar throes under their own prophets and mentors. I had never heard of the Mormons, nor was I even remotely acquainted with Brigham Young University. What I was acutely aware of, though, was an overwhelming desire to come to the United States to further my education. The liberal arts have always entranced me; and of all the universities in the world, I thought the American ones incorporate the liberal arts most effectively into a rigorous undergraduate curriculum. When application season came, I applied to five of the best private schools in the country. A couple of months later, a family friend, himself a graduate of Harvard and an admirer of Latter-day Saints, brought up the possibility of going to BYU. On his lofty recommendation, I decided to give it a shot, only to be told in a curt official notice that BYU doesn't allow men to wear facial hair for nonmedical reasons. Oh, and rule number two: hair must be worn short—no longer than collar length, ears exposed, neatly groomed.

That has to be one of the most amusing nonstarters. Not so much offended as baffled by the tone of the letter, I forgot all about BYU. But this family friend was irate. He pursued my case with some LDS friends in Salt Lake City. The misunderstanding was sorted out: of course I would be allowed to keep my hair and beard. A week later, I got a letter in the mail congratulating me on being accepted to BYU. Now I had a choice. The Honor Code tilted the scales in BYU's favor, and I moved into room 312 of V Hall, Deseret Towers. That was in the fall of 1992. In the spring of 1995, I received a letter announcing my eligibility to graduate that April, which I did with two majors, three mentors, four B's, and no job offers. But perhaps most importantly, with the art of preserving God in my life.

In the last several years, spent mostly in the United States, I have come to realize that even though God found me four years before I found BYU, I had not the skill to handle the fragility of his presence. The companionship of Deity is a blessing bestowed upon a disciple; this much I knew from my experiences as a fifteen year old. But I learned the hard way that this presence needs to be preserved and sustained, for the slightest inattentiveness results in its loss. I lost it several times during my time at BYU. Some days it was the pressure of a midterm; on other occasions a particularly bewitching young lady became the distraction; on still others the headiness generated by intellectual accomplishments got in the way. Perhaps it was a question of perspective, I figured, and hence requested my sophomore-year roommate, Marc Johnson, to chime to me as soon as the clock struck 11 P.M., "Look at the larger picture." Marc, the blessed soul, did it diligently the entire eight months we shared that not-so-spacious Penrose Hall room. It didn't work.

The quest for permanent, or at least a long-term, association with the Lord became increasingly convoluted. Maybe the spirit had deserted me because I had turned down the calling of the ward social events coordinator. I shared my predicament with the elders quorum president, Shawn Henderson, who listened sympathetically. He seemed rather surprised, for both he and the bishop had concurred on the validity of my reasons to decline the calling. (That was the first semester I attempted—rather disastrously, but that's another story—twenty-one credits.) I tried to make up for it by sedulously attending ward prayer every Sunday. They usually had root beer floats at the end, which gave my conscience a whole new warehouse of arsenal. But of course I didn't go there for the ice cream; I went for the bonhomie and the camaraderie and the warmth and the fuzziness and the . . . . Attendance in the activities of the ward didn't work either. More than anything else, I probably ended up distracting even further, with my polka-dotted turbans—ah, those were wild days—the already much distracted majority of eternal-partner-seekers.

Frank Susa, the pocket-sized dynamo from Rhode Island, furnished an alternative. Instead of the typical cheap undergrad pizza and (caffeine-free) coke birthday party, why not celebrate his twenty-first birthday by spending the evening with the children at a local orphanage? No prizes for guessing Frank's major. Philosophy, of course. Where else on a contemporary college campus can intelligent idealists still hang out? A service project, I thought, is bound to cure my malaise. It seemed to be working as long as the kids thought I was the genie—it's the turban, I tell you—and gave me a list of all the things they would have liked me to conjure up for them. I still have that list, scribbled in pink and green and blue crayons. Barbie dolls and fighter jets and red cars and palaces, but no mom and dad. Not a single child wanted mom and dad. Maybe they didn't think I was genie enough, or they, like the nine-year-old son of the second-grade captain in Dostoevsky's *The Brothers Karamazov*, had lost all hope. Except in this case, it was not my finger they wanted to chew, but my scalp. Someone figured out that I had hair down to my waist hidden under the turban. Before the orphanage administrator could blink her eyes, the little army had started to climb the six-foot-one-inch mountain with its eyes set on one goal: eliminate the peak and swing down the hair! I still hadn't found permanence, but I wasn't too worried about it that moment. Life seemed slightly more significant, and I'm grateful to have escaped alive, the rich crop on my scalp intact.

The significance of life — I use that phrase so effortlessly now. Yet it took James Faulconer, professor of philosophy, mentor, and dear friend, slightly over four years to get me to see life's significance, especially as it relates to discipleship, or the preservation of relationships with God. He stayed back after class — it was the second half of the history of Western philosophy, I think — one Tuesday morning to talk to me about a paper I had written for a course on Judaism. (Dr. Faulconer suffered, with fortitude that would make the pioneers proud, the torture of reading everything I ever wrote at BYU, from the first report I did for his honors freshman writing class to my commencement speech.) The conversation, meant only as an after-class courtesy chat, lasted almost two hours. Both of us missed the devotional. In addition, he probably missed a few important meetings, and I missed a north-lobby-of-the-library rendezvous with a prospective Friday-night date. I still recall vividly that hideous room where we stood talking, tucked away in a corner of the first level of the JKHB, surrounded by semi-circles of the world's most uncomfortable chairs. "You are a modern philosopher," Brother Faulconer said to me. "Thank you," I said, trying not to blush. "No, no," he clarified, a half-smile dancing around his lips, "that was not a compliment."

I love Brother Faulconer. He can be so delightfully cryptic at times. On that frosty Tuesday, he cryptically told me that in buying everything modernism was selling in the name of Descartes, I had been a sucker. The merchandise in question consisted primarily of the idea that the foundation of everything, including religion, is knowledge. Not right, argued Brother Faulconer, face aglow, arms waving like chopper blades. Religion teaches a *way* and not a knowledge, though it is usually assumed that the way will eventually result in a knowledge. Explanations of religious behavior — the Sikh practice of keeping unshorn hair, for example — therefore, are accounts that stem from a way rather than serving as justifications for the way. I was stunned. Faulconer was saying that the way that produces the accounts is more fundamental, more foundational, than the accounts themselves. Which is why there could be multiple equally cogent explanations. In other words, if one looks at the life that a disciple takes up — or, and this is classic Faulconer, the life that takes him up — one finds a flow, a gushing, dynamic truth that defies all attempts to reduce it to a set of propositions. The modern demand for the one, perfect explanation, then, is essentially misplaced. Our life, the Bauji reminds me, must change if we are to be Sikhs. Faulconer, in articulating and living life as the foundation of everything, including knowledge, taught me a crucial lesson in preserving God: discipleship is more about *being* than *knowing*. What better way to transmit the lesson than to stay back after class on a Tuesday morning and call your student a modern philosopher?

I now look to life, and not the passive principles of knowledge, for inspiration. Apparently, Dr. Faulconer taught me more than he intended that day. Subsequently, I have discovered that life is the only source of restoring the companionship of God. Life, that is, and not the mere motions of living. In moments when I can muster enough courage to jettison the secure, comfortable principles of the world and embrace life with all its mystery, I hear the laughter of my Lord as he leads, guides, and walks beside me. Mystery? Yes, for like Blake, I'm now at ease with not knowing some things, because knowledge is not of the foundation of everything, especially not of the religious life. And a religious life is what I have sought to live, ever since I met that retired army officer in 1988.

I couldn't possibly conclude this reflection without acknowledging that the very words that allow me to share these memories were acquired at BYU. The Lord's University taught me a new tongue, one that enables me to do three things: (1) delineate between spiritual discourse and worldly discourse; (2) recognize when I have slipped from the spiritual into the worldly and rectify the slippage; and (3) check my tendency to hijack the language of the spiritual to suit my convenience in the worldy. Amazingly, I can recollect the exact moment when the spiritual/worldly distinction became clear as daylight. The classroom decor was still as hideous, the building still the JKHB, the chairs still uncomfortable, but the professor this time was Arthur Bassett. This was my final undergraduate semester at BYU, and we were winding up Dr. Bassett's honors course on American humanities. The topic for the day was existentialism. Dr. Bassett walked in and in characteristic fashion proceeded directly to the chalkboard, where he scribbled, one atop another in a column, three words: *angst, absurdity, alienation* (the three A's of existentialism). The din subsided to a hush. Cheetos were put away, notebooks retrieved, pens positioned. A few of the forty or so in attendance stirred in anticipation; others resigned themselves, with an inaudible sigh, to the next hour, as if it were forced labor in Siberia. And, as always, there were those who chose to remain in la-la land. Dr. Bassett stood silently, a thousand unformed thoughts criss-crossing his brow. Suddenly, he turned back to the board and in another column of words, adjacent to the first one, wrote: *faith, hope, charity*. End of lesson.

Three weeks later, President Gordon B. Hinckley got up and introduced me to an audience of eighteen thousand. "An anthropology and humanities-philosophy major," he said, "Brother Singh is from New Delhi, India. The Sikh honor code requires him to wear a turban and a beard. He has been respectful of our faith, as we are of his." We had come full circle. From the terse you-can't-wear-your-beard-at-BYU notice to President Hinckley's cordial introduction, the journey had at once been full of both anguish and inspiration, suffering and salvation, despair and deliverance. "The World Is Our Campus," says the inscription at BYU's entrance. Where else would twenty-seven thousand Mormons train a Sikh to preserve the companionship of God?

Return to BYU for graduate studies in art history? *After* BYU had declined to display some of the sculptures in a Rodin exhibit? Nettlesome questions followed: Beyond the nostalgia of one's undergraduate years, what could possibly draw you to BYU for graduate work? Family and friends—Punjabis don't distinguish between the two—have reserved for themselves, by heavenly decree, the right to doubt and question another's decisions. And

I, confessedly, evaded their stinging questions, thinking my silence would somehow cause them to vaporize. They haven't.

Months ago while I was enrolled in a doctoral program at Brandeis University, I was compelled by an invitation to write the previous pages of this essay to construct a framework — necessarily conceptual, although not entirely subjective, in which case I would be able to write about it all — to make sense of what had occurred during my undergraduate years at BYU. I concluded then that the very language — the syntax, the structure, the style — necessary to be able to articulate my experiences and aspirations was learned at BYU. More than that, the aspirations themselves were given their substance by the incessant pursuit of excellence exemplified, with contagious panache, by my mentors. Sikh prophets created for me the possibilities of dreaming; my parents encouraged me to dream; but my mentors at BYU helped me forge the equipment essential to translate dreams into reality. To put it another, rather pedestrian way: if dreams have wheels, mine were rendered steel-belted at BYU.

Not surprisingly, in the two years that I was away from BYU the steel-belting took some hammering. The glorious community of disciple-scholars that I discovered and cherished at BYU was not found in the situation in which I found myself after leaving Provo. Brandeis's Crown Fellowships, abundantly financed and prestigious, with an impressive — make that *jaw-droppingly* impressive — body of alumni, exacted a price that I became increasingly unwilling to pay. The acquisition of knowledge required a renunciation of the spirit. To gain the intellectual, I kept finding, was to lose the spiritual. Put simply, what confronted me in graduate school was an atmosphere not conducive to sustaining the spirit. No matter how hard I tried, I kept losing its companionship. How was I to learn anything, except that I couldn't learn anything without the spirit in attendance?

I confess that there were moments in graduate school when I thought that going to BYU for an undergraduate education had been a big mistake. You see, colleges and universities of the sort that I was now attending were the norm; BYU was the exception. To my dismay, I soon found, however, that by starting out at that exceptional school, I had diminished my chances of ever making complete peace with the radically different ambience found at other universities. Miserable and slightly crestfallen, I sought the counsel of Jenny Pulsipher, a fourth-year Crown Fellow who was also a BYU alumna. Sitting at her dinner table, surrounded by much mirth and liveliness (it is amazing what life four children can bring to any occasion, mundane or otherwise), Jenny empathized with my "loss of meaning" experiences. But she said something that I could not get out of my mind: "Last night I stood on the back porch," she began, "with Sam [her youngest, then eight months old] in my arms. As I showed him the stars and sang a lullaby, I paused and said to myself: 'This has meaning.'" Alas, I had neither a wife nor children.

Six months later, I seriously considered dropping out of my graduate program. I was lonely, but I learned that I wasn't alone in feeling lonely. At the Starbucks on Massachusetts Avenue one cold night, as Heather Lau, my one-person community in Boston and the Relief Society president of the Longfellow Park Ward, and I sat sipping our honeyed milk, I lamented that the wait for a prospective wife was getting exasperating. With an "oh-yeah" look in her eyes, Heather leaned over and, with feigned circumspection, said: "There are one hundred and sixty of us in there. And what do you think we are doing? We are *all* waiting!"

Jenny's and Heather's comments reappeared in memory as I sat in my uncle's living room in San Jose trying to repatch my dreams. The classroom beckoned, for sure, and I knew it had to be art history and theory. But having burned my hands at Brandeis, this time I wanted to go where the mind could be developed along with, and not at the cost of, the soul. I also wanted community. And so I called the Visual Arts Department at BYU.

My circuitous educational journey has BYU as its origin and destination. I returned to BYU for a graduate degree because of the abundance of the spirit on its campus. Partaking of this spirit creates the courage to dream, and consequently there are dreamers aplenty here. So I returned to the machine shop to mend the tires, knowing that I must leave again to go elsewhere for a Ph.D. But this time I will leave understanding that unless one is careful, there is a negative correlation between advanced intellectual inquiry and spiritual preservation. When I went away the first time, I found that the more I pursued only the nuances of political, economic, and social history, the more the spirit eluded me. When I go away the second time, I will do so understanding that it doesn't work the same way if the two factors are turned around:

Beginning with the spirit, no depth of intellectual inquiry is outside of one's grasp. It is possible for disciples to do first-rate intellectual work, work that has meaning. Indeed, to use religion to excuse substandard academic performance and intellectual sloppiness is to strengthen the false dichotomy of faith and reason.

What is my dream? I want to be part of a *counter-renaissance* of men and women who call themselves servants of God who will reclaim from the world the arts and sciences. I dream that the abundance of spirit at the BYU campus will, even in the face of apathy and materialism, initiate a resurgence of learning where disciples will once again create the standards for meaningful intellectual inquiry. Of course this is a grandiose dream. But there are dreamers aplenty at BYU in body and in spirit as embodied in the history and unique heritage that is BYU's. If one is not careful, one can be infected with their vision. I stopped being careful a long time ago. That's why I returned to BYU for graduate studies in art history — *after* Rodin.

Transformations

If thou art merry, praise the Lord with singing, with music, with dancing, and with a prayer of praise and thanksgiving (D&C 136:28).

Act Well Thy Part

Melinda Cummings Cameron

Melinda Cummings Cameron was born amid the glamour of the film industry in Los Angeles, California, in 1948. Her father, Bob Cummings, was a movie and television star from the 1940s through the 1960s, starring in the number-one rated television show during the 1950s, THE BOB CUMMINGS SHOW. Melinda's parents reared her with honesty and family values in spite of the lure of glitz and glamour that surrounded her growing-up years. She came to BYU after a campus visit intrigued her with the beauty of the place. Her discovery of God at BYU is captured on film, and thousands of people have witnessed it without knowing that they were seeing the miracle of the Holy Ghost touch her life as she performed in PIONEERS IN PETTICOATS. After joining the Church during her third year at BYU, she married Kim Cameron. They are the parents of seven children and live in Ann Arbor, Michigan.

I was born while my parents lived in Beverly Hills, California. My father was featured in *The Ziegfeld Follies* with Fanny Brice and subsequently became a television and motion picture star in the 1950s. My mother was also in show business and had appeared in several movies before meeting and marrying my father in 1945. She relinquished her career to become the mother of my four brothers and sisters and me.

Let me begin by telling you more about my father and mother, because who they are and what they chose to do with their lives has had a major impact on me. My father was born Charles Clarence Cummings in Joplin, Missouri, in 1910, the son of a physician father and a religious mother. She called their only child, after ten years of trying, "my miracle baby." As a young man, my father was an outstanding student and swimmer, possessing a natural acting ability and a great love for aviation.

During the Depression, Dad left Drury College and a major in mechanical engineering after less than a year because of financial hardship. On a friend's advice that plentiful acting jobs existed in New York City, he moved there, eventually taking courses at the American Academy of Dramatic Arts. This training convinced him that he should pursue a career as an actor.

The demand for British actors in New York theater prompted Dad to go to England, acquire an English accent, and return to New York with a new identity — Blade Stanhope Conway. Dad was cast in *The Ziegfeld Follies* opposite Fanny Brice. During this time, Milton Berle took Dad under his wing and gave him a chance as Milton's straight man. When Milton discovered that Dad was not really British, but an impostor trying to preserve his job, he agreed to keep the secret. However, when a Hollywood talent scout offered Dad and Milton screen tests for an up-coming movie, and Dad got the part while Milton was turned down, keeping the secret provided a true test of Berle's friendship.

Once in Hollywood, Dad was cast in dramatic and romantic movie roles opposite some of the greatest stars in the Golden Years of Hollywood, such as Grace Kelly, Olivia DeHavilland, Ronald Reagan, Buster Keaton, and Ray Milland. He changed his name permanently to Robert Orville Cummings (Orville after Orville Wright, whom his own father once treated for an illness), and he became a major movie star.

My mother, Mary Elliott Daniels, was born in 1917 in Gaffney, South Carolina, the second of six children in a poor family. As a beautiful and brilliant woman and valedictorian of her high school class, she received several college scholarships but had to turn them all down because of indigent circumstances. She even wrote to Eleanor Roosevelt asking for a college loan, but she was turned down.

Mother won a number of beauty contests that resulted in her leaving home for New York City at age seventeen to pursue a career in modeling and show business. She supported her family back home in South Carolina, missing meals in order to send money to the family. Even though she was hungry, her high moral standards caused her to resist the advances of wealthy men promising a comfortable lifestyle.

Seeing her performance in a New York production, a Hollywood movie agent offered her a screen test. She was flown to

Hollywood and put under contract at MGM Studios. She spent her first years in Hollywood performing in small roles in major motion pictures, receiving studio training in acting, singing, dancing, diction (to help overcome her southern accent), and makeup. She was often tutored in the early mornings when the makeup artist had time for her and before the major stars arrived. However, when it was announced that Judy Garland or Joan Crawford was coming down the hall, Mom was whisked out of the makeup chair and into a corner of the room until there was time for her again. She spent numerous makeup sessions just listening to some of these famous women, observing the stress they experienced and pace of their lives. The demands they faced and the expectations placed on them by their careers took a heavy toll on marriage and family. Most of these relationships were conducted via telephone.

When I became a young woman, my mother shared those experiences with me. She told me, "I determined that if I could ever find someone to marry, I would not have a career so I could have a strong marriage and family." On another occasion she said, "It really takes all one's effort to have a happy marriage and family. I've known couples who put their marriages and careers before their children, and their children were a disaster; or women who put their careers before their husbands and children, and their marriages did not last; I have never known anyone who was able to do all three and stay together."

As a young girl growing up, I experienced the glamour of the Hollywood lifestyle — the travel, parties, exciting people, fame, fortune, and the promise of an exciting career. Traveling with my parents to Europe, for example, enabled me to meet Alan J. Lerner who said he liked my name so much that he planned to write a song about it someday — which he did in *On a Clear Day You Can See Forever*. I traveled to Japan on movie location with Shirley MacLaine and to London on location with Leslie Caron and Warren Beatty. Having an hour conversation with the Beatles was a highlight and a lifelong memory.

I have wonderful recollections of attending girls school with Candace Bergen, Jimmy Stewart's twins, and Lisa Halaby, now Queen Noor of Jordan. I attended summer camp with David Cassidy *(The Partridge Family)* and Patti Reagan, and acted in plays at Beverly Hills High School with Richard Dreyfus and Albert

Brooks. I also observed the price one pays for a lifestyle of popularity and notoriety. We had a constant intrusion of visitors in our home, and our lives were constantly interrupted because our house was on the Movie Star Bus Tour—a nuisance to me but evidence that Daddy was popular. My mother told me as a young teenager never to write anything in a note or a letter that I didn't want printed in the *Los Angeles Times,* and I was cautioned to be careful about what I said on the telephone.

On several occasions, my mother had to depend on nurses to look after us when she traveled with my father overseas. I remember how it felt to be cared for by a paid care-giver who had little patience with me and did not hide her favoritism or unkindness when Mother was not around to see it.

Family events were often held in front of a camera, with Mother trying to find a way to have us really do the activities we had just staged for a magazine article or TV show. These included taking trips, demonstrating lawnmowers, using play equipment, and eating and drinking various foods and beverages. After a hard day at work, Dad would come home and say to me, "Never marry an actor. It's a rotten life."

In the mid-1960s in Hollywood, scripts being offered to my father began to change. They became racy and even required some nudity. Many movie contracts reflected this change in the fine print by indicating that nudity or risqué outtake material could be required at the producer's discretion. Dad became more and more discouraged with the movie business and turned to live theater. He starred in several successful theater productions in the East and became interested in investing in theaters-in-the-round. One such theater was being built just north of Salt Lake City. Dad brought our family, along with the family of a close friend to meet the board of directors and participate in the grand opening celebration for the new Valley Music Hall. We were hosted by a member of the board of directors, M. Russell Ballard, who agreed to take us on a sight-seeing tour, which included the campus of Brigham Young University.

My mother had seen the campus on a previous visit to Utah, and my older brother thought the security of Utah would be a good environment for me. Mom was thrilled to again meet Janie Thompson, director of BYU's Program Bureau, and some of the Curtain Time USA tour members, recently returned from a world tour. I was so impressed with the group—their freshness and their happiness—but I was especially impressed with the feeling of peace I felt while touring the campus. These were feelings I had rarely felt with my friends in Beverly Hills or among the Hollywood crowd. I wondered, "Why is everyone so happy here? What is this feeling? Are they just putting on a show for visitors?"

My high school friend—I shall call her Diane—and I were offered college applications as we learned about the special standards at BYU. The code of conduct—which included honesty, integrity, modesty in dress and behavior, keeping the Word of Wisdom including no alcohol, cigarettes, or Coke—reminded me of my parents' teachings. All these ideas seemed to resonate with me, and I began to be drawn to this wonderful place. We all went back to California, but I never forgot how I felt that day at BYU.

Diane and I both began acting, and during my senior year in high school I started a professional stage career, preceded by acting classes from Agnes Moorehead and a recording contract offer from Jules Stein. I went on tour with a professional stage production of *Generation* opposite my dad. He was taking a big chance with inexperienced me. In fact, he declared on opening night in Palm Beach, Florida: "Because you are my daughter, people will expect more from you than they would from just any new actress. You'll have to be great on the first try. And, by the way, my career depends on it."

With that, we performed opening night, and our positive reviews and sellout audiences in each city during our summer stock tour began to convince me that acting was probably my best career choice. After opening night in Miami Beach, competing with Frank Sinatra at the Fountainbleau, a movie producer named Huntington Hartford introduced himself and offered me an audition for a motion picture and a television miniseries. He arranged for me to meet his representative in Los Angeles at the end of our show's run.

Back at home in Beverly Hills, I met with Mr. Hartford's representative, and he explained the special nature of the audition. I would be "living with the producer." I was being given a chance for a major breakthrough as a film star; I just had to compromise my standards to get the part. I felt too young to make such a choice. As a professional actress, this was such an important opportunity. But as a young woman, even though I had experienced little formal religious instruction outside my home, I knew this was morally wrong. I wanted to stay pure and build a happy marriage someday, and I knew that I could never really have a secure marriage if I knowingly gave in to this solicitation.

I tried to explain myself to this veteran Hollywood gentleman, but I was met with little tolerance on his part. Some of my parents' friends who heard about my decision to say no to an audition for this new Mike Nichols movie, *The Graduate,* and the special television miniseries based on the novel *Jane Eyre,* reprimanded me. "Melinda, do you realize what a great opportunity this is? With your father's connections, this chance has been handed to you. Others work their entire lives to get such a chance; you should be ashamed that you're giving it up."

In spite of the pressure I felt to say yes, I also felt a strong internal encouragement to maintain my values. I felt in my mind a voice simply saying my name, "Melinda," prompting me to remember who I was and helping me recall events in my life when I had chosen to stay morally clean. The experience was so unsettling for me, however, that I decided to apply to attend college rather than to jump back into professional theater. I applied to and was accepted by BYU in the fall of 1967.

After a few hours of orientation in Deseret Towers, I was introduced to my new roommate, Elaine Black, from Blanding, Utah. The differences in our backgrounds were immediately apparent. She had grown up in a large LDS family of modest means in Blanding, a town that had fewer people than my high school graduating class. She had never traveled far from home, and she delighted in rural activities and loved country and western music. On the other hand, I had traveled all over the world and had attended command performances in the presence of royalty, and Hollywood celebrities frequented our home. As time passed, however, Elaine turned out to be the perfect roommate and one who would influence my life immeasurably.

On several occasions while standing in meal lines at the Morris Center, some BYU students would come up and cattily ask when I was going to take the missionary discussions or be "dunked in the water." Elaine would brush it off in a cute way that made me feel comfortable. Later she told me she had prayed to room with a non–Latter-day Saint, but added, "I had no idea it would be someone like you!" I'm sure it was challenging for her to share a room with someone whose life seemed so complicated and whose value system was devoid of the principles of the restored gospel and of the Holy Spirit. But Elaine's testimony of the gospel was revealed in quiet ways by the way she lived each day — she prayed each morning and night, attended her church meetings faithfully, wrote letters of appreciation to her family for the privilege of attending BYU, and gently offered to answer any questions I had about the Church. I began to see a pattern in the way she and other BYU students lived their lives in harmony with their testimonies, which they frequently shared at dorm prayers each evening.

These quiet but powerful examples of the fruits of the gospel were supplemented by my first Book of Mormon class. I remember the first day of class, in which it became clear that I was the only non–Latter-day Saint in the room. When our instructor asked if anyone was opposed to offering a prayer, an LDS girl in the back raised her hand and indicated that she did not want to be called on to pray. I was surprised at the seeming contradiction, and my thought was, "Why not? Don't you believe this? Then why are you here?" I thought prayer was linked inextricably to Church membership. I came to realize that not all BYU students were like my roommate, Elaine.

As the semester progressed, I tried to abide by the standards that I had promised to live upon enrolling at BYU. Whereas my friend Diane had labeled the University's behavioral and dress standards, dormitory curfew hours, and required religion classes as "juvenile," I had committed to conform to the standards, and I intended to keep my word. One result was that I began to feel small promptings from the Spirit, and my understanding of eternal truths began to increase. However, that brought about a certain sense of personal anxiety that I would be responsible for this knowledge as I learned more. Contemplating joining the Church was troublesome because of the great problems it would cause in my family. In Beverly Hills circles, Mormons were comparable to a strange cult, and no one expected that I would actually become a Latter-day Saint. This quandary prompted me to apply to other colleges, as an escape, so that I could leave BYU before I learned too much.

On the other hand, I did not want to be a quitter. I blanched at the thought of giving up simply because things were becoming uncomfortable. Besides, I told myself, what I was learning was not bad for me; in fact, I felt that I was better because of this new knowledge. I didn't need to become a Latter-day Saint just because I was learning principles that were helpful to me. After all, I still needed to know what course I should pursue in my life. Was my earlier decision to pursue professional acting the right one?

During the summer after my freshman year, I entertained U.S. troops in the Orient on Janie Thompson's Program Bureau tour, "Startime BYU," and saw the priesthood of God at work when two returned missionary tour members pronounced a priesthood blessing that saved a life. I was tutored by Janie Thompson, who had herself made great sacrifices in her life for the gospel. She gave up a career as a professional singer in New York, followed the promptings of the Holy Ghost, and accepted a position at BYU to build the student entertainment groups. Along the way she refused several proposals of marriage because they did not include the temple. Through Janie's example on tour as well as in rehearsals on campus — which included morning and evening prayers, devotionals before each production, testimony bearing by tour group members, singing hymns, and seeing heaven's hand on many occasions while on tour in foreign lands — I was taught to acknowledge the Lord's hand in every aspect of my life.

I learned through Janie about my need for complete reliance on him when making life plans and difficult choices. I also became deeply involved in dramatic productions in the College of Fine Arts at BYU. Several individuals touched my life in unusual ways. For example, I was cast in a leading role of *The Barretts of Wimpole Street,* directed by Dr. Preston Gledhill. A week before production, I contracted the worst case of laryngitis I had ever experienced. I was unable to speak for the week prior to opening night, and the cast members specifically prayed for me to get well, some even fasting for me. As I saw the cast and crew kneel in prayer to begin and conclude each rehearsal and performance, I knew my miraculous recovery opening night was not by chance.

One of my acting classes was taught by a person who also became a mentor and tutor, Dr. Charles Metten. He challenged each of us to draw from ourselves the greatest performance of our lives as we acted our final exam scenes. I had been touched by Dr. Metten's great talent, energy, and gospel insight as he taught.

Now, as I watched other students perform their final scenes, I felt a similar power exuding from several of them. It was a power that I knew I lacked, but I strongly desired to acquire it.

Dr. Lael Woodbury was another highly influential instructor. He pointed out the responsibility directors and producers have each time they select material to produce. One principle I will never forget was taught in connection with a discussion about academic freedom, performing in productions with questionable material, and attending lewd movies just to know what others are watching. His personal standard, which was not shared as a prescription but as wise counsel, was stated this way: "I never want to be responsible for putting an evil thought into someone else's mind." That simple principle was to serve as a guidepost for me throughout my life.

The following year, still as a non–Latter-day Saint, I was invited to audition for a film being produced in connection with general conference, *Pioneers in Petticoats.* Filming began that winter, and we shot scenes over several weeks in locations in Provo, Salt Lake City, and Heber Valley.

Approaching the end of the shooting, I was working on some lines for a scene near the end of the movie. I felt awkward with the dialogue, and it seemed as though I couldn't really make the words a part of my character. I just wasn't able to get comfortable with the lines. Having little experience with personal prayer, I was encouraged by my roommate, Elaine, to pray about my concern. That seemed like a reasonable alternative given my quandary. So when she left the room, I locked the door, drew the blinds, and knelt by my bed. I offered a sincere but awkward prayer, then waited. I looked up. I think I expected to receive a Joseph-Smith-in-the-Grove kind of experience, but nothing happened. I felt no different.

I spent the next few days before filming that scene praying constantly for help with the dialogue. Each time I offered my petition, however, I received no response. I became very troubled by this, because I had heard many stories about others' answers to prayers, miraculous occurrences, and heavenly interventions. I was troubled by this lack of response. I began to think, "If Heavenly Father is really there, if he really cares about me, surely he will realize how much I need some assistance." Additionally,

I felt invested in the success of the movie, but I worried that my dialogue problems would alter the quality of the final product.

We began filming, and I silently prayed as I walked to my mark on the set. I began to speak the dialogue that by now had become so familiar to me. Then something very unusual happened. As I said the lines, I received an overpowering impression, a witness, that President David O. McKay, the living prophet at the time, was the Lord's prophet, and that this church, The Church of Jesus Christ of Latter-day Saints, is the Lord's Church, restored to the earth. I felt a consuming, warm feeling, and my tears flowed naturally. As we finished filming the scene, I noticed that several of the young women in the cast were also crying. I asked one of them, "Why are you crying?" She replied, "Melinda, we know that you know."

It has taken several years to fully appreciate the events that I experienced on the set that day and the sacred nature of that special witness. I realize that it was not by accident that I was reared in a home that prepared me to recognize the promptings of the Spirit. Without the example of special parents, I am certain that I would have been unprepared to feel the Holy Ghost and to recognize true principles. I am so grateful to my parents for their teachings and, especially, to Heavenly Father for knowing just the right time to answer my prayer.

As I was preparing to be baptized, I was fearful that my family would not accept my decision and, of special concern, would not allow my younger sister to attend BYU the following year. I came to understand again, however, that my responsibility was to keep the commandments and to act consistently with true principles, and that Heavenly Father would help me with my family. He did. He helped them to accept my decision. My family even permitted my sister to enjoy the blessings of BYU. A year later, after moving to Provo, she also accepted the gospel and was baptized. It was all a miracle to me.

A few weeks before my baptism, I was listening to the radio while getting ready for a ward Relief Society meeting. The broadcaster announced a news flash: my friend Diane had committed suicide. I sat numb as I listened to the grim details. My childhood chum. My classmate in school. My playmate at family gatherings and parties. My friend who had chosen professional acting as a career. Then it hit me. Both of us were offered opportunities to study at BYU, but only I chose to attend. That could have been me.

Let virtue garnish thy thoughts unceasingly; then shall thy confidence wax strong in the presence of God (D&C 121:45).

Playing the Games

Earl F. Kauffman

Earl F. Kauffman was born in Wiesbaden, Germany, where his father was stationed with the United States military. His mother is a native German. He was reared in San Antonio, Texas, where he played soccer and became a kicker on the high school football team. As a student at BYU, he played on the football team and was named to the All-WAC team as a punter, received WAC honorable mention as a place kicker, and received votes for All-American as a punter. He graduated with a bachelor of science degree in health and worked as a counselor in a treatment facility for troubled youth. Currently he works for the Department of Corrections of the state of Utah as a counselor in the long-term unit at a state youth correctional facility. Mr. Kauffman is married to Tara Laws, and they are the parents of four children. They live in Lehi, Utah.

Why did I come to BYU? It's a long story. I graduated in 1988 from Converse Judson High School in Converse, Texas, near San Antonio. In high school I had a talent for kicking the football, although before high school I had never played the game. I grew up playing soccer. My parents counseled me, "Wait until you are older, bigger, stronger before you go into a sport where you might get hurt." However, I played football as a high school freshman and liked it. When I reached the next level, I was hesitant since I really wanted to go to college, and I thought I should drop football and focus on my grades. But when the school year started and I watched our team struggle, I told my dad that even though I made a commitment not to play, I wanted to. He told me that he'd support my decision and that I should call the coach.

I immediately earned a starting position, had a successful high school career, and received a lot of publicity. Then the recruiting started. Different colleges expressed interest in me as a kicker. My first thoughts were that I wanted to go to Nebraska or to Penn State. The only thing I remembered about BYU was the National Championship in 1984. I was one of those people who thought it was a fluke and that BYU shouldn't have won it. I was basically a skeptical national fan. But out of the blue, BYU began sending me letters.

My interests narrowed to schools that were willing to offer a scholarship. BYU was one of them, but I was hesitant to take a recruiting trip. I didn't want to go all the way to Utah. My dad counseled, "Just take the trip. It's free. Enjoy yourself. It's a beautiful part of the country. There are Mormon people out there." I may have heard the word Mormon before, but I'm not sure. Dad's advice made me think twice. As I was recruited, news began circulating in the local papers about contacts from BYU. Surprisingly, friends who were LDS started saying, "We hear that you're thinking of going to BYU." They had probably told me in the past that they were LDS, but I had forgotten. Their interest raised my interest. I thought that looking more carefully at BYU would help me better understand the LDS culture. In the end, I took trips to BYU and two other schools.

When I first came to campus, I had a really good feeling. I loved the mountains. It was January or February, and snow was everywhere. At the other schools I visited my hosts took me to clubs or bars. In high school I didn't drink, so I wasn't particularly impressed. When I came to BYU on my recruiting trip, I also went to a nightspot, but it was different. There was no smoke. At home I loved to go dancing at country places, but I would come home smelling of tobacco. It was horrible. But at BYU it was nice. I also didn't smell alcohol on anyone's breath. I almost felt like a five-year old again. Everything seemed new and fresh.

Now as I look back I realize that I was feeling the Spirit. But at the time I was thinking, "Yes, this feels neat. BYU is a neat place." BYU felt like the university that I had pictured in my head as a kid, a place that is special. Students study seriously. There aren't people hanging out of windows at parties and the like. It has a special atmosphere. But I was still hesitant.

I finally narrowed my choices to BYU and TCU. At the time I had developed the habit of prayer from watching evangelists on TV. I had learned how to open a prayer and close a prayer uttering Jesus Christ's name. I was praying regularly, knowing in my mind that if I kept asking enough, I could get things that I wanted. The official signing day was close. On the day I decided I had to make a decision, my dad was gone for the evening and I was home alone. I said a prayer. In front of me there was a BYU sticker and a TCU sticker. I prayed, "Heavenly Father, where should I go to school? I want to go to the right place and make the right decision." When I closed my prayer and opened my eyes, I saw the BYU sticker first. It simply stood out. So I grabbed the sticker, stuck it on the counter top, wrote my dad a little note, "I'm going to BYU," and went to bed. I didn't think much about the spiritual effects of my decision then.

Between my signing in February and my arrival at BYU in August, my LDS friends from high school started seeking me out. One of them had told me about the Church's moral standards. She said, "I don't do this and I don't do that, and this is why." I remember thinking back to the year when we were sophomores. She would come into class, and I would joke with her, "Hey, Mormon girl, want to sin?"

In Texas the Church runs a lot of TV commercials. They seem to appear every fifteen minutes. In responding to one, I received a cassette called *Our Heavenly Father's Plan.* I was expecting someone to talk about different principles and was disappointed when it turned out to be songs. I also got my own copy of the Book of Mormon. I had expected a manual which would list rule number one, rule number two, and so on. But when I opened it up, I saw scriptures like I had seen in the Bible. Unfortunately, the Bible had always intimidated me because I couldn't understand it, so I closed the Book of Mormon, set it aside, and didn't think much more about it.

The night before I left home to go to BYU, my friends said, "Don't let those Mormons get you!" I said jokingly, "Oh, I won't!" That was my intent. I would be a person outside the culture, looking in and checking everything out. As time went on, however, my curiosity got the better of me. Moreover, when I finally arrived at BYU, the feelings that I felt during my recruiting visit returned. One of the first players whom I met and became close with was the center, Bob Stephens. I can't remember whether I asked a question or whether he engaged me, but I started half-heartedly asking about the Church. When I became bored with the conversation, I said, "Bob, if I ever decide to get baptized, I would like you to baptize me," not thinking that I would ever do it.

Another influential person on the team was Keith Lever, a backup kicker. He was a really spiritual person. He was always willing to answer my questions. He became a great friend. I admired the traits he had. Among my character flaws was a foul mouth. I'm now embarrassed at the language I once used. I noticed how well Keith conducted himself. I had admired those who used clean language all my life but was never willing to make a change myself. Seeing his good traits, I started asking him questions. At some point, Keith gave me a *Gospel Principles* manual, and my reading led to more questions. I finally decided to open the Book of Mormon and read a little. I noticed how comfortable it felt compared to my effort to read the Bible. It was exciting.

There was a snowball effect. I would be in the weight room working out, and a question would pop into my head. I would say, "What about this principle?" Almost immediately there would be nine or ten guys by my side, and there would be a missionary session in the weight room. I was living in the dorms with a lot of young men who were preparing for missions. I was feeling the Spirit but not realizing what I was feeling. I would ask a question and the dorm room would fill up with guys wanting to practice the discussions. In fact, we used to joke around that I was a "dry Mormon," a name they used to call me all the time.

My most influential classes were in religion. I could feel the Spirit in most of my religion classes, but I struggled because everything was so new. I had no knowledge of the Bible. So when I studied the New Testament, it was difficult. I was focused on learning religion as a general academic subject. I was trying to understand the information. It was that way with the Book of Mormon and the Doctrine and Covenants. But I had spiritual experiences in every class because of the environment. We could freely discuss the way we lived our lives. Brother George Pace was the teacher for my Book of Mormon class. I struggled. I didn't want to go to him and say, "I'm not a member, I don't know anything." So I worked hard. But in the end I had to go to him and say, "I have no knowledge of this. It's all brand new to me." He responded with genuine kindness. He really worked with me. I learned a lot because of the approach he took in class.

When I signed with BYU, the coach who recruited me, Claude Bassett, said, "There are some LDS people in your area of Texas. If you need a summer job before you come to BYU, let me know and I will introduce you to them." Eventually, I went to work for a man named Ron Kimball. I also met his daughter Tiffany. One night she asked me to go to a Church dance. In time, we became close friends. The second week after I arrived on campus, the Kimballs came to Utah for a visit. They introduced me to the Johnsons. The Johnsons were very nice and accepting of me. When Ron Kimball's daughter moved to Syracuse, Utah, to live with her aunt and uncle, we would meet each other at the Johnsons' home. To the children I was the "BYU football player." They always insisted that their parents invite me over. So when Tiffany came to their house for dinner or for a family occasion, the Johnsons would always invite me. Because of the people I associated with at BYU, my personality did a full turnaround. My language started to change. Looking at photos of myself, I believe that I was changing in physical appearance as well.

When I went home for Christmas, I couldn't get the Church out of my mind. I talked to my father about it. He was hesitant, thinking my interest was because of peer pressure, or the environment. He asked me to think about it for a while. But after I returned to school for the second semester I called my dad and said, "I really want to get baptized." He responded, "Hold off for me. I want you to make sure this is what you want." The semester ended and everyone went home for the summer. It was a sad time for me because I realized that the friends I had made were going to be gone on missions the next year. I was going to come back almost as a new student again.

When I returned home at the end of my freshman year, I told my father everything I had learned. As I told him new things, he would come back the next day and ask, "Did you really say this?" My father has always questioned me to make sure I knew what I wanted. He would turn my interests around on me to see whether I genuinely wanted them and would defend them. If I held to my interests, he would support me. But this time the questioning went on all summer, and I came to the point where I thought that my dad was going to be disappointed in my decision to join the Church.

My father grew up a skeptic. His father would get him up on Sunday mornings and say, "You've got to go to church. You need church in your life. Here's a dollar to put in the plate." As a consequence, while my parents were married, we would go to church on Christmas Eve for Midnight Mass and occasionally at Easter. My mother was good at exposing us to religion. I remember as a young child she helped me develop the ability to see people who were doing right and people who were doing wrong. Looking back, my life seems to fit the analogy that I was a little matchbox car in Heavenly Father's hands. He guided me through all the turns to bring me to where I needed to be, avoiding pitfalls that would have steered me from the Church. It was not always by my effort that I was able to avoid such things. As I look back, Heavenly Father had a plan for me: "No, Earl, you are going to avoid these things. I'm not going to hold your hand the whole way, but I will guide you in positive directions."

The way I was raised also helped me to be receptive. My parents were very open. When I was young, my father sat me down, "You know son, you are getting close to high school. If you want to drink alcohol, let me know. I want to know these things. I'm not going to get after you if that's what you choose to do. I just need to know." I remember as a sophomore saying, "I want wine-coolers, Dad." So he bought some. After awhile, I thought it was dumb. But I had the opportunity. I can remember going to parties and friends would have their alcohol. I would carry a drink in my hand. But I would take all night to drink it. At a New Year's Eve party, I finally told my friends, "I'm going to make a New Year's resolution. I'm not going to drink again." I saw no need for it. My parents encouraged me in this decision, and I went through high school known as the kid who didn't drink. I actually enjoyed parties more than my friends did because I enjoyed watching them look stupid. There was something else that kept me where I was. I was deeply saddened to see a lot of girls let alcohol lead them into morality problems. They would come to me later and express their sadness and disgust. Hearing these regrets all the time affected my view of what life was all about.

All of the summer after my freshman year, I continued to pray and to do the right things. One morning toward the end of the summer, my father came in my room and said, "Well son, I thought that being in that environment had placed you under peer pressure, and that's why you wanted to join the Church. I have hammered you all summer. There's been nobody to back you up, and you are still defending your desire to go that route. You have my blessing. Go ahead."

When I came back for my sophomore year, I contacted the missionaries. They said, "You need to take the lessons." I responded, "I want to be baptized. You don't need to waste your time." I went through three or four lessons and then said I wanted to wait for my father to come to be part of the baptism. So I called my father and asked him what games he was going to come to and scheduled my baptism accordingly.

Bishop Gary Lundberg and his wife, Joy, were very influential when I came back to BYU for my sophomore year. The prior year I had gone to church with friends. Therefore I knew that church meetings were held at a certain time in the Martin Building. So I showed up one Sunday at the beginning of my second year. Bishop Lundberg was the new bishop. After a couple of Sundays, I told him that I was going to be baptized. I don't think he knew I wasn't LDS. We hit it off quickly. We came to enjoy a really strong relationship.

Another person who had a major impact on me was Chris Pella, the special teams coach. He is a very down-to-earth guy. He knew I wasn't LDS, but he recruited me and was a fine example to me. Even though he scolded me when I became hotheaded on the field, when he didn't have to wear his coaching hat he immediately took it off and was the friend, the father figure, the support. When we would see each other, he didn't always ask, "How's the leg doing?" Instead, he asked, "How are things going in school? How are things with Tara?" He always expressed interest in how my life was going, not just in football.

Coach LaVell Edwards also had an influence on me. As the head coach he could not focus on just one group of players. He had to get to know everybody. Even so, he was very supportive of what I was doing. He was the father figure to whom you knew you could always go. At first he was almost intimidating. When he came to my home and recruited me, I thought, "Wow! LaVell Edwards!" He has a rather stern look, and a person is not sure what to say to him. But as soon as he and my dad started talking, he was a totally different person, laughing and joking. Every time I walked by his office I would glance in. He was "Head Coach

LaVell." Even so, I felt that I could go in anytime if I needed something. For his part, he would take the time to ask how things were going for me.

When I first came to BYU, the punter was Pat Thompson. He and I had similar punting techniques and the same build. Coach Edwards usually looks at the ground when he is walking. I would say, "Hey, Coach." He would reply, "Hey, Pat, uh Earl." For a long time I was "Pat, uh Earl." I once had a conversation with him and saw him in a different light. I saw him more spiritual. He told stories about how he grew up. He grew up as a hard-nosed football player, doing those things that I did when I was younger. I could see myself in him. Like others who surrounded me, I came to see Coach Edwards as a person put in his place by the Lord to influence me, even if it was only for five minutes. Such individuals were all a part of the whole experience.

I was baptized in November. The baptism took place in the double chapel above BYU on Ninth East, now the home of the BYU Sixth Stake. So many people came that we filled the chapel. I felt great knowing I had so much support. At the baptismal font only close family came to the front. It was such a good feeling. Someone opened the curtain, and I looked up and saw my dad, and there were tears in his eyes. Bob Stevens baptized me because I had made that promise to him. As I came out of the water I saw my dad first. Excitement and joy seemed to be flowing out of him. For me it was an overwhelming experience. As I recall it, I can almost feel the water rushing around me.

I met my wife, Tara, my sophomore year, a few weeks before I was baptized. I remember inviting her to my baptism. She gave me a funny look. She had thought I was a returned missionary because of the guys I associated with. I wasn't a freshman. So she thought, "What did Earl do to have to be rebaptized?" When I met her, she wasn't fully comfortable in the ward where she was. Because I didn't know that a person was to go to the ward where that person resided and because I just thought it was like church where I grew up—a person went where he or she wanted to—I said to her, "Come to church with me." So she became acquainted with the Lundbergs and developed a good relationship with them.

I found myself always looking to Tara because I was a new member. In fact, anyone whom I knew to be a member I immediately began to watch to learn more and to see whether I was doing the right thing. I carefully watched her example. There's a funny little story. I was coming back from church services one day and decided to visit her. She lived at the Glenwood Apartments. She was lying out tanning. I yelled through the fence, "What are you doing? It's Sunday!" I was only joking. But as she and I talked later, she said, "You know, from that point on I never tanned again on Sunday." We had a positive effect on each other.

Ours was a typical courtship. Tara doesn't call it typical. She says we set a record at BYU for dating longest before we got engaged—just over a year. Tara kept giving me pamphlets of talks that the prophets had given that said, "Don't wait for financial security. Don't wait to finish your education." But I came up with excuses of why we should wait and wait.

She knew our relationship was right almost immediately. I was still uncertain. Actually, I felt the promptings of the Spirit. But I wondered, "Is it my conscience? Is it the Spirit? Is it something else?" I wasn't quite sure. I was still trying to get more experience with knowing what the Spirit was saying to me. One night Tara and I were sitting in the library studying. I was in a kidding mood and started to play with some paper. I rolled it up and made a little ring. Then I took a little piece of paper, crumpled it on top, and made it into the shape of a little diamond. Then I colored it. I got on my knees and said to her, "Will you marry me?" Her eyes lit up. Right there I had to make a decision, "Is this what I really want?" I realized that I wanted her. Acting on a clear impression, a few days later I went to Fred Meyer and asked a clerk, "Do you have a ninety-day return guarantee?" He said they did. So I said, "Give me one of those rings." Then I picked up some flowers and put the jewelry box in the flowers so that it blended in. Needless to say, she was excited.

At first I really tried to do missionary work with my father. But it came to the point where I didn't want to push him over an edge. I have learned to be satisfied with the tools I have given him. Now I share my life experiences with him. "I blessed my daughter today," or "In church we did this today," or "When we went to the temple today. . . ." He and my mother had a bad relationship after they divorced. They didn't speak for years. Recently he walked up to her and said, "Let's bury the hatchet." He suddenly wants to make things better with people, to let go of anger. He has become a defender of my choices.

I think I would have been baptized into the Church at some point in my life. But I don't think I would have been as receptive as I was at BYU. In high school I was probably introduced to the Church by my friends but just didn't pay attention. At BYU, I was immediately receptive. I attribute my openness to the environment.

Friends have asked whether I wish I had gone to another school where an athelete could find more national recognition and have a better chance to become a professional football player. Friends have seen me struggle for years trying to play professionally. Whenever I went to a football camp outside of Utah, I found myself in a totally different environment. I had the distinct feeling, "I'm the only Latter-day Saint here." Consequently, I tried to act the part of who I was. Correspondingly, my athletic concentration dropped off because I was so focused on being a good example. When I was on the practice field, of course, I was trying hard. But my worrying about who I was and how I was acting actually influenced my performance. The situation may be different for others. But while I could say that I wish it were different, I'm glad it is this way.

Now I look back and think, "It may have been nice to play professionally, but I would not have what I have now." I have a wife to whom I've been sealed in the temple. I have three children—a fourth one is on the way—and a nice home in an area where I can be around the influence of BYU all the time. As I tell young people, I have certain tools and I can choose to use them or not. If I had gone to another school, I wouldn't have those tools. In my life, BYU itself made a huge difference. I'm glad it is this way. My life has changed tremendously, and all for the better. I could have had a lot of money, but money wouldn't have changed me into who I now am. As much lure as there is at a school with a bigger national reputation and enhanced chances of playing professional football, I know that had I not chosen BYU I would never have met my wife, I wouldn't have the children I have, and I wouldn't have the perspective on life I have. If I had to make the decision again where to play college ball, I would come to BYU.

During my playing days, it was almost a spiritual experience being out there because I felt that sixty thousand people were saying, "You're doing great! We support you. You may miss a field goal, but we're going to invite you on Sunday to speak to our youth." I have spoken at a lot of firesides since I was baptized. The one thing that I tell the youth is that it doesn't matter how many touchdowns you score, or runs you score, or games you've won. When you go back to see your Heavenly Father, he's going to ask, "How many people did you help? How many lives did you save?" He doesn't care that I kicked a winning field goal. It's meaningless in the eternal scheme. I am grateful for my change in life. I have tingles all over my body when I think about it. My experiences at BYU brought a vision of life. My angle of looking at life changed. Football, of course, is what brought me to BYU. I now count my blessings. If I had not been able to kick a funny oblong ball, I would never have heard BYU knocking at my door, and I never would have replied. I would have been eternally shortchanged.

*Therefore, verily I say unto you, lift up your voices
unto this people; speak the thoughts that I shall put
into your hearts, and you shall not be confounded
before men; for it shall be given you in the very hour,
yea, in the very moment, what ye shall say. . . . And
I give unto you this promise, that inasmuch as ye do
this the Holy Ghost shall be shed forth in bearing
record unto all things whatsoever ye shall say
(D&C 100:5–6, 8).*

And Back Again

Allen E. Bergin

Allen E. Bergin had set himself on an academically challenging course of engineering at the Massachusetts Institute of Technology and liberal arts at Reed College when he happened to visit a friend in Provo who had transferred to BYU. That visit changed every-thing. Dr. Bergin received a B.A. from BYU in psychology in 1956 and an M.A. in 1957. He completed his Ph.D. at Stanford in 1960, followed by a postdoctoral fellowship at the University of Wisconsin Psychiatric Institute and a distinguished career at Columbia University and BYU. Dr. Bergin has been a sounding voice in integrat-ing moral and spiritual themes into professional psychology research, theory, practice, and education, where his international reputation has affected the profession for good. He has been heavily involved in community service and interfaith activities. Dr. Bergin and his wife, Marian – a psychotherapist and clinical social worker – are the parents of nine children and thirteen grandchil-dren.

I came to Brigham Young University in 1954 mainly because I was in love with Marian. She was a faithful Latter-day Saint who had just transferred to BYU. In addition, I was curious about Mormonism. What I could not foresee then was that BYU would provide a uniquely nurturing environment for me. As a student, I would receive my testimony, become engaged, marry, start a family, learn the value of church service, and set my feet firmly on my career path in psychology. Years later, after I joined the faculty, BYU would offer a platform for my colleagues and me to launch a series of studies on clinical psychology and religion that would be part of a movement to transform the guiding assump-tions of the field. Naturally, along the way many people sup-ported me, not the least of whom was Marian.

She and I had both been students at Reed College in Portland, Oregon, a strongly academic liberal-arts school. At that time in my life, I was in a moratorium period, searching for direction. I had left my physics and engineering pursuits at the Massachusetts Institute of Technology (MIT) for Reed in order to explore the liberal arts. It was my sophomore year, my first at Reed. There was a program wherein a student could get a B.S. from MIT and a B.A. from Reed in five years, and that is what I was going to do. The first weekend I was in Portland, I met Marian at a get-acquainted dance.

We became very attached to each other that first year. I went to church with her a few times, and we enjoyed long walks and deep conversations frequently. The following summer she went home to Ogden, and I went to Alaska to work with my father, who was a construction superintendent. I took a large box of books— LDS books as well as books on evolution, philosophy, and Eastern religions. I was studying everything. I read the Book of Mormon; I even prayed about it, though I was not religious in the ordinary sense of the term. Actually, I read all four standard works that summer, and several other Church books as well. By the end of the summer I had definitely been affected by my reading and praying. However, I went to church only once, at the Fairbanks, Alaska Branch. My brother and I drove ninety miles to check it out. I was working six days a week, nine hours a day, on construction. Whatever free time I had I read and studied. Our house was literally out in the wilderness—no one was there but my father and mother and my brother and sister. My father was the supervisor of one part of a large project. I worked for him and made enough money to support myself for a full academic year.

At the end of August, as I was planning to return to Reed, Marian made the surprise announcement that she was transferring to BYU. She seemed to have decided that her religion was more important than our romance! I thought, "Well, I don't have any big commitment to Reed." I wasn't doing very well in school, and my focus in life was vague and ambiguous. So I took a trip to BYU and saw Marian. I was really taken with the campus and the people. Her aunt, Marge Wight, was President Wilkinson's secretary. President Wilkinson had already told Marian that if she would transfer to BYU, he would give her a scholarship, and she had agreed to transfer. I had never heard of Brigham Young

University. I didn't know anything about Utah. I was from the state of Washington and knew nothing about Mormonism until I met Marian.

Before I left MIT I had gone up on the roof of my dorm searching for answers and prayed the agnostic prayer: "God, if you're there, what is this all about?" That's how I received the impression to go to Reed. The same thing happened in coming to BYU. I went alone up east Center Street near the State Hospital. I didn't know it was the State Hospital, but I drove up there because it was a quiet spot. There I viewed the impressive mountains and the lights of the city; and because of a special, dramatic experience, I felt I should go to BYU.

So I applied immediately. It was only a week or two before classes started. I was accepted, which would be unusual now. I returned home to Spokane and then went to Portland to collect all my stuff. I checked out of Reed and checked out of the joint program at MIT.

When I first enrolled at BYU, everyone told me I should meet Professor Bob Thomas in English because he was a Reed graduate. So I went to talk to him. I was very impressed by his combination of faith and erudition. On the spot I decided to enroll in his Book of Mormon class.

During this period, Marian and I started to experience problems in our relationship. Conflicts and doubts about each other arose. So we broke up. Our breakup freed me from the complications of romance so I could focus on religion. But we were in the same Book of Mormon class. Not surprisingly, this created a tense situation. Through it all, I had a lot of talks with Bob Thomas. Those conversations were very important in keeping my feet on a proper path.

During that time, psychology professor Robert Howell had a significant influence on me. He was a clinical-type person, but he taught a course called History of Experimental Psychology. As I shifted from physical science into psychology, I moved toward experimental psychology because it had grown out of a marriage among philosophy, physics, and biology. Howell's course was wonderful for me because we analyzed the orienting assumptions behind modern science as they applied to human behavior. We covered the relevant great philosophers and scientists who had set the stage for twentieth-century empiricism. I had studied many of them before, but this time psychology and religion were both added to the mixture. It was as if everything in my life — science, philosophy, psychology, and religion — was altogether in that one class. I probably spent more time on that class than any class I have ever taken. I loved it. I buried myself in it. I was not a Latter-day Saint at that point, so dozens of intellectual issues I had been struggling with, in their confrontations with revealed religion, began to be sorted out in a rigorous way that I could respect. What is more, conversations with other students in the class, who were comfortable with their faith, had a profound impact on me.

Equally important were general authorities' Devotional talks every Tuesday. What an ideal learning environment for an investigator to hear apostles and prophets speak every week! Their messages left a deep impression on me and challenged me to rethink my values, commitments, and lifestyle. Under the circumstances, how could a sincere seeker not be persuaded? I also attended church off and on and then decided to go to general conference in October. A friend (who had dated an LDS girl at Reed) and I went to general priesthood meeting. We didn't know much, but we heard President McKay speak. Hearing him left another deep impression on me. It was a powerful weekend. Even so, I was so imbued with philosophy and science that it was very difficult to make the leap of faith. I studied all the issues long and hard. I talked with my roommates, two of whom were returned missionaries, and I continued to meet with Bob Thomas.

By the end of the quarter Marian and I got back together. In December, I asked her to marry me, decided to become a Latter-day Saint, and chose to become a psychology major. It had been the most complex, dramatic, and life-transforming period in my life. The BYU atmosphere, collectively and individually, had met my needs perfectly. If ever a person had become a new man, it was I. The founding mission of the University truly found full expression in my life and being. Looking back on it, I only regret that we do not currently have more room for inquiring, wandering non-LDS students!

I was baptized in March 1955, and Marian and I began attending the Manavu Ward after we married in June. We didn't marry in the temple because I had not been a member for a year. Bob Thomas felt we were ready for marriage and assured us that the temple sealing would be forthcoming soon enough. Indeed, our bishop was impressed to approve the sealing two months before the one-year period, an exception that is no longer available.

During the last year that we were at BYU, I became the deacons' advisor while attending the Manavu Ward. I had an illustrious group of boys in that quorum, including one of Ernest Wilkinson's sons and one of Roy Doxey's sons. But there was also a group of inactive boys in that part of Provo. So I read the manual. Some might say I was naive. I thought, "Well, as a Mormon you do what it said in the manual, and the manual says you reactivate the inactives." So I took my deacons quorum presidency to all those homes and reactivated all but one of those boys. They were twelve or thirteen years old. Marian and I came back a few years later and visited the Manavu Ward. There were three priests administering the sacrament with whom I had worked. They were all going on missions. It was exciting for me to feel that I had given something back in a place where I had received so much.

Because of all that happened during my junior year, my first year at BYU, I found myself scrambling to meet the requirements for a psychology major while deciding what I was going to do with my life. But my senior year went well. I received all A's every quarter; the department gave me a teaching assistantship and invited me to come back on scholarship for a master's degree. I felt I needed to get through this stage, so I did the master's degree in nine months, including the thesis. I finished by the next summer (1957) and then was accepted to graduate school at Stanford. By then I had three years at BYU, two years in the Church, and I had become excited about the gospel because I had spent so much time studying it. We also had our first two children, David and Sue, and began our family life as Marian chose to devote herself to family and dropped out of school.

In 1960 I finished at Stanford, where our third child, Cyndy, was born. Then I took a postdoctoral fellowship sponsored by the National Institute of Mental Health at the Psychiatric Institute at the University of Wisconsin Medical School. Carl Rogers, a famous psychologist with whom I wanted to work, was there. Our fourth child, Kathy, was born there. After a year, this man, who had obtained his doctorate at Columbia in the 1930s, recommended me and three other people for a professorship at the Teachers College Columbia University doctoral program in Clinical Psychology. I went to Columbia for an interview and, by some inspired combination of events, was offered the job on the spot.

Marian made it clear that she didn't want to go to New York but was willing if it was the right thing to do. I didn't really want to go either, but I had felt a strong impression and did want to become established as a leader in my profession. I said, "Let's do it for five years." We stayed eleven, during which time we both devoted major time to church service. Marian also gave birth to our fifth and sixth children, Eric and Ben, in New Jersey, where we lived, and she continued to anchor the family. Over those years, I became a full professor and enjoyed many opportunities, including several research grants. I published as widely as I could. In addition to journal publications, I published one major book. Several books were in process.

During those years, BYU faculty and administrators had tried to entice me to come back many times, including while I was still a graduate student at Stanford. I kept in touch, but in the 1960s BYU had a small psychology department and no accredited doctoral program where I would fit in. However, the numbers were starting to expand as BYU grew. Every year or two someone wrote to me, but I just never felt drawn back.

After about ten years at Columbia, a lot of problems arose in my department and at the university. Many of the difficulties followed the 1968 riots protesting the Vietnam War and the Columbia students' occupation of the administration building. The faculty split on how to respond to the crisis. In addition, there were wide differences of opinion about the war. By the time the university started to settle down, a lot of relationships had been broken. Some people decided to leave. In my program, in particular, there were serious problems. The director of my area, a very famous person with whom I was writing a book, decided to leave. That was demoralizing. Then somebody else earnestly suggested that our program be closed down entirely, even though it was a very prominent program. To escape the confusion and turmoil, I started looking at jobs at other universities.

I was interviewing at other places in the East and Midwest when the BYU psychology department sent a letter. In fact it said, "The former chairman of our department is retiring and we would like you to consider coming." I decided to take a look even though I was skeptical because I was unsure about the new doctoral program at BYU, and I previously had not taught undergraduates, which was an important responsibility. Applied psychology was strictly a graduate program at Columbia Teachers College. There were two hundred doctoral students and about three hundred master's students in half a dozen specialties. It was like a professional school. I didn't really want to go somewhere where I couldn't do what I had been doing.

When I visited BYU, Bob Thomas had become the academic vice president and Dallin Oaks had been the president for a year. The two of them greatly impressed me. I thought, "I will test this." The dean of social sciences was Martin Hickman. He asked, "What would it take for you to come here?" I said, "Number one, I only teach two classes a semester." He said, "Okay." "Number two, I want such and such a salary." He said, "Okay." Whatever I asked, he said yes. I thought, "My gosh, I should have asked for more."

It had felt right years before when I had left my Reed College and MIT connections for BYU. On this new occasion, before I returned to New York, I met with Bob Thomas and enjoyed another of our long talks. He had baptized me, ordained me an elder, and was my spiritual godfather, so to speak. I already felt pretty convinced about coming back to BYU. After our conversation, he hugged me and said, "So you think this is it?" I said, "Yes, I think this is it." When I returned home, we fasted and prayed as a family and decided to accept BYU's offer. Everybody in the family seemed to feel good about it until they got to Provo. The adjustment was especially difficult for our teenage daughters, but the boys loved the outdoor opportunities.

We had been gone from Provo for fifteen years. Our return in 1972 was nice in many ways because I had the administration's support. But when I was assigned an office in the Faculty Office Building, separate from the psychology faculty, someone quizzically remarked to me, "Do you remember the Old Testament story of Joseph and the coat of many colors?" It became clear that colleagues thought I was receiving special treatment. For my part, I was not entirely happy because I felt that the department was a little backward, not up to date, and not doing enough research.

To solve my dilemma, I started to collaborate with some of the younger faculty. One of them, Mike Lambert, has now become a senior person in our specialty and is a major international scholar. The Oaks administration was in favor of the sort of cooperative and productive research work that Mike and I under-took. It was just that there was tension between people who had been hired under other agreements specifying that they would mainly teach. I could see their point and came to respect those faculty. But I also wanted to see the department become a major player on the national scene; during the 1980s and 1990s this finally came to pass. The BYU psychology department is now first-rate.

The gospel has made all the difference to me professionally, especially in the sense that the BYU environment has been so reinforcing of my development as a person and a scholar. It seemed that at BYU I could bring together research and religion at a new level. Our new locale in Provo also became the setting for the birth of our triplet sons, Patrick, Daniel, and Michael, and for Marian's eventual return to school. She is now a clinical social worker and psychotherapist in private practice, where she harmo-nizes spiritual and professional approaches in treating LDS cli-ents.

At Columbia, and even at Stanford, I had tried to bring religion and psychology together and to coordinate them. In another subject, chemistry, for example, I don't know whether one would see the connections, except maybe in theory. But in psy-chology there is a major overlap between the goals of psychology and the goals of the gospel in terms of social development, mental health, and personal growth. In the era of the 1950s and the 1960s, when academic departments were anti-God, especially in psy-chology, I got nowhere. The best I received was approval at Columbia in the late 1960s to teach a course on values in psychol-ogy. I decided not to teach that course. Instead, I decided to incorporate its essence into a course that I was already teaching. But we would get into serious arguments in the class when I introduced conservative moral values as possibly being beneficial for mental health.

Liberal moral values and antireligious attitudes manifested themselves in other settings. For example, we had a case confer-ence every week. A therapist from New York City would be invited to come in and present a case. Often moral issues would come up, such as, should this client be encouraged to have a sexual relationship with her friend? I remember specifically one episode in which the presenting therapist said he would consider therapy to have been a success with this very isolated, shy young woman when she had a sexual relationship with a young man. In his view, that action would be a sign that she had come out of her shell, so to speak, and could be intimate and could express herself. I challenged him very vigorously on his ethics, his morality, and the potential negative consequences of achieving such a goal. He was shocked by what I said. He thought that my response was ridiculous. There were more than thirty people in the room, graduate students and faculty, and not one person supported my position. (Afterwards, one student who was a Catholic said privately that she supported my position.) One faculty member did say, "I disagree with you very much, but I admire your courage." She sensed what it took to respond as I had.

Now the field has changed. Between 1980 and 1990, there was a tremendous shift toward basic moral values and the role of spirituality in mental health. My colleagues and I at BYU have been part of the publishing, speaking, and challenging that have brought about the change. There has also been a coalescing of groups, with new journals and organizations devoted to psychology and religion. Even though this is not yet a dominating trend, it has earned a respected position and is here to stay. However, in the beginning (say, 1980), the movement was very controversial. I was invited to speak in many places because people wanted to debate the religious issues. Not surprisingly, some of those experiences were very negative.

For example, I was invited to give a keynote address in Amsterdam to the Dutch Psychotherapy Society at its fiftieth-anniversary celebration. I said, "The subject of psychology, values, and religion is what I want to talk about." The members knew what I intended to discuss. At the conference, I gave a straightforward, value-oriented talk, and supported religion as a mentally healthy thing, arguing in favor of traditional values as anchoring lifestyles that could prevent many mental and social problems. During my speech, people yelled at me from the audience. A fellow twenty feet away from me jumped up and shook his fist. The first part of my presentation lasted an hour and a half, and then we took a break. During the break no one spoke to me.

In 1980, Amsterdam was one of the drug capitals of Europe, and the city had deteriorated since I had been there in 1968. At the beginning of the second session, I said, "I've overheard a lot of nasty remarks about what I've had to say so far. I would like to ask you a question: If you don't think values are important, where do you think all of these deviant people walking the streets of Amsterdam come from?"

At that point people really let loose on me. The two discussants ripped into me. One was a psychiatrist and one a psychologist. One of them said, laughing, "I think the Bible is a pretty interesting book, but it doesn't have anything to do with mental health." Then he said, only half in jest, that I had ruined their birthday party. At another point I thought I was going to be physically attacked. As a result, I did not go to the banquet that evening; I went back to the hotel and ate alone. It was a terrible experience.

A Dutch journal of psychotherapy was supposed to publish my address. When I finished the final draft, I sent it in. Not surprisingly, the editors refused to publish it. It seems that my name was used in vain for several years thereafter.

There were other, contrasting experiences, such as one at the University of Washington, where some of the faculty felt affirmed and legitimized in their personal faith. They came up and hugged me and said, "You know, I will never teach psychology the same way because obviously there's a different, richer philosophy." These were "closet Christians" who decided it was acceptable to come out. In the 1980s such experiences happened over and over again in the United States and other countries, and not just from my influence. Many people started speaking out, saying psychology had been ideologically oppressive, dogmatic, and insensitive to the beliefs of the populace at large.

The standard position at that time was exemplified by a notable psychologist in New York, Albert Ellis, who published a critique of one of my articles and said, "Religiosity is in many respects equivalent to irrational thinking and emotional disturbance. . . . The less religious they are, the more emotionally healthy they will be."[1] In this period, my BYU colleagues and I, and others elsewhere, published evidence about how most clients are religious and come from religious cultures. Essentially we said, "You're interested in diversity. You're not accounting for religious diversity."

I took Albert Ellis's statement as a challenge and decided I would study BYU students. I thought this effort would be an acid test. Here we have devout people, and the question is whether they can be both devout and rational. That question seems ridiculous to people like ourselves, and to those from other religious traditions. Psychologists simply did not realize how far they were from what most people thought. If most people had understood psychology's antireligious bias, they would have stopped funding psychological research.

In this light, I pursued several studies of BYU students, with graduate students helping me. Basically, we gave undergraduate students many mental health tests and clinical interviews. Then we took the theory of Albert Ellis and administered a measurement based on his work that is called the Rational Beliefs Test, a measure for neurosis, giving it to a group of BYU students. They came out quite well on that test, as well as on other tests. They were consistently equal to or better than national norms for mental normality.

I thought that another acid test of whether religiosity can be normal would be to examine a group of returned missionaries. The group of returned missionaries whom we selected were taking an advanced Book of Mormon class. We did psychological tests on thirty-three returned missionaries, testing for depression scores and the like. They came out with the lowest average depression score of any sample I had ever seen. We then published all of our research results.

We decided that we would never publish in religious journals or pastoral counseling journals. We published in mainstream psychology journals. Sometimes it was difficult. There would be arguments with the editors; they would reject an article out of hand. I would send it to another journal. The strategy paid off: each study was published in a good journal, some were published in the best journals. Other people, doing similar research, started doing the same. Gradually, the debate regarding religion and individual values dramatically changed in our favor. Finally, in 1989 the American Psychological Association gave me the Distinguished Contribution to Knowledge award for this work and the earlier work which I had done at Columbia on therapy research. Other awards followed from several national and international professional societies. These "official" stamps of approval, given to me and other colleagues, have opened the way for a new philosophy and a new kind of research to blossom.

BYU and other religious schools gave people like me a base of operations and support, in a word, reinforcement. I could not have done this kind of research at a secular university at that time. I could not have found funding. At BYU the College of Family, Home, and Social Sciences kept giving me money every year. Things have changed sufficiently that today many organizations will give money for research on values and religion, including government agencies and private foundations.

BYU now has a significant name in this work. Let me illustrate. Scott Richards was one of my students in 1983, and now he's a professor at BYU. In 1997 we published a book entitled *A Spiritual Strategy for Counseling and Psychotherapy*. The publisher was the American Psychological Association, and it has become one of their best sellers. The Association also invited us to edit a second book that is titled *Handbook of Psychotherapy and Religious Diversity*. We have invited expert therapists from many major religious traditions to write about how one would counsel people within their particular religious tradition, such as Muslim, Jewish, and Hindu. Contributions will also represent several Christian groups. Naturally, we have a chapter on Latter-day Saints.

Sally Barlow and I have also published a chapter in the new *Handbook of Religion and Mental Health*, edited by Dr. Harold Koenig of the Duke University Psychiatry department. The chapter summarizes research that has been done over the last fifteen years on LDS religious and mental health issues. The book's last section is titled "How Do You See Mental Health from the Religious Perspective?" The editor chose seven religions: Judaism, Catholicism, Protestantism, Unity religions, Islam, Buddhism, and Mormonism. That's it. No others are represented. Notably, we were classed among seven major world religions. I was amazed.

For a person like me it has been wonderful to be at BYU. I have been hampered only in the sense that there were some faculty who held to traditional psychology and didn't like the idea of bringing in a spiritual perspective. Rather contrary to BYU's mission, they felt it was important to make a reputation in the way that the rest of the profession does. There is nothing wrong with that in itself, but there was a period of tension between me and a few faculty members who felt that psychology should remain purely as a traditional social science. But that issue has been resolved. I like the changes that have occurred. I like the feeling that God is more in the classroom, laboratory, and clinic at BYU.

As much as BYU's religious tradition has nurtured my work and soul, there are a few obstacles to finding God there. One of these is the pressure to conform to certain behavioral standards. All of these are part of what I would call extrinsic aspects of religion, and they worry me. In our studies, we have tried to distinguish between intrinsic religiosity and extrinsic religiosity, as originally defined by Gordon Allport at Harvard University. We have found that intrinsically religious persons choose to be faithful to God for their own internal reasons. Such persons are healthier mentally and spiritually. I fear putting pressure on our youth in general and our BYU students in particular to meet external contingencies of reinforcement. In other words, "If you do these things, then you get approval or certain rewards." To be extrinsically rewarded or conditioned can get in the way of a genuine religious life. It would be unfortunate if we were successful in creating an image of righteousness without the heart and soul of it. In our research and in my experience as a bishop and stake president on campus, I fear that I have seen too much religious role-playing—that is, doing the right thing for the wrong reasons.

I don't have all the answers to the dilemma of how to maintain standards and encourage independent exercise of agency at the same time. Perhaps a statement we made in one of our published articles about BYU student mental health is pertinent here. After observing cases of perfectionistic depression, shallow religious conformity, and emotional blandness in some subjects of our studies, we noted the following: "The healthy features of intrinsic religiousness will be better actualized when the institutional and familial environments allow for honest recognition and acceptance of moral imperfections, thereby emphasizing growth relative to moral principles rather than an outward perfectionism that reinforces rigidity and ensures lowered adaptability."[2]

However such matters are ultimately resolved, and I do believe they require resolution, the fact remains that BYU has attracted an unusual community of believers. It is governed by spiritual inspiration to such an extent that the social system is collectively an unusual, even distinctive, source of positive human development in the quest for eternal life.

Notes

1. Albert Ellis, "Psychotherapy and Atheistic Values: A Response to A. E. Bergin's 'Psychotherapy and Religious Values,'" *Journal of Consulting and Clinical Psychology*, 48, no. 5: 635–39.

2. Allen E. Bergin, "Religious Life-styles and Mental Health," in *Religion, Personality, and Mental Health*, ed. Laurence B. Brown (New York: Springer-Verlag, 1994), 85.

. . . the Lord knoweth all things from the beginning;
wherefore, he prepareth a way to accomplish all his
works among the children of men; for behold, he hath
all power unto the fulfilling of all his words.
And thus it is (1 Ne. 9:6).

The White Picket Fence

Kevin and Lita Little Giddins

Kevin Jones Giddins grew up in New Jersey and has performed as a leading dancer throughout the United States. He has been involved in television commercials, film, theater dance, and music since graduating with a B.F.A. in dance from Ohio University. He received an M.A. from BYU in choreography. He is currently working for Franklin Covey as a consultant/trainer and teaches dance at the MBS Training Center in Southfield, Michigan, where the Giddins family currently lives. Lita Little Giddins was born in Chicago, Illinois, and raised in Southern California. She has been involved in the recording, commercial, film, and musical theater industries. She is a graduate of BYU, with a B.A. in socio-cultural anthropology and an M.A. in clinical social work. Recently she has been working with Michael McLean on his musical production, THE ARK, and she continues to seek opportunities to use her social work and artistic skills. Both are converts to the LDS Church. Both were recruited to BYU, in part, to perform with the Young Ambassadors, where they met. They are the parents of three children.

Kevin:

We all have different images of BYU. To the outsider looking in, BYU may be just another place to attend school; but to me BYU is much more. BYU helped me capture some of my goals and made my dreams come true, along with dreams that I had never imagined. To some, the following account may seem corny — a fabricated story complete with a house and white picket fence. For me, a white picket fence represents the "good life" — a house in the country, family, space for the dog to roam, etc. For my family in the East, however, a white picket fence represented something completely different. My parents feared that if I came to BYU, I would marry a "*white* picket fence." My aunt told me that we in the black culture have every shade of the rainbow. "Why would you marry white? Who are you going to find at BYU?" While I did find someone to marry at BYU, I also found both myself and God. Neil Simon said something to the effect that "in order to know who you are, you must know who you were." For one to know how I found myself, God, and my wife at BYU, one needs to know who I was.

On 17 December 1961, I was born to a boy of seventeen years and a girl of sixteen—Jacqueline Giddins. My birth mother wanted me to have both a father and a mother but realized that she wasn't in a position to care for me in the way that she would like. She decided to put me in foster care with a private New York agency. Thus, although I was born in New York as Kevin James Giddins, I was reared in the suburbs of New Jersey by two wonderful parents, Edmond and Elizabeth Jones, and was raised as Kevin Giddins Jones. It was only when BYU required that I provide a birth certificate as proof of citizenship that I found "Giddins" had been misspelled.

There are eleven children in the Edmond and Elizabeth Jones' family. I am number six. I grew up loving my family, school, life, and God, although I didn't know him as my Heavenly Father at the time. My parents saw to it that all of us were conditioned to attend Sunday school and church regularly. My mother was Baptist and my father was Catholic in his early years. However, my father swore that he would never raise his children in the Catholic church. The memory of nuns disciplining him was too vivid. Conveniently, there was a Baptist church within a few blocks of our home, so almost by default my family attended it. My parents, however, influenced us not to believe in the Baptist church but wanted us to understand that it was the teachings of Christ that we were to follow. Family life in the Jones home was very close, and, because of our family's size, life seemed like a party. After each family gathering, the coffee table would be pushed to the side and the music and dancing would begin.

I attended Ohio University. I was there for two weeks before I discovered that I was actually at the wrong place. I had intended to enroll at Ohio State University but didn't really understand the difference between the two institutions and ended up in Athens and not Columbus. It was at an OU football game when I first realized this. I was cheering for the team by yelling "Go, Buckeyes!" when someone turned to me and asked, "Buckeyes? These aren't the Buckeyes, these are the Bobcats." I felt my heart drop. I left the stadium in a daze, returned to my dorm room, and called my mother, who responded, "The wrong school? Your father drove eight hours, dropped you off, and you have been there for two weeks. You might as well stay. An education is an education." And so I stayed. The mistake was, in the end, an important event for me because I came to realize that something or someone else was directing my life.

It was at Ohio University that I fell away from the principles that meant so much to my parents. A moral drift started when I was in high school, and I found myself falling farther and farther to the point where I was not able to distinguish right from wrong, good from evil, or eternal from temporal. But it was also at OU that I began to search for a better life. One night, while taking a walk, pondering and praying for strength to overcome my weaknesses, a feeling came over me. Even though I feared that it might be too late, I still had a desire to do what was right and to listen. I didn't know how to do that. Satan knew me and always tempted me by using the most clever tactics: my friends, my art, and my weaknesses.

I graduated with a degree in fine arts and communications and began working professionally in the entertainment industry. I opened the door as fame and fortune were knocking. With temporal success came more temptation and peer pressure to the point where I felt like I was dying from within. I wasn't living the life I was brought up to live. I knew I needed to change, but I didn't know how. I fell continually, always promising to do better: "Tomorrow I'll be better." "I won't do that again." "I promise. I promise." "Okay, this time it is for real." "Okay, to show I am serious, I'll fast." After two hours: "Okay, maybe not a complete fast; I'll only have water." After four hours: "I'll only have one meal." I simply didn't have the discipline nor the spirit needed to get my life back in order. I fell again and again.

Frustration, guilt, fear, and anger became part of my daily life. No one would have guessed that the happy-go-lucky successful college graduate was fighting within himself and terribly unhappy. I hated my habits and my life and, even worse, I couldn't control them. No one knew, except God.

I was working at Opryland when I met a couple on vacation from Utah. I was warned that they were Mormons, but they seemed okay to me. One of them was a director of the Young Ambassadors and he invited me to go to BYU the next fall to perform with a touring group and also to teach dance. Although Utah was never in my life's plans, at the time it seemed to me that it might have some things to offer. Opportunities that led me away from Utah were popping up every day. In addition, my parents shared with me their warnings and informed me of their fears. They told me of an incident involving two black men who were killed in a park in Salt Lake City. They expressed concerns about white supremacists and told me of their fears concerning Mormons. They missed me and wanted me to come home rather than moving farther away. My mentors and friends also told me that I was making a big mistake. Financially, it was a mistake to move to Utah since it meant less income, and I didn't know anyone there. Utah also meant "Mormons" and no coffee. The only voice of encouragement was my pastor. He told me that he was certain that I was a good Christian and would not be converted to Mormonism. (He was, however, a BYU football fan.)

In my confusion, I prayed one of my longest prayers. I asked the Lord to help me make the right choice, to provide light. As I worried over the decision, the light came to me frequently: the Mormons called often to see how I was doing. But I was really confused. I began to fear a ringing phone because it might be Mormon friends calling yet again. I wanted to tell them that I didn't want to move to Utah. But after they had planned for my arrival and my other options had fallen through because of my lingering over this decision, I really didn't have a choice.

I was both nervous and excited about the move west. I would have to sign an agreement to live the standards of their university: socks must be worn with shoes, and shorts were not to be worn at all. Conservative clothing, no smoking or drinking, no sex. This was definitely not the normal college experience. (It made me wonder what Mormons did for fun on the weekend.) Going to BYU was going to be very, very different for me, yet I knew I needed this difference. I saw BYU as a kind of military school and recognized that I needed the discipline and a new way of living. Getting religiously involved with the Mormons was out of the question, but I would take their money and a scholarship.

Going to Utah was a major decision in my life. I followed what I now know to be the Holy Ghost. I take, however, no credit for being in tune with the Spirit—I could not identify what had led me to Utah until after I found God there. My Father in Heaven brought me to Utah just as he brought me to the foster home of the Joneses and just as he brought me to OU rather than OSU. Some might say that it was chance, but I know that God was involved. As difficult as I was, he showed me that my ways were not his ways. So, not knowing the reason at the time, I found myself in Utah.

I was in Utah only two days before I felt that something was different about BYU. At first I thought the entire male population was very strange. I had never seen so many macho men with cheesy smiles, shaking hands, changing diapers, carrying babies, crying at movies, and walking around on Sunday mornings with what appeared to be little briefcases. This was clearly a very different place. Yet I was received with open arms. I was amazed at the special something that the young people on campus seemed to have. Their generosity seemed too good to be true. My room-mates were respectful of my beliefs and trusted me. I waited for them to misplace or lose something of value and then suspect me of stealing it. I waited for them to ask me to play basketball, as if it were a game that all blacks played. But they didn't. I was not expecting them to say, "My brother, we love you." But they did. I was overwhelmed to know that my fears and stereotypes were misguided.

Soon after arriving I decided to attend a Mormon service. I went expecting to find a quiet, non-responding congregation listening to their pastor. To my surprise, this Mormon church service was longer and louder than the Baptist church services I was used to. It wasn't the brothers and sisters shouting "amen" that made it louder, however. It was crying babies. And their cries were echoing around classrooms. This was a very odd paradigm shift: sitting one day in a biology class with students taking notes and the next day in the same room in a sacrament meeting with mothers and fathers standing at the back rocking babies. Neither the content of the meeting nor the parents quieting babies made a lasting impression. The wonderful examples of families, of fathers caring for their children and changing diapers, did. I had always planned on having a family and I would think to myself,

"If only I can make it without wasting my talent and life, one day I want a nice family and home with white picket fences and all." I actually imagined those dreams coming true that first day at church.

I discovered, however, that there were some people in church, at BYU, and in Utah who had problems. One returned missionary informed me that he hated "this happy valley" (referring to beautiful Utah Valley). If he only had the taste of that "valley of the world" that I had experienced, I thought to myself, he would think twice about such a superficial judgment.

Within the first two months, I was stopped several times by the police while driving around Provo. The first stop was for what the officer said was a "routine check." The second stop was because I had a light out. The third time because I made a "California stop" at a red light, which was valid. However, the fourth and fifth times. . . . Each time I was actually impressed with the officer's disposition, even though I was being stopped for questionable reasons. The police were always polite and gracious, always smiling and courteous. I received no citations, but I expected better.

There were a few other negative experiences. Elsewhere, I would have been told, "We are not hiring at this time." But in Utah, even when they were hiring, the door was closed. If I had been respected as an individual, I would not have been led on and on (with a smile). I applied for jobs waiting tables, but when I walked through the door, it was clear that the managers had no intention of hiring me. I had a bachelor's degree and many years experience in the East as a waiter and restaurant host. One manager told me, "You are the best applicant that has ever applied. The next opening that we have is yours." But when no call ever came, there were reasons to believe that he had no intention of hiring an African-American waiter.

But even though there were negatives in this adventure to the West, there were too many positives to let me be pushed away. Even though there were imperfect people, I knew that BYU was something very special. It was still a gem hidden away in the mountains of Utah. And even though I found some ignorant and backward people in Utah, they were more than balanced by wonderful, kind, and thoughtful people.

I came to campus not knowing exactly what I was getting myself into. I met roommates who seemed a little too friendly, met teachers who seemed to be too interested in me, and walked across a campus without the litter usually found on college campuses. The air seemed cleaner and skies at BYU seemed bluer. When you take a homeboy born in New York and raised in New Jersey and plop him on the BYU campus, it's an almost out-of-body experience. And, of course, there were all of those white faces.

I was involved with the Young Ambassadors as one of twenty or so clean-cut BYU students who sang, danced, and more importantly, carried a spirit into their performances. Most of the men were returned missionaries and most of the women were marrying those returned missionaries or, if not, going on missions themselves.

Early morning I would wake and find my roommates praying or reading scriptures. At my first Young Ambassadors rehearsal, I was astounded when someone said, "Let's start with a prayer." This was refreshing to me: starting every day or meeting or rehearsal with prayer. They actually referred to the start of a rehearsal as a "devotional." Everyone would sing a song, have a prayer, read out of a book called "Mormon," and share a spiritual thought. Then we would begin the rehearsal. Going through this kind of experience every day, I didn't have a chance! Before I knew it, I was beginning to change.

The Young Ambassadors would give firesides with music and short talks or thoughts. All members of the group participated, whether Mormon or not. They often asked me to speak, and I did. I felt like a new person at those firesides. I felt like I was becoming like those people, maybe even becoming Mormon, or at least a practicing Christian. I didn't know what it was, but I did know that what was happening was changing me. I was still Kevin Giddins, but the attitudes, beliefs, and convictions of those BYU students impressed me. Those students knew who they were and knew where they were going. Doing so brought power, and I felt that power.

The faculty at BYU were off the "unbelievable scale." I was often invited to dinner at their homes. I can count on one hand the number of dinner invitations I received at Ohio University, and none were from faculty members. By contrast, in addition to my intellectual and academic development, the BYU faculty were concerned with my emotional and physical well being. Being in their homes and seeing their families made me homesick. But it wasn't for my family in New Jersey. I was missing something that these people had.

It didn't take long. Within the first month of my arrival in Utah, I knew that I wanted to join The Church of Jesus Christ of Latter-day Saints. I knew that the Church had something special, and I wanted to be part of it. However, I wanted to become a member as part of a "Christian experience." This term is used in the Baptist church when a person changes membership from one Christian church to another. I had already been baptized and, since it was clear that my new friends were Christians, I simply wanted to shift my Christian affiliation. My Utah friends told me that there was more to it than that. Little did I know that the process of becoming a member meant meeting the missionaries!

My friends had to convince me that the only way I could join their church was to talk to these nineteen-year-old boys. This I could not understand. My idea of missionaries was the older women of my Baptist church spreading good will to the needy. I envisioned missionaries helping the hungry people of a distant country. When my friends informed me that the missionaries would teach me about the Church, I was further confused. I had already taught a lesson in an Aaronic Priesthood class and was participating actively in a ward. (One Sunday, the teacher of the priests had handed me the lesson manual and asked me to teach for him the next Sunday because he wasn't going to be there – apparently, he thought that I was a member.) I knew about the Church and I knew all about being a Christian. I had been attending a particular ward regularly and the ward members treated me as if I were already a member. I thought, "Why confuse the issue by learning about something that will come in time?"

In the end, I gave in and agreed to meet with two missionaries. My friends informed me that these missionaries would teach me about the gospel and the Church's beliefs. When I met them, I thought of them as merely teenagers in suits and ties, and the only reason I was willing to listen to them was because I respected my friends. I did it to be nice, as a favor to them.

The discussions didn't get off to a particularly good start. I was a bit insulted when the missionaries proceeded to show me pictures of Jesus as they recited, "This is Jesus Christ." I interrupted them and said, "Wait a minute, you guys. I hope you don't mind me speaking boldly, but I already know who Jesus Christ is. He is my Savior. He died for my sins. I too went to Sunday School as long as I can remember. Tell me something I don't know." They smiled and said, "Great!" Then they added, "Jesus died for your sins." These fellows obviously didn't get it. Each time I would ask a deep question or a question about differences in our beliefs, they would respond, "Good question! We'll get to that in the third discussion on the Restoration." After repeatedly hearing, "Good question, we'll get to that later," I began to feel a little frustrated.

This whole ordeal started to confuse me. I just wanted to formally join the local LDS congregation, but I found myself getting into something quite different. I started asking a lot of questions. Even though these meetings with the missionaries seemed very odd to me, I couldn't resist the fun-loving time we spent together. After our fourth discussion, the elders asked me if I would set a goal. Essentially, they said, "We plan with all of our investigators a future date to work toward being baptized." I told them I was already baptized. They responded that my pastor wasn't called of God. This irritated me a good deal since I had, and will always have, fond and loving memories of the Baptist church and my pastor. After long—very long—nights debating with the elders and my friends about this Mormon concern for authority, I finally understood that my pastor was a good man who is doing a good service in calling others to repentance, but that he had not been ordained by an authorized priesthood holder. I also began to realize that Mormons believed in all the teachings that I knew and cherished from my Baptist influence. This gospel that they were sharing with me did not take anything away but, instead, added to my understanding.

The Lord literally prepared and preserved my life to receive this gospel. I know today it was the memory of love at home, knowledge of God from my Baptist upbringing, and the clean-cut, all-American activities and organizations that I was part of in school, that helped me to realize what I wanted in my life. When I saw the love of family the first time I attended church at BYU, something hit me. When I attended LDS services, something hit me. When I saw young people on the BYU campus and interacted with them, something special hit me. I was stunned when I went out one Friday night with friends in Provo. There was no drinking, no smoking, and no fighting. The joy of dancing without the strong influence of Satan was wonderful. And finally, during the time I was meeting with the missionaries, I was overwhelmed by the Spirit at a fireside given by one of the Young Ambassadors' directors, Janille Christensen. Her talk centered on her life, family, and testimony. She talked about how she had been led by the Spirit. I knew then what I had to do to be successful in my career and life: Repent, be baptized in The Church of Jesus Christ of Latter-day Saints, receive the gift of the Holy Ghost, be led by the Spirit . . . and call home and tell Mom and Dad what they needed to do. Who would have thought that the Young Ambassadors, this singing/dancing group (to some), was actually a conduit that focused my life on what mattered most to me. Like the prophet Joseph Smith said, "I knew it, and I knew that God knew" that I knew it, "And I could not deny it" (JS–H 1:25). When the missionaries told me about the pre-earth life, I knew that puzzle pieces were coming together: I came to understand that I was a child of God and that life has a specific purpose.

At BYU I met many people, students and faculty, who lived their beliefs twenty-four hours a day, seven days a week. Hence I couldn't get away from this feeling of what I needed to do. I was living in and around the Spirit in Utah, at BYU, and in LDS homes. The Young Ambassadors were a great fellowshipping influence.

But Satan put three obstacles in my way. The first was ignorance: "Now don't be offended, Kevin, but does black people's hair get wet?" "You're a good dancer who has been blessed with wonderful muscles that white people just don't have." "I've never dated a black man. My parents would have a cow if I did. But, I think it would be fun. And I would show them that we're all the same." I was able to put these kinds of comments aside because I was focused on what mattered most. I didn't allow myself to get distracted by matters that had little, if any, bearing on my eternal goals.

The second and largest stumbling block was the issue of priesthood authority. My Baptist pastor was not like many other preachers. He attempted to teach from the scriptures. And in good faith, he taught his congregation the best way he knew, with humility and a Christ-like attitude. I now realize that those qualities alone don't authorize a man to be God's agent without his permission. However, my young missionaries erred when they told me preachers in other churches were only out to get gain and didn't have the authority of God to preach. My pastor was such a good man. Later, after humbling myself, I realized that he did have the light of Christ, but that he needed more. The LDS Church has truth—the complete truth—and even though to this day I believe my Baptist pastor had a vision to preach the gospel, his calling wasn't complete. With regard to priesthood authority, I came to understand that I can't second-guess God, "For my thoughts, are not your thoughts neither are your ways my ways, saith the Lord" (Isa. 55:8).

Peter in a vision was commanded to take the gospel to the Gentiles. Until then, the gospel was not being taught to the Gentiles. Just as Peter received revelation about the priesthood, so too did a modern-day prophet in 1978. Why did Jesus not go to the Gentiles? Why this or why that? "Trust in the Lord with all thine heart; and lean not unto thine own understanding" (Prov. 3:5).

I found that it wasn't important to understand why the blacks couldn't hold the priesthood for a time, or why the Jews were once the only "chosen people" and the Gentiles weren't permitted to learn about the gospel or have the priesthood. Yes, it was important to look at history in order to learn and appreciate the blessings from God. I knew about the attitudes in the 1800s and beforehand that put people in chains. I also knew something about LDS Church history, and I was aware of misinformed and ignorant statements by our pioneers. Even so, I came to understand that there is a time and season for all things. Maybe the reality is that the white members of the Church weren't righteous enough or ready before 1978. But for me, it became most important to know simply that "All worthy male members of the church have been extended the priesthood" (Official Declaration 2, Doctrine and Covenants), and that, "Ye are all children of God by faith in Christ Jesus. For as many of you as have been baptized into Christ have put on Christ. There is neither Jew nor Greek, there is neither bond nor free, there is neither male or female: for ye are all one in Christ Jesus. And if ye be Christ's, then are ye Abraham's seed, and heirs according to the promise" (Gal. 3:26–29). My Father in Heaven showed me, through the Spirit, that the natural man can't begin to understand the things that the Spirit of God knows. The second obstacle was removed.

The last obstacle was family tradition and the feeling of leaving a wonderful, loving church. What would I say to a family who loved me, supported me spiritually and financially, and shaped me into who I am today? How could I talk with them? Disappoint them? But I was reassured to know that I was not becoming a member of just another denomination. I was accepting the *religion* of my *faith*. The step that I was contemplating was to a new way of life, not merely a religion on Sunday. I had wandered and, in many ways, lost my way. But in the end, I had come to a place of promise. I knew and felt that The Church of Jesus Christ of Latter-day Saints was truly the right way to go. My mother always told me, "Kevin, there is one thing that the world can't take away from you — what you think, feel, and know." I knew that the Church and its teachings were true, the Holy Ghost had testified of that. The fruits of the Spirit are love, joy, and peace (see Gal. 5:22) and I had felt it. The Holy Ghost had confirmed it: "One Lord, one faith, one baptism" (Eph. 4:5). I came to the same conclusion as Nephi: I had been born of goodly parents. They were not members of the LDS Church. Still, they taught me in all of the Christian learning of their fathers. I knew from their teachings that I had to go and do as the Lord commanded, for I knew that the Lord would not give any commandment to me unless he had prepared a way for my family to accept, and come to embrace my decision to join his Church. I can remember that evening when, after reading 1 Nephi, I closed my scriptures, got on my knees, and prayed to my Father in Heaven, thanking him for the knowledge and power to follow his principles. I knew I would be honoring my parents and my family by doing what was right even though they had no clue that my decision to attend BYU would lead to the fulfillment of my dreams: inner peace and the knowledge that Jesus Christ has established his gospel and the Father has established a pattern that I can follow in leading my eternal family forward. Today my brothers and sisters introduce me as "Kevin, our Mormon brother with a beautiful wife, perfect kids, and a wonderful life." I add, "complete with a white picket fence."

But this dream of a white picket fence is intricately intertwined with a blessing given to Lita Little and a promise to me, as I was about to leave on a mission, that I would meet my wife within the next two years. Lita's part she must tell.

Lita:

I found God long before I got to BYU. But he brought me to BYU so that I might meet Kevin, a man whom he had prepared and brought to BYU as well. The story:

When I met Shawn Dennis and his sister, Kim, in a choir class at Rialto Junior High, it was the beginning of my beginnings. I was fifteen years old and had accumulated quite the collection of spiritual seeking experiences from various churches. Due to the friendships that slowly developed between the Dennis family and myself, I unknowingly began to involve myself in yet another experience which would prove to be my most prized collection of them all.

I couldn't help but be curious about their way of life, their attitudes and behaviors, and, in particular, their ideals and beliefs. To be completely honest, I thought my newly found friends were a bit "out there," but their zealous convictions seemed to work for them. Whatever the case, I grew to value any time that I could spend with them. They were so accepting and fun! And when they prayed, and asked for God's blessings to be with me, I felt that he was really listening.

My curiosity got the best of me and I began to ask questions. Lots of questions. Well, before I knew it, I was having dinner with the Dennises and a couple of tall, nicely dressed guys named Elder Gross and Elder Jones. They talked with me about many truths that sounded familiar and made perfect sense. But when they told me about the boy "prophet," Joseph Smith, and that there was a living "prophet" on the earth at that time, President Spencer W. Kimball, time seemed to stand still. As Elder Jones held up their pictures side by side, I knew that I was looking at men of God.

Throughout the course of my visits with the Dennis family and the Mormon missionaries, I gained a personal witness of the value and worth of what I was learning. The spirit of God testified to me of the complete truth of their words and that I had a responsibility to obey in the face of whatever difficulties or opposing forces life would hand to me. That meant I needed to get baptized. My mother, however, did not agree. So, I waited. For three and a half years I waited, and the Dennis family stuck by me. They rallied around me with unwavering support, remarkable sensitivity, and Christlike love. I will never be able to express in this lifetime my feelings about this family who helped place eternity in my view.

When I became eighteen, my desire to be obedient was stronger than ever and I was baptized on 7 October 1979 by Dad Dennis. That was a wonderful, long-promised day! Shortly thereafter, I received a patriarchal blessing promising me a life of being "led by the spirit," if I kept the commandments. All events and experiences mentioned by Kevin were miles from what I dreamed of doing with my life. You see, unlike my wonderful husband, my dreams leaned more toward the "worldly" side. My focus was to secure a stable career in the entertainment field, all with very righteous intentions, of course. BYU did not fit into the temporal scheme of things in obtaining that worthwhile goal.

This is not to say that BYU didn't try. Shortly after my high school graduation. Rex Pugmire, the son-in-law of a good friend in my stake, was recruiting for BYU. He was a wonderful guy and an excellent recruiter, but I just wasn't interested. Instead, I had to follow an intense, undeniable power directing me to take a different role. I didn't know why I felt so compelled to attend Citrus College. What I did know was that I needed to become a member of Ben Bollinger's touring group, the Citrus Singers. My Father in Heaven would, sooner or later, reveal the rest.

With this group I began an intense tutorial of singing, dancing, acting, and constant prayer, and it was from that junior college that I received my associate's degree in fine arts. What a tremendous mentor and instrument Ben Bollinger was in the hands of the Lord. I treasure him and my experience with his group deeply. I felt completely prepared to graduate and to move on to bigger and better things. Believe it or not, I seriously had come to think that my mission in life was to become "the black Marie Osmond."

I was wrong. That mission was made more clear to me when I was set apart as a full-time missionary in the Missionary Training Center. A fine brother set me apart and gave me a blessing. At the conclusion of that blessing I received some shocking counsel. This brother concluded by stating the following: "Now, Sister Little, your Father in Heaven wants you to know that your husband is being prepared for you. You must be careful not to be hasty with your choices. You must be sure that your future husband is the one that Heavenly Father has prepared for you. " (I wish I could remember the name of that fine brother. I'm usually so good with names. I must have gone into a state of denial.) There I was, twenty-five years old, willing to set aside a promising career in the entertainment world (I had an agent and everything), and a wonderful single life that I had come to enjoy because I wanted to be obedient. Then I was flat out told that my *husband* was being prepared for me! Whose dream was this anyway? Unknowingly, Kevin was traveling across country toward BYU to join the Young Ambassadors and begin his preparatory adventures in "Mormon" country.

After the conclusion of my mission to Leeds, England, Rex Pugmire approached me again about attending BYU. It was the end of winter, 1988. It was ten years after my high school graduation, and five years after having graduated from junior college. The very idea of going to a big university unnerved me for a couple of reasons. First, while I was a good student throughout the course of my educational experiences up to that point, five years is a long time to be away from school. And second, members of my family didn't go to college. I couldn't set my sights on anyone in my family who had embarked upon the college experience or had completed that experience successfully. I suppose it's human nature to fear those things you don't know a whole lot about. A case in point was my mother's attitude about my joining the Church. She knew very little about the Mormon Church, and what little she knew or had heard was not all correct. So, in essence, she was as petrified for me joining the Church as I was for myself at the prospect of returning to school. But I knew that if I did all I could do to keep the commandments of God, I would be "led by the Spirit, not knowing beforehand the things which I should do" (1 Ne. 4:6). In the summer of that same year I became a student at BYU.

Life at BYU was more fun than I ever could have imagined! In addition to taking classes, I felt that it was my responsibility to get involved in all the extracurricular activities of the community — church, young single adults, seeing the sights. Did I mention dating? Well, that too. I found dating to be a fascinating phenomenon! I enjoyed going out with interesting, fun people. My undergraduate degree was in socio-cultural anthropology. Different people were my thing. I believed they enhanced my educational experience. That meant that some — to be honest, many — of those people were of various shapes, sizes, and colors. I just love finding out all about people. I didn't think much of my dating interests until I was in a marriage preparation class that I was counseled to take.

Let me set the scene: A young male student raises his hand and asks, "What's the attitude of guys who date interracially?" The professor responded by saying, "It's a form of dating down." (The answer was based, presumably, on a view that guys like to have the upper hand.) On cue the entire class turned and looked at me, the only person of color in the entire class, sitting in a corner seat. I got an education that day! What really stuck with me was the idea that even if people didn't feel that interracial dating was a form of "dating down," the fact that there were people who thought that people could think that was a problem. And if that was the case, then how could Zion spread forth and the kingdom of God ever come to be established? I turned to my Father in Heaven for comfort and reassurance. I found it.

Shortly thereafter, I found myself being led (or maybe being compelled again) to become a BYU Young Ambassador. The purpose of joining the Citrus Singers had been revealed. They helped to prepare me. I had developed skills that allowed me to walk through an open door without fear. As a returned missionary, I was intrigued and excited about the missionary opportunities this group encountered. The most recent was the conversion, baptism, and missionary farewell of some black guy named Kevin. Every single person I met would say, "You have to meet him!" Of course, my attitude was "Whatever. . . ." But meet we did. And the rest is history. No, the rest is eternity.

Why the Young Ambassadors? They helped me to get back to the basics. I worked hard to prepare myself spiritually to be a worthy tool in the hands of the Lord as we toured to many parts of the world. My soul got refocused. I didn't need a secure career in the entertainment field. I needed a secure relationship with my God. And did I need to be another Marie Osmond? The answer is obvious. I did not. He will use me to fulfill my mission for him if I obey his words.

I needed to find Kevin. I did. He proposed on stage at the conclusion of *The Wiz*, entering in a puff of smoke with escorts carrying pillows with gifts: one with a queen's crown. He asked me, "Lita, will you be my queen and come with me to the celestial kingdom?" A second one with the Tin Man's heart; "This is my heart, I give it to you." A third with roses. And the fourth, with the ring. Some would look at our relationship and assume (at BYU), black girl–black guy, they must go together—a match. However, I accepted, not because he wanted to marry me because I was black, nor I him because he was black, but because he loved me and I loved him.

But I then needed to gain a better understanding and a deeper appreciation about his dream of a "white picket fence." I view it differently now—like a spiritual metaphor. It represents the peace and rest and joy hoped for in dwelling eternally as a family in the glorious presence of the Lord. Jesus has promised that in his Father's house are many mansions (some with white picket fences presumably), and that he is preparing a place for us (John 14:2–3). I don't know what color the fence will be, or what size, or any of the specifics. But I do know that Kevin and I have a hope of securing a place that the Lord has prepared with *our* family.

Whose dream is it anyway? It's certainly not mine. It's not even Kevin's dream really. The dream belongs to our God to fulfill his work and his glory. His will be done. Jesus Christ has made all our dreams a humbling possibility. I cannot begin to express my feelings regarding the incomprehensible worth he has placed upon the souls of all humankind (my soul too) through his completion of the Atonement. Why did he do that? So that we all might be lifted up. The word "all" is one of my most favorite throughout the many passages of scriptures. "All shall see the salvation of the Lord" (Mosiah 16:1). "All shall rise from the dead and stand before God" (Alma 11:41). The Creator died for "all men, that all men might become subject unto him" (2 Ne. 9:5). "The Lord esteemeth all flesh in one" (1 Ne. 17:35). There is nothing "down" about any of us.

How did I find God at BYU? By finding his power within me. Lorenzo Snow made a statement that speaks to the very depths of my soul. He said, "It is the privilege of Latter-day Saints . . . to have the supernatural power of God, and in faith, day by day to secure from the circumstances which may surround us that which will be beneficial and advance us in the principles of holiness and sanctification, that we may as far as possible be like our Father." I ache for that privilege because there is nothing "down" about me. I am a child of God, and he really does love and value me deeply. And I am loved by a pure-hearted, extraordinary son of God who asked me to be his queen that I might go with him to the celestial kingdom. He gets what this is all about. My daily plea is to do all I can do so that this power might increase — allowing me to rise to the highest stature of divine womanhood in God's Church and kingdom, picket fences and all. May he continue to lead me and guide me by the power of the Spirit to do his will.